# TERROR
## TO THE
# WICKED

# TERROR
## TO THE
# WICKED

America's First Trial by Jury
That Ended a War
and Helped to Form a Nation

## Tobey Pearl

Pantheon Books | New York

COPYRIGHT © 2021 BY TOBEY PEARL

All rights reserved. Published in the United States by Pantheon Books,
a division of Penguin Random House LLC, New York, and distributed
in Canada by Penguin Random House Canada Limited, Toronto.

Pantheon Books and colophon are registered trademarks of
Penguin Random House LLC.

Library of Congress Cataloging-in-Publication Data
Name: Pearl, Tobey, author.
Title: Terror to the wicked : America's first murder trial by jury,
ending a war and helping to form a nation / Tobey Pearl.
Description: New York : Pantheon Books, 2021.
Includes bibliographical references and index.
Identifiers: LCCN 2020027983 (print). LCCN 2020027984 (ebook).
ISBN 9781101871713 (hardcover). ISBN 9781101871720 (ebook).
Subjects: LCSH: Trials (Murder)—New England—History—
17th century. Murder—New England—History—17th century.
Criminal procedure—New England—History—17th century.
Jury selection—New England—History—17th century.
Classification: LCC HV6533.N22 P43 2021 (print) |
LCC HV6533.N22 (ebook) | DDC 364.152/309744—dc23
LC record available at lccn.loc.gov/2020027983
LC ebook record available at lccn.loc.gov/2020027984

www.pantheonbooks.com

Jacket image: *Destruction of the Pequot Settlement,*
© Look and Learn/Bridgeman Images; (watercolor background)
Flavio Coelho/Moment/Getty Images
Jacket design by Jenny Carrow

Printed in the United States of America
First Edition

2 4 6 8 9 7 5 3 1

FOR MY CHILDREN

# Contents

# A Note on Historical Context

During the time the events in this book took place, King Charles I reigned over England, Ireland, Scotland, the southern New England colonies, and the Virginia colonies.

The American Indian tribes featured in this story—Narragansett, Wampanoag, Pequot, and Nipmuc—are all traditionally grouped under the category of Eastern Algonquian, designated by a shared set of traits in their respective languages. Indigenous words throughout this text are Eastern Algonquian.

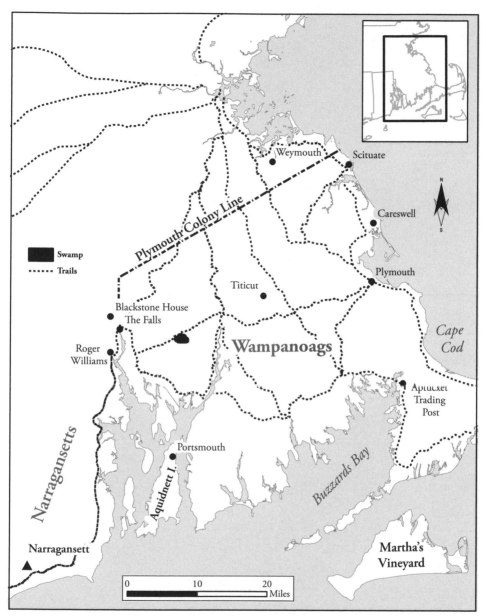

Weymouth

Scituate

Plymouth Colony Line

Careswell

Plymouth

Titicut

Wampanoags

Cape Cod

Blackstone House
The Falls

Roger
Williams

Aptucxet
Trading
Post

Swamp

Trails

Narragansetts

Portsmouth

Aquidnett I.

Buzzards Bay

Narragansett

Martha's
Vineyard

0        10        20
                    Miles

This map incorporates seventeenth-century coastlines and landmarks as interpreted from archival records by historical geographers Bill and Kristen Keegan.

# Cast of Characters

**PENOWANYANQUIS**—Nipmuc trader

**WILL**—Governor Roger Williams's young American Indian slave

**WINCUMBONE**—Will's mother

**MONONOTTO**—Sachem (chief), who fought with the Pequot, Will's father

**MIANTONOMO**—Sachem of the Narragansett tribe, territory bordered Providence, Rhode Island

**MIXANNO**—Narragansett, son of Canonicus and nephew of Miantonomo

**MASSASOIT (OUSAMEEQUIN)**—Sachem of the Wampanoag, territory bordered Plymouth Colony

**NINIGRET**—Sachem of the Niantic tribe, Massasoit's plotting foe

**ARTHUR PEACH**—Pequot War veteran, Edward Winslow's indentured servant

**THOMAS JACKSON**—Peach gang member

**RICHARD STINNINGS**—Peach gang member

**DANIELL CROSSE**—Peach gang member

**GOVERNOR THOMAS PRENCE**—Governor of Plymouth Colony

**REVEREND JOHN LOTHROP**—Unofficial religious leader of Plymouth Colony's Scituate settlement

**FORMER GOVERNOR EDWARD WINSLOW**—Plymouth Colony, Arthur Peach's master

**FORMER GOVERNOR WILLIAM BRADFORD**—Plymouth Colony, ordered the use of jury trials

**GOVERNOR JOHN WINTHROP**—Governor of Massachusetts Bay Colony

**GOVERNOR ROGER WILLIAMS**—Governor of the settlement of Providence, Rhode Island

**JOHN THROCKMORTON**—Peach gang trial witness

**STEPHEN HOPKINS**—Plymouth Colony's notorious tavern owner

**DOROTHY TEMPLE**—Stephen Hopkins's indentured servant, Arthur Peach's lover

# TERROR

## TO THE

# WICKED

# INTRODUCTION

Plymouth Colony—July 1638 (Julian calendar)

The threat facing Penowanyanquis, a young Nipmuc tribesman on a trading mission, must have felt oddly familiar. The serenity of the forest was notoriously fleeting. His elders passed down countless stories involving brave sojourners unexpectedly tested by angered gods, tricksters, mischief makers, or monsters—and the man coming toward him, Arthur Peach, was a monster.

The Nipmuc cautionary legends that addressed such menaces often began with the same words: "Long ago, it was this way." The words evoke a group of listeners settling in to hear a tale both otherworldly and exigent in the moment they are spoken. They are fitting words for this story. In many ways the foundation of our country, certainly the underpinnings of our jurisprudence, took root in these bygone events. Peach's attack on Penowanyanquis provoked Plymouth Colony's first significant murder trial. The dramatic legal proceedings, culminating in a trial by jury, formed part of a daring and risky experiment for which the timing could not have been worse.

The attack on Penowanyanquis took place against the backdrop of the Pequot War, a series of battles fought during the late 1630s between the Pequot tribe, who lived in present-day Connecticut, and besieging colonists. Penowanyanquis had been trading for the Narragansett tribe, whose territory stretched across present-day Rhode Island and who were steadfast foes of the Pequot. Everyone had a stake in the fighting, and each regional tribe was touched by the combat. The notion of a fair jury verdict in the trial of a settler accused of murdering a tribesman—during wartime, in which the killing of indigenous people was indiscriminate and sanctioned—seemed improbable. Colonists and American Indians alike wondered what measure of legal righteousness could exist in the absence of peace.

Jurors would be called on to hear the tale of Arthur Peach and Penowanyanquis, both of whom were archetypes of vanishing populations. Penowanyanquis was a member of a unique group that would soon disappear to history—pre-contact Eastern Woodland American Indians. Born far west of New England's coastal colonies, Penowanyanquis came of age as a child during one of the last times and in one of the final places not yet touched by colonists.

Peach, too, represented a dying breed. He was at the tail end of an epic, ruthless survival quest that had brought him out of Ireland into England, perhaps by way of the battles being fought in the Netherlands, then to the Virginia colonies, a site of more warfare, and on to Massachusetts Bay Colony, present-day Boston, where he became a soldier in the Pequot War, fighting in brutal combat in present-day Connecticut. As conflicts raged, Peach moved to yet another location and another role. He landed in Plymouth Colony in the final wave of settlers and indentured servants referred to as the "Great Migration," populating the New England colonies by the thousands in the 1630s.

In many ways, the Pequot War and its sweeping reverberations brought the two men on a deadly collision course. Discovering their stories requires an understanding of that war and its dark origins.

To hear many of the colonists tell it, the Pequot War was not a foreseeable event. Such a war of aggression would have been inconceivable to the earliest Puritan settlers, some of whom boarded the *Mayflower* fresh from experiencing hellish persecution and aggression. They had been hunted down and imprisoned in England, and many of their friends and loved ones were killed. These men and women professed their intention to live a peaceful existence in the New World, where they would treat indigenous people equitably. The oppression and torture the Puritans suffered in England provided conviction for these ideals.

To remember the worst of what they endured, colonial settlers needed only to reflect on London's notorious Star Chamber court-room and its countless examples of brutish tyranny. The lovely room in the palace of Westminster, known for a high ceiling gilded with large stars that appeared to float from heaven, produced terrors almost too sickening to describe. One colonist described Puritan defendants facing gruesome penalties for protesting "not only against stage plays . . . [but also] against hunting, publique festivals, Christmas-keeping, bonfires and maypoles." Puritans did not celebrate Christmas, a holiday they believed distracted people with its frivolous trimmings. The rulers of the Star Chamber—not a jury of peers—found the dissenters guilty. Each man's ears were cut from his head.

The convicts who had their ears cropped were then branded with the letters "SL" on each of their cheeks—"Seditious Libelers." Authorities ordered them banished to dungeons on the outskirts of the kingdom. Their jailors, who would be the only people to ever see them again, would know them by their branding. In the grimmest of silver linings, at least they had avoided the common practice of nose splitting, where the castigated endured the eruption of pulsing blood and unfathomable pain.

The desperate men and women fled the specter of death and torture to the New World, but in the very act of flight they risked their lives. Half the original *Mayflower* passengers died during their first winter. The settlers who disembarked from that first vessel were, in the words of one passenger, met with the "grime and grisly face of povertie coming upon them like an armed man." Illness combined with deprivation had been more than most of the *Mayflower* settlers could withstand. A New England winter challenged Englishmen and -women accustomed to milder weather. The settlers had arrived on the cusp of the frigid season without adequate clothing. To make matters worse, that first winter brought historically cold temperatures, a climate phenomenon later known as the "Little Ice Age." The brutal weather hampered efforts to secure food and shelter and to fight off illness.

Venturing into the uncharted woods to procure resources could prove deadly. One pair of early settlers became lost while frantically collecting thatch to cover their roofs before the January snow took hold—deep snow bringing dangers the colonists had only begun to comprehend. Darkness descended quickly as fellow settlers "hallooed," calling out for the pair of missing men to no avail. With no shelter, the lost men spent a bone-chilling night pacing around a tree as two mountain lions roared, one stalking them. At the break of day, they made their way back to the settlement, where one man's shoes were cut from his frostbitten feet. Despite being lame and barely able to walk, he was so desperate to finish his shelter that he went back into the woods with his dog; it was not long before two wolves took an interest. The dog quickly hid "betwixt his legs for succor." The settler hurled a stick at one wolf and hit the animal, which darted away before returning moments later with a companion, "grinning at him a good while." The man managed to rejoin his fellow settlers, but he died from apparent exposure soon after. In the first year, in the tally of one contemporary, "of 100 and odd persons, scarce 50 remained. And of these in the time of most distress, there was but 6 or 7 sound persons."

Plymouth Colony governor William Bradford later recounted the travails of those formative days. "Many sold away their clothes and bed coverings [to the Indians]; others (so base were they) became servants to the Indians, and would cut them wood and fetch them water for a capful of corn; others fell to plain stealing, both night and day, from the Indians . . . In the end, they came to that misery that some starved and died with cold and hunger." One settler gathering shellfish in the mucky sand surrounded by bleak straw-colored marsh grass and clutches of snow "was so weak as he stuck fast in the mud and was found dead in the place." When a critically ill settler's desperate wish to quench his thirst with a "small can of beere" could not be granted, colonists responded with empathy, lamenting that even if the dying man were "their own father he should have none."

Incredibly, the *Mayflower* passenger Captain Myles Standish not only survived death but never fell ill. Standish, and the few other healthy men, women, and children, "spared no pains, night nor day, but with abundance of toile and hazard to their own health, fetched [the sick settlers] wood, made them fires, drest them meat, made their beds, washed their loathsome clothes." Governor Bradford acknowledged that he "and many others . . . were much beholden in our low and sicke condition" to the settlement's "captain and military commander." Standish had even managed to use a notoriously faulty, slow-to-fire weapon to kill an eagle at a great distance; the ravenous, grateful settlers described the bird's meat in glowing terms: "hardly to be discerned from mutton." He was willing to take a calculated risk, and he could deliver results. Standish's desire to help had been forged by grief, when after arrival in the New World his wife, Rose, became one of the first to pass away.

While the heartiest settlers, such as Standish, propped up fellow colonists, the long-term survival of the English entirely depended on assistance from the indigenous people, namely the Wampanoag and their powerful chief, or *massasoit*, Ousameequin, known later simply as Massasoit. Early cultural exchanges projected goodwill and tremendous gratitude as delegates from the tribes showed the English how to endure the cold climate and thrive in their new environment. Wampanoag families lived and intermingled with neighboring settlers, freely walking in and out of colonists' homes, since they disdained the Western custom of knocking. The Wampanoag shared recipes, natural remedies, and farming and fishing techniques, helping settlers acclimate.

Encounters with indigenous people remained generally positive during the early colonial period. One newcomer described a charming scene of cross-cultural interaction. "A youth in our company that could play upon a gitterne [lute]" delighted tribal audiences with "homely music." They gave "him many things . . . tobacco, tobacco-pipes, snakes skins of six foot long." Indigenous men and women "danced twenty in a ring" to the young man's music. Enchanted, they sang out, "*Io, Ia, Io, Ia, Ia, Io.*"

Even common cultural muddles in the New World were smiled upon. One Englishman who walked in the woods to the north often recounted his own story. Unexpectedly, the sojourner had come upon forty or fifty Indians. The colonial traveler called out the common English greeting, "What cheer?" The English used this expression to inquire after the latest good news. Baffled, howling with laughter at the meaningless sounds, the tribesmen repeated the salutation "so loudly the woods rang with the noise."

These early years in the colony led into a productive stretch of subsistence farming and modest trade as settlers adapted to their new home. Colonists even built a fishing weir. Tribes had used the technology for thousands of years, gathering sticks to build a long, narrow, rough-hewn dock that culminated in a figure eight of two interconnected circles; builders placed a single rectangular opening at the far end of the first circle. Fish entering had no way out.

Settlers hoped to expand the fishing trade into a larger-scale industry, constructing a Western-style "fishing stage" where a fast-moving river ran into the ocean. In the spring, "there come so many shad from the sea which want to ascend that river, that it is quite surprising," observed one settler. With their intricate trellised platform, colonists snared ten thousand to twelve thousand fish. One colonial traveler noted that up to "2 or 3 spoonfuls" of fat could be obtained from the fish heads. "Good eating for one who is fond of picking heads." Plymouth settlers wanted for nothing. The new neighbor to the north, Massachusetts Bay Colony, improved the fortunes of Plymouth Colony settlers even further.

The rapidly expanding Massachusetts Bay Colony demanded a constant supply of livestock and goods. Plymouth settlers found themselves in a strong position to barter and enrich themselves—days of starvation and poverty receded into the past. As colonists moved from hand-to-mouth existence to relatively affluent status, land became a sound investment. One optimistic settler called for his fellow colonists, who were arriving in droves by 1638, to "seek out a convenient place or two or three." Word had spread that "Cap-cod, New Plimouth, Dukes bury, and all those parts" welcomed new settlers.

Colonists prided themselves on the virtuous nature of their purchases. One Englishman urged his New England contemporaries, "If any of the savages pretend right of inheritance to all or any part of the lands granted in our patent, we pray you endeavor to purchase their titles, that we may avoid the least scruple of intrusion." Indeed, King Charles II exhorted his New World subjects not to lose sight of the fact that "Indians were members of the same 'miserable drove of Adam's degenerate seed' as the English, and thus 'our brethren by nature,' with the same potential to be subjects and citizens." The king further noted that his "well-beloved . . . [English] subjects" lived "in New England by grants from the Native Princes of that Country." Colonists took these admonishments to heart.

The book *La Leyenda Negra* was widely distributed and read among the English populace. It contained gruesome details of Spain's ruthless conquistadores, who had plundered the lands and killed the people they had encountered in the Southern Hemisphere. A conscious sentiment took hold among English settlers to behave honorably, further urged on them by the most powerful and learned men in England. As persecuted religious dissenters, Puritans often took pains to do what they perceived as morally right.

A utopian element lay at the foundation of the New England colonies; as one historian notes, Massachusetts Bay colonists "were striving to build the best possible society on earth," respecting civil liberties. The same could be said for neighboring Plymouth Colony to the immediate south. Puritan colonists zealously aspired to this objective, professing their insistence on equitable land trades with the indigenous people as they launched into a frenzied period of purchases.

Settlers yearned to own land outright in the English sense, and they were willing to pay. They craved permanency, a desire heightened both by their arrival in a new place and by recent changes to land access in England. During the sixteenth and seventeenth centuries,

English peasants were affected by the privatization of common lands once used by shepherds to graze their flocks. The changes pushed the disenfranchised toward working in factories or the risks of searching out New World opportunities. This transformation in public land use also reinforced "the sacred status of property." For all of these reasons, the colonial leader John Cotton, for example, felt eager to reassure his own children that "they [would] dwell in a place of their own, and move no more."

New World settlers provided comprehensive deeds for their land purchases from tribes, but the careful language at the end of one surviving deed reflects a ticking time bomb. This particular settler restricted access to the land to himself and his family, making a point to add that "the only pp [people's] use . . . [will be by] the said Gyles Rickett his heirs and Assignees for ever." The clause embodies the center of emerging friction between indigenous men and women and colonists. Tribes that sold land to settlers had little understanding of English property law. Accustomed to shifting territorial claims by rival tribes, they found the idea of restricting access to land connected to their gods incomprehensible. Many settlers took advantage of the cultural misunderstanding.

Quachattasett, sachem of the Manamet, signed away his interest in his tribal land in the seventeenth century, agreeing to carefully drafted legal terms that terminated his rights in the territory. The legal document stipulated that "all woods timber or whatsoever is in the land or upon the land in any respect appertaining there unto, I the aforesaid Quachattasett do . . . alienate from my self my heirs executors and assignees and fully and absolutely deliver."

Future events demonstrated that Quachattasett never realized the implications of the decidedly English document he had signed. Back in court not long after signing the first deed, he requested clarification for himself and two of his tribesmen, demanding that they "shall have liberty of wood and timber for firing and other uses out of the bordering woods." In the context of New England intertribal relations, it was entirely reasonable to assume that acquiescing control of a given territory would not preclude the right to pass through the land of an ally when hunting and gathering. For the English, the matter was not so clear. Settlers were forced to grapple with this vexing ethical dilemma. What did it mean to own land in the New World? Was it distinct from controlling territory in ways more familiar to the indigenous people? The devil was in this detail, and there would be no peace without resolving the issue.

Another seventeenth-century tribesman, put into a desperate situation that forced him to sign a land deed, hoped to protect his children's rights to live, hunt, and sustain themselves. He improvised language to add to the deed: "I do not sell this land . . . I bequeath it all to my four children . . . as long as the earth exists . . . only they use it." A Wampanoag commentator described the English landgrab succinctly: "*Yeunuh wussukquohwonog wutche nummukkoukounganun Englishmananog yeh ahquombi*," which translates to "This writing is about our being robbed by the English at this time."

When New England colonists witnessed the unlikely sight of a snake and mouse fighting in present-day Watertown, Massachusetts, they watched in disbelief as the humble mouse, after a "great combat," gained the upper hand and killed the snake. From the settlers' perspective, this morality play reflected the Puritans overcoming oppression—they identified with the mouse, not the snake. The travails of local tribespeople never crossed their minds as they watched the surprising tableau.

The apex of the Great Migration in the 1630s further exacerbated the displacement of American Indians. Settlements pushed into the western reaches of present-day Massachusetts—a vast region that was Nipmuc country, Penowanyanquis's homeland. Colonists convinced themselves that their incursions into the stronghold of their tribal neighbors benefited the indigenous people. Settlers drew parallels to the Roman invaders who so long before had conquered the lands that became England and brought advanced civilization: "Had not this violence, and this injury, been offered unto us by the Romans," the coarse English might have remained "rude, and untutored, wandering in the woods, dwelling in caves, and hunting for our dinners (as the wild beasts in the forests for their prey)."

On the Careswell estate, where Arthur Peach worked as an indentured servant, a similarly pharisaical perspective pervaded the mindset of the household. Josiah Winslow, a ten-year-old boy with a mop of light brown hair, came of age soaking up the views of his elders, like his father and Peach's master, former Plymouth Colony governor Edward Winslow. As an adult, Josiah viewed his interactions with New World indigenous people as beyond reproach. Josiah took up arms during the later King Philip's War, exhibiting a manic level of bloodthirstiness. He led approximately one thousand men into battle. When Josiah became governor later in life, he remarked without a hint of irony, "I think I can truly say that before these present trouble with the Indians broke out"—King Philip's War—"we did not possess one foot of land in this colony but what was fairly by honest purchase of the Indian proprietors."

In fact, Josiah Winslow represents one of the worst culprits to carry on unscrupulous dealings with local tribes. In 1671, when Josiah sued an American Indian for nonpayment of a horse, he demanded ten pounds for a horse valued at between two and four pounds. He won judgment in the stunning amount of twenty pounds, which likely crippled the tribesman with debt for the remainder of his life. Settlers followed the letter of the law in most cases, carefully adjudicating even seemingly trivial matters to uphold the appearance of justice—but disastrously failed to account for standards of morality. No wonder they went to bed fearing late-night raids.

Many years after the trial of Peach and his accomplices, one of the men who had served on the jury, Gabriell Fallowell, found himself again in court on a matter concerning a tribesman. Fallowell was beside himself when "Harry the Indian" and his son inadvertently ensnared a cow and steer belonging to Fallowell. His unpenned cattle had wandered into land Harry considered open-hunting territory. Fallowell did not acknowledge—perhaps never even considered—his shared responsibility for the mishap.

Settlers' free-roaming cattle contributed to the destruction of the indigenous people's way of life: crops belonging to local tribes were damaged, hunting opportunities stymied, and, adding insult to injury,

American Indians landed on the losing side of courtroom battles when the worlds collided. In fact, Harry may have killed the animals in revenge for the destruction, a known practice at the time. The court ordered him to compensate Fallowell over the course of two annual "Indian harvest[s]." The long-term payment plan was no mark of generosity—it was a realistic strategy to allow Harry sufficient time to pay the onerous judgment.

In the winter of 1634, Pequot tribesmen made a bone-chilling trip from their territory along today's Connecticut coast to Massachusetts Bay Colony. They carried gifts for the old Puritan leaders, who sat in hard-backed chairs in cold, unadorned rooms and dryly accepted the tokens of friendship. With the peace offerings, the Pequot showed they had no interest in war with the settlers. While the olive branch helped maintain cordial relations between tribes and settlements for a time, events ultimately took a turn. In the summer of 1636, with settlers desperate to obtain more land and pressing westward into Pequot territory, a violent clash sparked the ire of colony leaders and gave pretext to quietly pack up the gifts and return them to the Pequot. This proved an unassuming but fatal foreshadowing, given the inconceivable horrors soon unleashed. It also underscored the underlying motivation for war on the colonists' part—land. This displacement of indigenous people from their land, concurrent with the influx of thousands of English, reflected no mere by-product of migration but a purposeful construct called "settler colonialism," the success of which ultimately depended on the subjugation of one group over the other.

The fighting started in earnest in 1636, and English soldiers chronicled horrific scenes of carnage: "So many souls lie gasping on the ground so thick in some places, that you could hardly pass along." The Battle of Mistick Fort in 1637 had shown the Pequot a new kind of war—one that aimed not just at winning battles or wars but at the annihilation of an entire people. Skirmishes between tribes typically resulted in low fatality counts. A colonial soldier contemptuously observed that, with their style of combat involving "changing a few arrows," the indigenous people "might fight seven years and not kill seven men." The Pequot War demonstrated a possibility unheard of in the New World: genocide.

Former governor Bradford did not mince words in describing the Mistick Fort slaughter. The four hundred Pequot deaths had resulted in "a fearful sight." Colonial soldiers' sword arms grew tired with the sheer volume of killing. They decided on a more brutally efficient means: torching the whole Pequot settlement. The victims died as if "frying in ye fryer . . . ye streams of blood quenching ye same." Roger Williams, founding settler of Providence, Rhode Island, noted with restrained disgust at the time that the Pequot had been "subdued." The Pequot War changed everything. Certain camps of settlers began referring to their indigenous neighbors as "savage," "beastly" "hell-fiends . . . not to be trusted." Earnest interactions gave way to mistrust, suspicion, and hatred.

While the number of battles had decreased by the time Arthur Peach attacked Penowanyanquis in the summer of 1638, the Pequot War dragged on with no end in sight. Peach's assault presented the ultimate provocation, one that threatened to rekindle the worst combat and engender a collective reckoning. When twelve colonists came together as a jury to judge Peach, their efforts represented the first fully developed, documented jury trial of the era, surpassing previous limited undertakings in the most volatile context possible.

Even without having served on a criminal jury before, the New England farmers who made up the population of Plymouth Colony understood—from past persecutions—the horrors of a society without a jury system. Relatively young, skilled, educated, and literate at twice the rate of the English population as a whole, these earliest settlers had the chance to rise to a singular occasion. Those colonists ultimately assigned to carry out the trial would assume their duties with grave purpose, their outlook colored by a complex mixture of puritanical religious dictates, lingering medieval mores, relatively newfound ideals of humanism, and an Early Modern England still influenced by the last gasp of the English Renaissance. Indigenous people, too, became integral to the outcome in the court, testifying, strategizing, even tampering. It was anyone's guess how this assortment of change makers would produce a verdict poised to reshape the war and the New World.

Their story, too, begins like this: "Long ago, it was this way."

# EARTHQUAKES AND OMENS

"They thought to avoyd ye pursute."

—*Plymouth Colony governor
William Bradford*

Arthur Peach felt for his rapier. This weapon, his only material possession in the world, was a reassuring accessory on this journey in the peak of summer 1638. Everything else around him had deteriorated, but the metal blade remained sharp, cool, and clean. For several days, he and his companions, fellow indentured servants, had been traversing an unfamiliar forest with insufficient supplies. Now, the hellish forces of exposure and hunger wore on him and the three other men—and he had reason to fear that these men questioned his leadership.

The formidable stands of oak, maple, and pine trees obstructing his view of the sky were broken up by the wetlands of Misquamsqueece, north of present-day Seekonk, Massachusetts. They stopped in an eerie spot filled with curious markings—including a foreboding imprint forged into stone known as the "Devil's Footprint." Elongated and worn deep into the dark rock, it was simply an ancient indigenous corn mortar, though Peach had no way of knowing this. Peach and his companions may have overheard the similarly sinister name for the watery region, the "Devil's Swamp." To this day, the desolate wetlands provoke the local belief that the place itself could "foster pain and evil."

The men's choice to camp on the border between the Wampanoag and Narragansett territories provided an opportunity to avoid both tribes. If Peach and his companions had ventured farther east or west, they would have been confronted by indigenous men. Their location fell with precision on a natural border; six years later the spot would become the center of a large-scale land boundary dispute between the colonies.

Relentless mosquitoes and slow-moving dragonflies hinted at the proximity of swampy waterways. Peach must have wished he were back in the lush expanses of his native Ireland, however contested and bloodstained. As he rested his head on a bed of dried-out pitch pine needles, he could reflect on the surreal events that had brought him to this abysmal place.

Earlier in the summer, on June 1, 1638, nature itself had seemed to promise remarkable things to come. First, Peach noticed the ground in Plymouth Colony shaking under his feet with such ferocity that "with a report like continued thunder . . . chimnies were thrown down, and the pewter fell from the shelves." In describing the trembling earth, some said "that the Holy Ghost did shake it in coming down on them." The Providence patriarch Roger Williams described the accompanying din as a "kind of thunder." That was just the earthquake itself. The aftershocks rumbled on and off throughout June, and then on the twenty-fifth of that month, in a crescendo of God's mysterious works, the light drained from the moon, turning its eclipsed form from opalescent to the russet color of battle-dried blood that Peach knew well. The fantastic omens tantalized young adventurers looking for new opportunity.

The servitude contract Peach had entered into with the Plymouth powerbroker Edward Winslow two years before would end when he turned twenty-five, permitting him to live as he pleased from that point on. By 1638, Peach had two years to go: nothing in the grand scheme of things, but a lifetime to a restive youth. Breach of his servitude would trigger severe punishment if he were caught, but

Peach never dwelled on consequences. After the panic-inducing lunar eclipse, he set out as if pulled away by unknowable forces or the nearby tides, leaving behind debts on top of his indenture contract.

Indentured servants had no right to leave the colony without expressly granted permission, and before fleeing Plymouth, Peach compounded his transgression by convincing three fellow servants to join him on his mad dash. Now, just a few days into their journey, the very presence of the companions by the campfire complicated matters for him. Reasons for impatience multiplied. So far, Peach had failed to provide much sustenance or even to navigate the woods properly. By the time they had camped in Misquamsqueece, he needed a way to prove himself a leader. A distant sound demanded attention. It was impossible to differentiate between predator and prey, at least until it—man or beast—moved closer. With daylight on them, Peach could have hunted for food, but for the moment he conserved his waning energy.

In addition to the earthquake and eclipse, a less celestial but equally moving circumstance had pushed Peach out of the settlement into this wilderness. He had a sweetheart, a servant in a different household in Plymouth. He found love when it seemed least possible, during a moment of epic despair when he had been consumed with his plight in life.

Peach had been living at the sprawling Careswell estate in Marshfield, Edward Winslow's manor, on the outskirts of Plymouth Colony. Poor and landless, Peach had agreed to work for the high-ranking leader, who had served twice as governor in the colony. Peach's placement with Winslow promised access to opportunity, but in practice the role did not suit him. Nor did the work. Peach hailed from a long-established family of adventurers and warriors; he wanted to own an estate, not serve one.

A few short years earlier, a manor like Careswell would have been largely unheard of in Plymouth. As the settlement transitioned from terrifying ordeal to the drudgery of subsistence farming, hunting, childrearing, and worship, the quiet life of most of the religiously devout Pilgrims settled into a quotidian existence—but for a few, life became grander. The clapboard facade at Careswell may have been un-assuming, but the building, with views out to the ocean, rambled on well beyond the needs of any New England family. The expansive stretches of farmland included a lavish range of peas, wheat, and corn crops; Winslow had created a type of estate living that was entirely novel in the New World.

The ambitious settler had taken pains to show his status. Winslow came from a well-established family in England, part of the merchant class, and he was an "old-comer"—one of the first to settle the area. He had arrived on the *Mayflower*. Careswell would have marked him as a member of the landed gentry class, a term that had no real mean-ing in New England. Winslow could not have afforded such an estate in the Old World, but he had taken a gamble coming to Plymouth and stood on the cusp of making a fortune.

The vast size of new estates such as Careswell could only be sup-ported by an array of servants like Peach, purchased through indenture contracts. The Pequot War, which began in 1636, provided another labor source. Soon Plymouth's masters would be challenged with the dilemma of whether or not to "buy" indigenous slaves, tribespeople who had been taken as prisoners of war in the fighting. The moral lines quickly blurred between indentured servants, prisoners of war, and those who were penned and awaiting sale. The distinctions among the three would only become clear a lifetime later, to the horror of mothers and fathers who had fallen into the most hopeless category, slavery, which was inheritable—their children and their children's children doomed to the same fate.

As an indentured servant, Peach fit a clear role on Careswell, but property owners such as Winslow remained perplexed by tribesmen and -women. During Winslow's early days in Plymouth Colony, he dismissed the idea that the indigenous people believed in God. Tribal spiritual leaders corrected his misperception, and he took quill to parchment to set the record straight: "Therein I erred, though we could then gather no better." It meant something to Winslow to understand the beliefs of the indigenous people around him, particu-larly on this point. To a Puritan, a faithless soul would be met with confused disdain. A believer, on the other hand, even a non-Christian, could be humanized.

Just to the north, in present-day Boston, Massachusetts Bay Colony governor John Winthrop had no compunction regarding the issue of slavery. When he later wrote out his will, he allocated his estate in clear terms: "I give my son Adam my land called the Governor's Garden . . . I give him also my Indians." While Peach did not face the horrors of enslavement, the indignities of servitude plagued him. And the influx of Pequot slaves may have further roused his anger. Peach had served as a soldier in the Pequot War, likely engaged in armed fighting in 1637, just one year before his flight into the dark forests. Peach despised his enemy combatants and had no desire to work alongside them.

Plymouth bitterly disappointed Peach. While New England indenture contracts dating as late as 1634 promised, in bold hand, "one hundred acres of ground" in exchange for service, by 1636 Plymouth Colony restricted the acreage given in indenture contracts to a comparatively paltry five—and there was an easy way out for the government to leave the obligation unfulfilled. The colony declared that land would be available only to those subjectively determined to be "fit" to receive it. Soon after, Plymouth's leaders further degraded prospects for indentured servants by stipulating that land given to indentured workers would come out of their masters' acreage rather than from the colony. The bait-and-switch trapped Peach in what proved to be the latest dead end, inciting a dangerous state of rage. To make matters worse, as servants' disenfranchisement increased, freemen grew wealthier and more powerful.

Arthur Peach faced the reality that, despite his newly lush surroundings with the Winslows, the "end-payments" for his servitude amounted to little more than "two suits, one for the Lord's day and one for working days." Just a few years later, the number of men willing to sign up for such servitude terms plummeted. Peach was part of the final large wave of servants helping to settle New England. It was precisely the year of his flight, 1638, in which the first generation of indenture contracts expired, with few takers to replace them.

Arthur Peach's master, Plymouth
Colony governor Edward Winslow; a
rare portrait of a *Mayflower* passenger.

While caught up in the push and pull of events larger than himself, Peach met another young servant, Dorothy Temple. Like Peach,
she was twenty-three years old. If Dorothy, on arriving in Plymouth
Colony, thought she had landed in the center of the most rigidly
puritanical settlement in the New World, her expectations were soon
upended by her bohemian master, a *Mayflower* passenger who was the
polar opposite of Edward Winslow.

An opportunist who broke the Puritan mold of the early Pilgrims,
Stephen Hopkins boasted a larger-than-life presence. Hopkins's small
wattle-and-daub (or woven lattice) cottage had an unassuming, humble facade and two sleepy, slender-horned cows, Mottley and Smykin,
grazing out back. But what went on inside roiled Plymouth.

Over the roughly constructed plank fences that separated garden
plots around each house, neighbors inserted themselves into one
another's affairs. Little transpired without a witness. Everyone in
Plymouth certainly observed the spectacle of the Stephen Hopkins
home—or, more accurately, the Hopkins tavern. The bleak abode
was a kind of single-structure red-light district, marking the center
of town on the corner of the "highway." Its owner played host to
raucous men who wanted to drink and unwind. The noises reverberated through the settlement, including the raspy echo of wooden
game pieces coasting over the surface of the Hopkins dining table,

perplexing and alarming Pilgrims unacquainted with shuffleboard, a tabletop game at the time.

Settlement leaders were nonplussed, and something between irritation and exasperation emanated between the lines of the various court orders. Hopkins, the court recorded, was "suffering servants and others to sit drinking in his house, contrary to the orders of the Court, and to play at shuffleboard," and "oppressing" the colony with the sale of alcohol at high prices.

Hopkins's standing as a *Mayflower* original may have spared him harsher scrutiny from colonial leadership. In addition, leaders such as Plymouth Colony governor Thomas Prence and Captain Myles Standish prized Hopkins's usefulness on diplomatic expeditions, which complicated how to handle his religious apathy and his indiscretions. With the courtroom a limited option for redressing small grievances, frustrated settlers often lost their tempers with each other. As one enraged young man bellowed to an elderly neighbor who had upset him, "God damn me if thou wart not a old man I would beat thy teeth down thy throt." Hopkins and his household would have been subject to plenty of private reproofs. In a settlement where the servant class comprised the lowest rung of society, the libertine environment that Hopkins established for male and female servants alike offended almost everyone.

Still, the games continued unabated, enticing a certain type of young man who sought spirited leisure time. The "lusty" Peach fit the bill. He took plenty of detours to the hard-packed dirt path that wound through the village center to Stephen Hopkins's home, lured by the sounds of howling and cheering. Settlers soon learned that Peach had "rune into debte," perhaps the product of poorly executed shuffleboard wagers. Dorothy Temple, one of Hopkins's indentured servants, served warm beer in bowls and tankards; visitors and patrons also ordered wine and "strong waters," relaxing as she cooked and cleaned.

For all of the colony leaders' lofty expectations of appropriate conduct for servants, Hopkins took a more nuanced view. Unlike some higher-born settlers, Hopkins knew what life was like as an indentured servant. He had been one himself, inadvertently becoming a part of literary history along the way.

At nineteen years old, Hopkins had exchanged years of his life for the promise of future land when he departed from the other Plymouth, back in England, on a 1609 journey to Jamestown, Virginia. It was this voyage—along with Hopkins's outsize personality—that caught the attention of William Shakespeare, who was at work on his final solo-written play, *The Tempest*. In 1610, the now well-established and financially comfortable dramatist dug around for inspiration for a character that might add a missing flourish to the production. Shakespeare needed a figure whose buffoonish tomfoolery counterbalanced the serious messages he conceived for a play that explored the intrinsic worth of the individual. He acquainted himself with the account of a real-life harrowing tale by the poet and historian William Strachey called *A True Repertory of the Wracke*, a text detailing the recent ruin of the *Sea Venture* on Bermuda's reefs. The narrative yielded the exact sort of model he had been looking for in the form of the unstoppable, cocky Stephen Hopkins. Shakespeare's version of Hopkins, the future tavern operator, who appears as Stephano in *The Tempest*, often imbibed to darkly humorous effect. ("Here's my comfort," Stephano slurs, raising a glass.)

Stephano's soused-up comic relief carried the day for many in the audience of *The Tempest*'s debut on All Hallows' Day at Whitehall Palace. Shakespeare waited on tenterhooks for the reaction of one person in particular, the person whose opinion counted the most: King James I. While the counter-authoritarian subtext of *The Tempest* may have been lost on the leader of the English-speaking world, the story's central drama of shipwreck struck the right nerve to please a monarch who lived in terror of his ship sinking.

Contemporaries had plenty of clues to decode Stephano as Stephen Hopkins, who had been shipwrecked in Bermuda. Hopkins was sentenced to death after the shipwreck for dangerously advancing the intriguing idea that the naval officer's "authority ceased when the wreck was committed." In a pitiful state, Hopkins had begged and pleaded with all who listened, making "so much moan" about his case, arguing that his wife and children faced destitution without him. His sad appeals were said to sway "the hearts of all the better sorts of the company." The exhausted captain, apparently in an attempt to shut Hopkins up, relented and commuted the sentence. Hopkins lived to see another adventure in the offing, his greatest yet as one of the first English arrivals to the New England colonies. The *Mayflower* passage would lead him to Plymouth Colony and to a man who surpassed even his own recklessness: Arthur Peach.

For Peach, Hopkins's tavern provided a haven to plot his escape from his servitude. If Winslow's brooding presence back at Careswell bordered on insufferable, Hopkins, with his freewheeling nature, unwittingly breathed life into Peach's impulse to rebel. The trailblazing entrepreneur demonstrated not only that it was possible to resist Plymouth Colony's social constraints but also that doing so could be lucrative. Hopkins, who infused his watering hole with his cult of personality, held out a natural attraction, having transformed from servant to master on his own terms and through grand adventure. In Peach's search of the next big opportunity, the Hopkins tavern offered him a place to plan and search for his fortunes.

Away from the toil and isolation of the Winslow estate, Peach could speak freely with other servants, including Richard Stinnings, who matched Peach complaint for complaint about Winslow with his own gripes about his master, the local cooper Robert Bartlett. Bitter to find himself a servant with no chance to enrich himself in the style of his master, Peach opened his eyes to a possibility of another kind. Dorothy Temple tantalized him, even covered in her modest clothes. And while Peach has long been assumed to have been the lone Irish person living in Plymouth Colony in 1638, Dorothy was likely Irish, too. Peach and Temple, the two outliers in the small settlement, bonded.

Peach's encounters with Dorothy changed everything. His visits to the dimly lit tavern soon transformed from the occasional respite and grousing session to a chance to dream of a future with a woman. Though authorities forbade romance and marriage between servants, Peach and his lover consummated their relationship. It is possible that the young couple entered into an understanding of their own that mirrored official marriages. These understandings between indentured couples were so common that a few years later the Virginia General Assembly enacted an ordinance curbing secret, illicit marriages between servants.

It was a high-stakes romance. If Plymouth Colony authorities discovered the relationship, Peach and Temple risked being whipped and fined to the point of ruin. In an example of these laws in action, Massachusetts Bay Colony in 1634 prosecuted a young man for his seduction of the governor's maidservant, "pretending love in the way of marriage, when himself professes he intended none; and also for insisting her to go with him into the cornfield." It is easy to imagine young Dorothy, deprived of a right to a personal life by law, having trouble declining similar trysts in the cornfields near Winslow's Careswell estate with a dashing young former soldier named Peach. Male servants greatly outnumbered female; she had her pick, which suggests that he had looks and charm enough to stand out.

In addition to his other grievances and motivations, Peach's imminent flight from Plymouth also protected Dorothy from the discovery of their affair. Only after Peach left the colony—taking with him whatever emotional and financial support he offered—did Dorothy realize she was pregnant, a secret she kept from colony leaders. The men who followed Peach out of Plymouth Colony—or the Peach gang, as Thomas Jackson, Richard Stinnings, and Daniell Crosse became known—each sought a way out of his own dead end. To reach new beginnings, the escapees "rane away from their maisters in the night," leaving Plymouth behind and heading south toward the settlement of Manhattan—or at least they hoped they were heading that way. Peach must have taken extra care as he absconded in "secret going away." Leaving the Careswell estate, he headed a stone's throw west to an indigenous trail that by 1638 was known as the "Green Harbor Path." The route's proximity to the house must have caused Peach some amount of worry. Ten-year-old Josiah, sleeping within earshot, may have been the member of the Winslow household who would have most relished sounding the alarm; archeologists later unearthed a small whistle at the site of the Careswell Estate that was just the right size for a boy.

The path led farther away from Careswell, hugging the coastline to Plymouth Colony proper, where Peach surreptitiously met up with the other servants. Continuing south and deeper into the woods, the men then chose another trail that seemed untraceable, "for they went not the ordinarie way, but shaped such a course as they thought to avoyd ye pursute." But as daylight faded, their surroundings became difficult to navigate.

In contrast to the reassuringly domestic pinewood fences, smoke-darkened stone hearths, and warm clay walls of the settlement, the menacing black oaks in the forest provided poor shelter as the night wind whistled around the small band. The familiar sound of the ocean lapping up against the marshy coastline was long gone.

As they were resting in the dismal clearing of their campsite, the daylight hours brought back the overwhelming July heat and the painful reality of their current predicament. The men could see part of one of the labyrinthine forest trails but little else. As they smoked tobacco in the lonely woods, Peach heard an indistinct rustle for a second time. The four men caught each other's eyes as the sounds became louder. On the one hand, the escapees feared capture by their masters; on the other hand, the noise gave them hope. Deer often crisscrossed the ancient trail. The likelihood of successfully taking down nimble prey with the rapier Peach carried was slim, but the men's hunger pains pushed them to ignore the odds. Peach's companions held out hope that their battle-tested leader could overtake whatever drew near them from the wilderness.

2

# MURDER

—————————

"[I] will kill him, and take what he has from him."

—*Arthur Peach*

As the sound approached, Peach and his men peered into the warm day's hazy sunlight filtering through the trees, but instead of the soft outline of a slender doe, they spotted the contours of a tribesman. The man had a distinctive gait. Indigenous infants were bound, "toes in," to cradleboards, producing this characteristic walk. Surprised at the sudden appearance of the sojourner, none of Peach's men jumped into action to engage him. They did not try to trade for sustenance, to ask for guidance through the woods, or to learn the latest tidings from the area. Peach failed to play the leader and act. In their collective moment of hesitation, the tribesman passed by them without salutation, vanishing as though an apparition into the verdant woods. They missed their chance to turn the encounter to their benefit.

The bare-chested traveler could have been a tribal scout soon to be followed by others—rumors abounded among settlers of the ferocious and unsettling tactics the indigenous people used during attack, "barking like dogs and howling during battle." But the cricks and calls of the ancient New England forest revealed no indication of tribesmen signaling one another. As day turned to night once again, the servants could set aside any fears and hunker down, taking comfort in the fact that they hadn't encountered other Indians.

The man they saw had been approximately Peach's age and relative social status—indentured servants and young tribesmen shared the same low standing—but, intriguingly, he appeared to have a purpose. That meant he had come through the woods prepared for an expedition. Even without daring to believe that the tribesman carried something as precious as wampum, a little food alone meant strength, which meant salvation for them. As Peach waited for sleep that night, head on the hard ground, he made up his mind. He whispered his plan. "[I] will kill him," Peach said, "and take what he has from him."

The indigenous man who had swept past the Peach gang turned out to be the Nipmuc who would become known as Penowanyanquis. The last days of July were a difficult time to be apart from his close-knit family. This was the period of *chikohtaekeeswush* (the rising heat moon); the strawberry moon had waned. Many fellow tribesmen had also traveled toward the shore for the short-lived season of ocean fishing, after which all would return to their homeland for festivities and thanksgiving. The "Three Sisters"—the staple crops of corn, squash, and beans, given that designation for the protective spirits that watched over them—flourished. It was time for celebration, feasting, and courting. Such reunions with kin awaited Penowanyanquis as he fell asleep in his own bare-bones encampment some distance from the fugitive settlers.

While Peach and his companions entered the forest shirking the orders of their superiors, Penowanyanquis methodically fulfilled the directives of his. After he came across the Peach gang and restored his energy with a night of sleep, he continued on his way in a hurry. Though this territory belonged to an allied tribe, the Narragansett, for whom he was on a mission to Plymouth Colony's Aptucxet trading post, the next tract of land he was set to enter belonged to his tribal enemies, the Wampanoag. The Wampanoag tolerated the Narragansett even less than they did the Nipmuc. The Wampanoag and

Massasoit, their sachem, or chief, controlled the land on which the trading post sat, leasing it to Plymouth Colony settlers under the strictly negotiated terms of a celebrated international trade agreement. The 1627 accord established and sanctioned trade at Aptucxet, a first-of-its-kind arrangement in the New World that set the New England currency as wampum. Leaders from England, Plymouth Colony, and New Amsterdam, and the sachem Quachattasett of the Manamet, a subtribe of the Wampanoag, signed off on the comprehensive treaty, delineating land use near the trading post and regulating the exchange of beaver pelts.

The Wampanoag sachem felt threatened by the neighboring Narragansett, who had suffered less from the exotic illnesses brought to the New World by the English. Allying himself with the settlers, Massasoit hoped to repel potential Narragansett incursions. Massasoit offered Plymouth Colony almost unrestrained support, beyond what any other indigenous entity had proffered. By 1638, Massasoit chafed at the by-product of an arrangement that worked all too well. He faced the unpalatable situation of Narragansett traipsing into his land, not to fight but to trade. The savvy sachem wanted to restrict the lucrative transactions at the Aptucxet post not only to allow his subjects to prosper but also as leverage for peace within his tribe. Some of the lesser sachems Massasoit ruled over, like the ambitious Corbitant, stood at odds with their leader. They were displeased by his willingness to sell off land to the English and by his complicity in settlers' dealings. The wampum-generating indigenous fur trade appeased those who otherwise might rise up against Massasoit. As more members of other tribes usurped business at Aptucxet, Massasoit's position waned.

The Narragansett leader, Canonicus, understood Massasoit's position and tread carefully because of it. A few years earlier, Canonicus and his tribe had learned firsthand the perilous risk of encroaching on a rival's trading territory. In 1633, the Dutch and the Pequot signed a treaty allowing the Dutch to trade from the Pequot's optimistically named outpost, the House of Good Hope. The treaty explicitly permitted Dutch trade with other Algonquian tribes who crossed into

Pequot lands to sell their goods. While the Pequot had signed off on the deal to appease the Dutch, they were quick to preserve their trade monopoly by attacking and killing Narragansett representatives who arrived to trade.

Canonicus and other Narragansett leaders could not approach the Aptucxet trading post themselves; it fell to far more anonymous figures, such as Penowanyanquis, to carry out the sensitive trade mission on their behalf. Given that Penowanyanquis crossed Massasoit's Wampanoag territory trading the most sought-after commodity possible, beaver, for the most powerful regional enemy conceivable, the Narragansett, Massasoit must have been aware of the tribesman's presence. This alone meant that he traveled under threat of death. The beaver he carried on behalf of Mixanno, the son of a Narragansett tribal leader, symbolized a groundswell of tense geopolitics.

As Massasoit sold land to the English, and Narragansett edged toward a trade relationship with the same colonists, Massasoit's divided underlings had reason to stoke resentment at the sachem's leadership. The neighboring Narragansett would have been well aware of this dynamic. For this reason, the fact that Penowanyanquis traveled alone jumps out. It seemed entirely possible that the Narragansett goaded the Wampanoag to attack, using the Nipmuc tribesman as bait. If the trade went well, the result would be a financial success for the Narragansett; if Massasoit's men harmed Penowanyanquis, the Narragansett would succeed in a different way—provoking a strategic rift between the Wampanoag and the Plymouth Colony settlers. Within all this intrigue, no one could have foreseen the desperate actions of the fugitive waiting in the woods, Arthur Peach. Penowanyanquis traced the banks of Cusset Creek for nearly five miles before traveling inland to the outcropping where the Cusset and Manamet rivers converged. A verdant green undergrowth and sun-flecked trees enfolded the Manamet, which wound its way south of Plymouth Colony. The indigenous man stayed alert as he carried his wares in a deerskin-hide satchel slung across his chest. He likely had pulled back his long, dark hair to keep it out of his eyes, as was customary among tribesmen. By the time the narrow trail, hemmed in with ghostly hanging reindeer moss, finally opened onto a clearing, the traveler would have been footsore and weary.

The Aptucxet trading post, a saltbox structure built with "hewn oak planks," stood alone in the otherwise uninhabited area. A small hog pen and plot of land for corn provided the lone signs of cultivation. A few settlers, rough-and-tumble men capable of securing a good exchange and defending this isolated position, operated the post on behalf of Plymouth Colony. With its store of wampum ready to exchange for pelts, the site presented a tempting target for plunderers.

Penowanyanquis's bag weighed down his shoulder and back. The beaver pelts inside were much heavier than they appeared. North American beavers were bigger than their extinct European counterparts and had thicker coats to handle cold New England winters. It is possible that Penowanyanquis had hunted the beavers himself and offered to trade the pelts on behalf of the Nipmuc protectors, the Narragansett. Beaver make their homes in waterways and are notoriously difficult to track. Their large tails brush away their prints as they move, but those who live close to the animals' freshwater dams can easily spot them. The Nipmuc's clustered dwellings near such streams provided an advantage for hunting. Seated in canoes, tribesmen waited for long stretches with arrows at the ready until the animals surfaced for air. The pelts taken from the animals to fashion wide-brimmed felt hats for French royal courtiers were as glossy and soft as the silk with which they were paired.

The customs of France and other faraway nations were more real to Penowanyanquis than we might expect. The European settlers on all sides of his tribal lands had brought with them a spectacular assortment of precious and useful objects, including weapons, brass kettles, looms, coats, and boots, evoking very different worlds full of material extravagances and new technologies. The historical record reflects indigenous men eager to barter for these items, especially metal pots. With hollowed-out burls (the outgrowths on tree trunks) providing bowls that were both unbreakable and impermeable, and flat stones making ideal cooktops, the demand for kettles may at first glance seem perplexing.

Archaeologists have shed light on the interest, unearthing brass arrowheads scattered in seventeenth-century Pequot War battle sites. Previously, arrow tips had been made of lithic stone, but tribesmen had begun carving up and repurposing brass kettles into deadly metal arrowheads, each tribe establishing its own distinct shape. For a trader such as Penowanyanquis, learning new languages opened up an array of business opportunities and provided access to these valuable goods. Possessing passable English, which there are reasons to think Penowanyanquis did, made it easier to absorb the fascinating, exotic details of life on the other side of the sea amassed during the exchanges.

Whatever Penowanyanquis picked up about the Old World, the indigenous trader probably did not gather insight into the life of Louis XIII. Yet Penowanyanquis's mission into the heart of Wampanoag country turned, to some degree, on the whims of the man who had been king of France since turning eight years old in 1610. The king had the unusual affliction of a double set of teeth and spoke with a terrible stutter, which required him, on occasion, to "hold his tongue out" until he regained control of his words. Deprived of eloquence, the king's fashions made some of his loudest statements. By embracing a romantic style involving loosely hung fabrics and furs, Louis XIII created ferocious demand in France and much of England for beaver.

Though the European beaver began to go extinct from overhunting, North America promised a convenient new supply of the sought-after animal. By 1638, their pelts had become precious, and the demand outpaced the capacity of the land. American Indians, who enjoyed sleeping on sumptuous animal hides six to seven layers deep for warmth during cold winters, never in their wildest nightmares imagined stripping resources the way the settlers had done. In describing the ferocity of the Iroquois fighting over pelts during the Beaver Wars, one French Jesuit wrote that "my pen has no ink black enough to describe [their] fury." Penowanyanquis felt with his own rough fingers the luxurious softness of the fur—fit for a sachem or a king.

As Penowanyanquis approached the Aptucxet trading post, he took in the sight of the small saltbox set by the water. For those such as Penowanyanquis who were well acquainted with local vegetation, enough food sources presented themselves to keep him satiated long enough to reach the trading outpost. The nearby forests, including the one he just left behind, had been purposefully cultivated by indigenous people to yield abundant nut trees. The intentionally interspersed trees offered tended gardens shelter and helped create stunning vistas of sweeping, pastoral lands. Indeed, a contemporary describing the forest where Penowanyanquis walked, and where the Peach gang hid, noted with surprise that the woods were so well cleared they "could be penetrated even by a large army."

The young trader had likely subsisted for days on berries and bountiful nuts; he also had possibly eaten fish or turtle and *nokake*, the sweet, hearty cake-like food American Indians in the region carried for subsistence on lengthy treks through the wilderness. Still, the stench from the pigsty in the hot July sun would have signaled to Penowanyanquis the presence of a singularly delectable food source to which only settlers had access.

With each party in possession of something the other wanted, intense wrangling could occur, but trading between settlers and tribesmen usually proved a highly structured affair, marked by ritualized gift giving and pleasantries. The Nipmuc boasted rare weaving skills, forging baskets with strips of black ash or white oak, seamlessly woven and then stamped with vegetable dye in decorative motifs, featuring geometric patterns of natural elements, including suns and feathers, or turtles, which were central to their creation myth. The designs conveyed messages to basket makers even from other tribes—details that might reflect, in the words of one scholar, "the path one traveled through life"—but those subtle messages would have been lost on colonists. Settlers coveted the baskets because they had few means for transporting their goods. They were a perfect gift for Penowanyanquis to bring for the men at the trading post.

For their parts, the traders stationed at the desolate outpost probably offered the tired traveler salted or cured pork. In the end, Penowanyanquis exchanged his valuable wares, "three beaver skins and beads," for "five fathom [of wampum] and three coats." The beads Penowanyanquis offered likely came from the same repurposed brass that indigenous men had been using for arrowheads. Brass retained value for settlers, too, and they wanted it back when possible. The wampum Penowanyanquis received would have been polished beads made from clam or quahog shells, the common currency of the New England colonies. English and indigenous people alike accepted it as compensation for goods and services, with students at Harvard College even using it to make tuition payments. Fathoms of wampum beads constituted a fixed amount of currency; each fathom consisted of 360 wampum beads strung in six-foot lengths, and one fathom equaled about one contemporary English pound sterling. Wampum came either purple-hued or white, the darker being more valuable.

Penowanyanquis negotiated a good deal. In the mid-1630s, an English beaver hat ran about five pounds sterling, an exorbitant sum. The plague had hit London in 1636, temporarily driving down the price of beaver and resulting in cargo holds in English ports filled with rotted pelts. With Black Death sweeping the lands, not a soul had been present to welcome the barks. By 1638 trade had improved, and Penowanyanquis and his Narragansett partners benefited from prime selling conditions.

Leaving with thirty linear feet of the small shell beads, Penowanyanquis's cache of spoils would have rattled as he moved. He was as conspicuous and vulnerable as a man departing a bank into a dark alley with a bag of gold. Penowanyanquis followed the creek downstream and turned back toward the territory of the Narragansett who awaited him.

Traveling toward Mixanno's *wetu* (home), the young trader walked due west through pitch pine and scrub oak, the well-trodden path beneath his thin deerskin soles softened into silt. He likely walked on the Patuxet Trail, which is marked by a large outcropping of granite rock bearing three indigenous petroglyphs, sacred etchings carved into the stone. Penowanyanquis could see the powerful image of a human hand, fingers splayed, a marker of shamanism or a vision quest. Next to it was an eastward-pointing arrow and a sun. Both of these symbols likely indicated that he was leaving the ocean "dawnland" behind and heading inland. These stone landmarks, *sunsh nipámu*, along the trail guided him as he logged dozens of miles on foot on the long walk homeward. This landscape was rich with visual meaning for the tribesman, "a vast memorial terrain . . . continuously being cleared, refreshed, and narrated by those [indigenous people] who walked by." Peach and his men, in contrast, missed the significance of nearby landmarks and found the forest a daunting place.

Penowanyanquis at last reached the Narragansett Trail. The trail was one of the many ancient paths, as one scholar describes them, "deeply worn from centuries of travel by bare and moccasined feet, some as much as two feet deep in places." Today, in order to drive the many miles Penowanyanquis traversed, circuitous routes are unavoidable, but on these footpaths he followed a precise cardinal point west. Hundreds of years later, a Narragansett two-time Boston Marathon victor trained barefoot on these same convenient trails that crisscross the woods of present-day Rhode Island.

One obvious obstacle remained for Penowanyanquis: the Peach gang, whose camp he had spotted a few days before on the very footpath on which he walked. Though Penowanyanquis likely owned a lithic-reduced stone hatchet, fashioned from foraged rock, the earliest treaties between tribes and settlers dictated the well-established custom of trading while entirely unarmed—no guns, bows, or hatchets allowed. But Penowanyanquis could find comfort in the rarity of violence, outside of declared war, between colonists and his people.

For Peach and his companions, what would ordinarily have been trivial—the tribesman who passed them days earlier—was akin to an uncaught fish for a castaway. Now Peach's scheme took hold to attack the indigenous trader if he returned the same way. Peach hunkered in the campsite, which was at least protected from the fiery sun and had access to water. The trail was clearly an established thoroughfare, which meant that others might also pass. They need only wait.

Before long, a sound echoed through the woods, a reminder of Peach's days in Ireland: the percussive rhythm of horse hooves beating against the ground. Out of the forest gloom, a different sort of traveler than the earlier passerby burst into view. The rakish John Throckmorton, a prominent settler and the patriarch of a large family, appeared mounted on horseback. The escaped servants shot to their feet. Gaunt, wide-eyed, clothes dirty, arms out, specters of the strong men they had been just five days before, they approached the trail, once again lacking a clear plan.

Throckmorton was nothing if not decisive, and he did not like what he saw. He sensed the possibility of an attack. He knew that the value of his mount alone was enormously enticing, considering how few people in the colonies owned horses, a relatively new species on the continent—the ears would have even been marked and cut to show Throckmorton's ownership of the animal. The horse and rider thundered by the campsite, Throckmorton confident that his animal could knock down the beleaguered men if they dared pursue him.

The sun high, tempers rose as the gang settled back around their fire in the aftermath of another fruitless encounter. Peach must have reached the end of his rope. As a soldier, he had been accustomed to eating "corne, pease, oatemeale, beefe, butter, fish" and drinking "strong water" or "malt." He had also been in superb condition, facing grueling marches while shouldering weapons and provisions that weighed nearly sixty-five pounds. The strapping young Peach could have been one of the soldiers who took on the Herculean task of carrying metal cannons out into the wilderness during the Pequot War.

A few years earlier, men lost in the wilderness for a comparable amount of time as the Peach gang described "being almost senseless for want of rest." One seasoned traveler who attempted the same path described the debilitating route, noting that it surpassed any travail he had faced "so far this three or four years [of exploration], wherefore I fear my feet will fail me." The men's faces would be haggard, lips cracked, eyes ringed red from lack of proper sleep, and cheeks scorched black from the campfire, with near starvation clouding their thinking. Jackson, Stinnings, and Crosse had counted on

Peach's judgment when they fled Plymouth Colony under his direction. Now they faced a fight for survival.

In fairness to Peach, they had already secured their freedom. The only thing left to do was resettle somewhere far from the reach of Plymouth Colony's leaders, who must have been grousing at the loss of four able servants and the destabilizing precedent set by their getaway. As time passed, the danger of continuing on through the woods, where they risked apprehension, could be weighed against the advantages of waiting to see who else might come up that path. The latter plan rested on Peach's rapier.

At the next rustle, there was not a moment to spare. Losing another opportunity could well lose Peach his men; reaching safety on his own would test him even more than what they faced together. Penowanyanquis materialized on the path for a second time. While the trail was well traveled, the convergence of the indigenous man who had come of age in a pre-contact world and the four escapees from across the ocean, in the hinterlands of the sparsely populated New England colonies, represented a portentous twist of fate.

The beginning of their interaction is lost to history. *"Aquene!"* Penowanyanquis may have called out to the ragged men, announcing his approach by signaling peaceful intentions.

In a glance, as Throckmorton had, the experienced trader must have read the other men's desperation and the slew of unpleasant possibilities that came with it. In a bizarre vignette, Peach, despite being half-starved and bent on violence, played the welcoming and leisurely host, stoking the fire and waving Penowanyanquis over, his rapier dangling ominously at his waist. His companions gathered around him at the makeshift campsite as the tribesman joined them by the fire.

Penowanyanquis's trade experiences lent him some advantage with the group of four, men who in some ways resembled those at Aptucxet with whom he had successfully negotiated. He may have considered sharing his *nokake*. Most pressing, he had to gauge their intentions.

Peach rose to his feet and moved closer. He offered tobacco, a reassuring reminder of home for the tribesman. A tinge of relief must have passed through him as he reached forward over the smoldering fire for the pipe, heavy and warm to the touch. Then Peach transformed from host to hunter. He drew his weapon. Just as quickly, one of Peach's companions rebuked him, hoping to keep their leader from harming Penowanyanquis. As outgoing Plymouth Colony governor William Bradford later noted, Peach's friends reported after the fact that they "were some thing afraid."

Rapier readied, Peach thundered back, "Hang him, rogue, I had killed many of them!" In the time it took Penowanyanquis to realize that he had walked into a trap, Peach had thrown his weight into a devastating blow and stabbed him. Then he "made the second thrust, but mist him." The other three men leapt to their feet, with no way to turn back from Peach's scheme. One of the men—not specified in contemporary accounts of the events—joined the bloodshed and also "struck at him." Penowanyanquis bounded out of reach, "getting from them a little way into the swamp." But "they pursued him." Inside the dense thicket of the swamp, the thrashing blows of weapons devolved into a flurry of motion and screaming. Penowanyanquis tumbled down into the brackish water, writhing out of reach. Peach and his men tried to ensure that they killed Penowanyanquis, but even while wounded, the tribesman showed incredible agility. Once more "they mist him."

Adrenaline surely rising, Penowanyanquis sprinted and tripped through the warm, murky water farther into the depths of the swamp. Thick clumps of impenetrable reeds sliced his ankles. The injuries erupted in blinding pain. Blood gushed from his stomach wounds into dark liquid clouds around him as his body sank. One last time Penowanyanquis "heard them close by him" and tried to elude his pursuers. He ventured even farther into "the swamp, till he fell down again, when they lost him quite."

Penowanyanquis himself was likely quite lost at this point—and critically injured. He prayed for help. The dense vegetation obscured the sun and any means of navigation, and the enormous, lush leaves of stinking skunk cabbage plants underfoot emitted an unpleasant dizzying heat.

He may have reached the small island that existed at the time where he could hide himself for the night. If he did, he would have upset the gaggles of breeding black geese for which Seekonk was named—*seakihonk*, literally "black goose." The overlay of their wild honking and thundering wings would have registered as an alarm that had meaning for his ears alone. As dusk fell, end-of-summer fireflies hovered, providing pinprick orbs of glowing light. His eyes could track them as his breathing and movements slowed in the overnight chill. Unable to get warm and dry, in all likelihood he fell into a state of hypothermic shock. Massasoit called the bog where Penowanyanquis hid the "dead swamp"; the putrid water may well have been non-potable. The injured man either remained painfully thirsty as the night wore on or sickened himself by drinking the water.

Penowanyanquis left no record of the hours he spent hiding in the swamp, but a fellow Algonquian man born in the eighteenth century wrote about the panic he himself felt after getting lost in a similarly impassable environment:

> Shut out from the light of heaven—surrounded by appalling darkness—standing on uncertain ground—and having proceeded so far that to return, if possible, were "as dangerous as to go over." This was the hour of peril—I could not call for assistance on my fellow creatures; there was no mortal ear to listen to my cry. I was shut out from the world and did not know but that I should perish there, and my fate forever remain a mystery to my friends.

And so it was for Penowanyanquis. He was out of reach of Peach's rapier, but he remained lost, injured, and disoriented in a nightmarish scene.

Peach's boastful battle cry as he assaulted Penowanyanquis spoke volumes. In the fateful moment of bloodlust, his motivation to attack shifted from deprivation and need to anger—from theft to murder.

His peculiar justification—"Hang him, rogue, I had killed many of them"—indicated his conviction that killing Indians in the past empowered and entitled him to kill another one. One way to interpret the declaration is to conclude that Peach killed Penowanyanquis *because* he was an American Indian. And, indeed, Peach's indirect reference to the Pequot War reflected the ways in which violence in war carried over into everyday life and desensitized this particular man to its brutality. Soldiers such as Peach had aimed not just at winning battles or wars but also at the annihilation of an entire people. While skirmishes between tribes typically came with low fatalities, suddenly anything was possible, including random murders.

Ironically, given Penowanyanquis's apparent familiarity with English, it is possible that he had fought with his Narragansett allies in the Pequot War on the side of colonists like Peach. Many Narragansett took up arms with settlers against the Pequot, and this could account for whatever English-language skills Penowanyanquis possessed. It would be a dark twist of fate if indeed Peach's violent attack was directed against a former brother-in-arms.

Resentment fueled hate. In those past military missions, Peach's service protected colonial interests by fighting indigenous men. Yet Peach remained chained to superiors, a fugitive from their inhumane rules, while this indigenous stranger approximately his own age walked in freedom through the woods. His rage burned even hotter, surely, because his stature as a servant meant that he had to give up a woman. Had he known she was carrying his child, his rage surely would have been hotter still.

For Peach, Penowanyanquis's demise also funded the survival of his men. From hopeless and homeless, the escapee Peach reverted within a few minutes back to the wily, merciless soldier he had once been—glory days regained. It was an incredible reversal of fortune. With unclean hands he counted out each piece of the tribesman's wampum, currency that signified food, clothing, and freedom if it could get Peach and his men far enough away to leave their deed behind. The stolen coats may have become props for revelry, perhaps tempting the undernourished outcasts to try on for size the garments that had been destined for the great sachem of the Narragansett and his warrior son.

Any raucous merriment was soon interrupted, however, with yet another encounter in the desolate woods catching them off guard. The newcomers who descended on the Peach gang this time were Narragansett, men fully able to defend themselves if necessary.

No doubt Peach and his men pushed aside the stolen coats. As far as Peach knew, they had just killed these newcomers' brother, their tribesman, a fellow Narragansett. He would not have understood that Penowanyanquis was a Nipmuc, a lesser tribe that submitted to the Narragansett. Not that the distinction shielded the Peach gang. The Nipmuc fell within the Narragansett protectorate, which proffered the victim a special degree of protection. The power structure rested on keeping subsidiary tribes safe.

The Narragansett urged the strangers—who were apparently lost—to accompany them out of the woods to safety. The tribe's members were known for their benevolence. Strangely, the desperate souls rejected their offers of assistance, claiming that they were servants accompanying one of their masters, John Barnes, to Connecticut. Barnes, in actuality, was not the master of any of them—and, of course, was not in the woods. Nor were they heading to Connecticut. It was a clever stratagem on Peach's part. If word did reach Barnes in Plymouth, he would find his servants accounted for and chalk up the report to a miscommunication. Since Barnes was a powerful merchant and moneylender, Peach subtly warded off interference by using his name.

The Narragansett, however, remained baffled. Concerned for the welfare of the settlers, the Indians—with a parting plea that Peach and his companions make for safe haven at present-day Providence, Rhode Island—reversed direction in order to go that way themselves and alert their colonial ally, the formidable founding father of Providence, Roger Williams. (Local tribesmen referred to and treated Williams as "governor," even though he technically lacked that title.)

Members of the Narragansett tribe were already on edge that late summer of 1638. When the *naunaumemoauke* (earthquake) had struck earlier in the summer, the Narragansett women and children crouched down and swayed with the earth as it rumbled. Nearby trees shook. Scouts and warriors raced along the network of forest paths, creating a chain reaction as they carried news of the trembler.

Damage from the earthquake was not what disturbed the Narragansett; their lightweight edifices, often built in clearings, posed little risk of falling down. The real fear came from what the earthquake portended. Their ancient legends foretold the horror due to strike their tribe sometime after the earthquake subsided—a plague that might kill them all. The countdown to the death and destruction of their people began.

Tramping deeper into the eerie woods, the Peach gang remained on the move, though an intense foreboding of their own haunted their progress. The attack on Penowanyanquis had succeeded, but the sudden appearance of the Narragansett soon after had presented a wrinkle: their victim might be discovered at any moment. Peach pushed with his companions through the forest toward Providence, fearing that they would draw attention to themselves if they did not comply with the Narragansett tribesmen's advice. But the next man Peach came across in the woods entirely confounded him, neither presenting a threat nor offering assistance.

Isolated on the far outskirts of Providence, a figure emerged at the gnarled wooden door of a hand-hewn cottage. His home rested atop a small, cleared hillock with no settlement in sight. Through the door, every conceivable surface of his queer habitat could be seen covered with books, 184 volumes, the first substantial library in New England. It was as though some kind of oracle stood before Peach and his men. This mysterious hermit, in fact, was a product of a very civilized history.

William Blackstone was a Cambridge University–educated minister who, like so many others in the colonies, risked his life for his beliefs. A capable organizer, he had helped found the settlement of Boston, but after it grew in size he decided to leave with his books for quieter pastures, selling his land on Beacon Hill. He rode his bull all the way to the secluded area outside Providence called Pawtucket in search of "undisturbed solitude." There he fondly named his new home Study Hill.

His home in late July 1638 overlooked his expansive apple orchard of home-grafted Yellow Sweetings—his own creation and the first apple bred in America—which burst with green leaves and tender off-shoots, ready to blossom into delectably tart, blush-red apples when the weather cooled. With his beloved brindle bull grazing contentedly in the summer heat, the "Sage of the Wilderness" laid claim to almost all he needed. Indeed, Blackstone had a ready quip for the occasional settler who intruded on his serenity: "Could ye not leave the hermit in his corner?" One person proved an exception—someone whose presence he had ensured, at great expense.

The young tribeswoman who lived with Blackstone had escaped from his previous home twice, but the authorities at Massachusetts Bay Colony who apprehended her implemented a horrifying idea to keep her from running off again: they heated an iron tool until it glowed molten red and branded her slender shoulder with a symbol distinct to Blackstone. The ridges of the scar marred her skin, an enduring reminder of his ownership. She had always headed south toward the Narragansett when she fled. Blackstone's move to Study Hill in Narragansett territory may have been to appease his young captive.

When the ragtag fugitives happened upon this unlikely manor in the forest, the peevish Blackstone quashed any notion they might have had of holing up there before continuing to Providence. He did not want anyone to intrude. Just as the Narragansett had done, he urged the four men toward Providence—let the civic-minded Roger Williams aid them. The dark-cloaked recluse may have given the Peach gang a reason to make haste; according to Peach, the eccentric minister told them "some Indians said, that they had hurt an Englishman" nearby. These brazen tribesmen, Blackstone apparently warned, roamed somewhere between Pawtucket and Providence, the very area Peach and his companions had to traverse. When the men departed, Blackstone must have watched until they vanished from the sight lines of his perch on Study Hill. But they didn't make it far; once again, the Peach gang stalled with indecision and apprehension.

The day after the Narragansett tribesmen's encounter with the gang, a second cohort of Narragansett, three hunters, stalked the far side of the woods. Small, plaintive sounds emanated from a source low to the ground. A wounded or abandoned baby animal—if that is what it proved to be—would mean easy prey, both needing to be relieved of its suffering and providing food and skins for the tribe. The trio quietly pressed forward, taking care not to spook the animal. But the feeble arms of a wounded man stretched forth from the mud at the edge of their footpath instead. The injured Nipmuc man had "made shift to gett home." Hoping to return to his family and native land, he had dragged himself to a spot where he might be found by passing indigenous travelers. The Narragansett men stood shocked at the sight of the anguished Penowanyanquis "groaning in the path." Their hunt became a rescue.

Nothing about the man's bloody gashes indicated that he had been attacked by another tribesman, which might have ended with a fatal wound to the skull. Moreover, a bear would have mauled a man, and a woodland catamount would have pierced the neck of its prey. The haphazard stabbings to the midsection of Penowanyanquis's body told a different story.

The tribesmen turned away from the wounded man briefly to scan the woods. They had passed and heard no one else on their approach. Quickly, the Narragansett would have ordered the fastest among them, a sprinter able to run without breaks, to race toward Study Hill in Pawtucket. Little did they know their runner was heading right toward the attackers who had mortally wounded Penowanyanquis. The tribesmen decided to start by questioning the nearby Blackstone, hoping for clues to decipher the unorthodox act of violence.

It was likely during the Narragansett's interview with Blackstone that the Peach gang, still close by in Pawtucket, somehow became aware of the tribesmen's discovery. To their horror, the fugitives realized that Penowanyanquis still lived. Peach and his men embarked on the race of their lives. Governor Winthrop documented that "when Arthur and his company heard [questions about the attack], they got on hose and shoes and departed in the night." Only steps ahead of the tribesmen, they left at once for Roger Williams, who had not yet heard about the attack. Whoever arrived first at Williams's home would have the upper hand.

# 3

## The Children's God

"Taubotne Kuttabotomish newutche yeu
Kessuckok wunnegin."
(I thank you for this beautiful day.)

—*A verse of Nipmuc prayer*

Long before Penowanyanquis's lonely trek through the woods outside of Plymouth in 1638, the same tribesman found himself alone on another occasion of life-transforming import. Being alone was in itself unusual for the Nipmuc, whose *wetus* or wigwams were clustered near each other and who hunted and communed with extended family. Other tribes may have boasted significantly more members and acreage, but these Nipmuc lands boasted strategic importance.

The sacred area comprising the Nipmuc heartland contained the headwaters for almost every single major river in eastern Massachusetts and Rhode Island. These Nipmuc waters, in fact, fed the very swamp in which Penowanyanquis took refuge from his assailants. The "Fresh Water People"—as *Nipnet* or *Nipmuc* translates—controlled the water of the entire region. Interestingly, as the Nipmuc, like the Narragansett and the Wampanoag, sold off their lands to English settlers throughout the seventeenth and eighteenth centuries, they refused to part with a stretch of territory adjacent to present-day Grafton, Massachusetts, *Hassanamessit*—a refusal that remained a mystery until puzzled researchers noticed the pattern of headwaters, representing the mystical beginnings of all the region's waterways.

Their territory counted other sources of spiritual power. Near Hassanamessit, and once included in it, the Nipmuc could access an extremely significant astronomical viewing chamber built out of carefully selected rocks. With the seventeenth century's absence of man-made light, the night sky shone as bright and illustrative as a computer screen. Indigenous elders taught their young how to read informative constellations carefully, with their eyes drawn to one in particular, the Pleiades. Within the stone cavern, the viewers' eyes dilated further, and the Pleiades' stars revealed themselves all the brighter.

Stone cairns built out on the horizon along the exact sight line of the viewing chamber highlighted the ideal spot to view the Pleiades. The rise and fall of the constellation denoted the beginning and end of the planting season. We know the historical fall of Pleiades today as Halloween. In 1524, when the explorer Giovanni da Verrazzano wrote to the king of France to describe the southern New England indigenous tribes, he noted that they planted according to "the flux of the lunar course, the birth [first rising] of the Pleiades." This vista onto the stars empowered the Nipmuc.

This sacred stretch of land also lay in proximity to one other mystical source of remarkable power, the seismically active *Nashobah* mountain. Nipmuc understood that a potent source of energy came from the nearby elevation. Indigenous people believed that "four winds were pent up inside it." They heard eruptions. "Terrible roarings and growls and rumbles would issue forth." Nipmuc feared that "the earth might have cracked open and revealed the dark, boiling innards." Settlers also took in the dreadful booming noises and believed they were about to be attacked by "cannon fire coming from inside the hill." It sounded to them "as if an army were trapped there." Whoever held this subterranean force had an invincible weapon that powerful shamans could wield to their advantage.

While the sun may have risen first on the proud coastal Wampanoag, the Nipmuc held the stars, seismic power, and the fresh, drinkable waters of the region in their fold. They would fight to keep this land at all costs. To this day, the Nipmuc hold the only "four and one-half acres [that] have never belonged to the white man" in Massachusetts, Nipmuc Nation. This may be the only land in New England that has never been traded out of indigenous hands. It is still revered and still called Hassanamessit.

A river or pond that provided drinking water, fish, and turtles flowed near the *wetu* of Penowanyanquis's family. This small settlement was bounded together by a serpentine rock wall, irregular at the surface and in its meandering structure. Unlike the walls colonial settlers constructed, indigenous stone walls included built-in seats for rest and reflection and gaps for wildlife and gusting breezes to pass through. Nipmuc culture and language reflected appreciation of nature. In the Algonquian language that Penowanyanquis spoke, there is no gendered classification of words like those in Romance languages. Instead, the Nipmuc language divided words as either animate or inanimate. The Nipmuc tellingly spoke of their treasured stones and rocks as animate—living, breathing, soulful objects of nature imbued with spirit. Indeed, their spirit stones, *manitou*, resemble elfin forest sprites. From forest glens, *manitou* peek out at visitors; they stand guard over sacred sites. Penowanyanquis and the Nipmuc lived among these stones, respecting them, using them for essential structures, appreciating their protection.

Intertwined in Penowanyanquis's story is the Nipmuc reverence for nature—particularly, spirit stones or *manitou*. This is an example of one in eastern Massachusetts.

Settlers who encountered Nipmuc and other Algonquian tribes noted the emphasis on family, observing parents as "very loving and indulgent to their children." One of the only surviving eighteenth-century documents written by a Nipmuc woman features the letter writer pleading for a reunion with her mother. Nipmuc mothers, while busy cooking and farming, swaddled babies with soft milkweed diapers and bundled them into the tightly woven baskets for which the tribe was famed, then trussed the infants into the branches of swaying trees to lull them. While busy with their labors, the young women sang a melodious traditional Nipmuc lullaby reminding themselves to place those precious babies only in the strongest limbs of the trees—a lullaby that according to Nipmuc lore came to be translated into English as "Rock-a-bye Baby."

Children in the era of Penowanyanquis's youth faced a series of rites of passage and transformations, in some cases signaled for or prompted by the individual as he or she grew up. Personal transformations affected basic facts of one's identities. For example, Penowanyanquis almost certainly grew up with a different name. Names were relatively fluid in Algonquian culture, and at times changed based on life events. As Roger Williams detailed, the Narragansett tribe even had expressions for those tribesmen who forgot their temporary names and for those who had no names at all.

For almost four centuries it has been wrongly understood that "Penowanyanquis" was the name of Arthur Peach's victim—the name of one of the most significant crime victims in colonial history. Careful scrutiny reveals that *penowe* is the term for "foreigner" or "stranger" in Algonquian dialect, the likely source for the descriptive appellation "Penowanyanquis." When he cried out for help as he lay bleeding, he may have used the word *penowanyanquis* to convey to the approaching Narragansett that he was on foreign land. He was a stranger away from his tribe, and he wanted to return home in his moment of despair. One current member of the Wampanoag Confederation describes the critical bond between indigenous peoples and homeland that surfaces in tribal naming: "We name ourselves after the place that is our nurturing, that sustains our life." The name Penowanyanquis, by contrast, was a repudiation of his dire and solitary physical circumstance.

What is certain is that at home Penowanyanquis was called anything but that. Within his clan and on Nipmuc territory, he had never been a stranger.

Back in his childhood, evidence suggests that the future-named Penowanyanquis found himself on a vision quest—one of the rare times an individual Nipmuc would be on his own—taking him far afield. He may have crunched gratifyingly through crisp *sochepo*, or snow, his feet bound with deer hide, the rest of his body mostly unclothed and exposed to the bracing air. He would have been accustomed to being outdoors year-round. (Roger Williams observed having "often seen the natives' children run about stark naked in the coldest days.") He was fit and would have been described as *yo cuttaunis wunnetu* (a fine child).

Like all Nipmuc boys, Penowanyanquis had been nurtured and carefully instructed on the survival skills needed to navigate his environment. He could effortlessly tell time and orient himself by reading the sun's position. He could also navigate using the dazzling starscape, gauzy layers of infinite white pinpoints. The nighttime "heavenly lights" clustered in familiar terrestrial forms overhead, just as the clouds bunched together to create images.

Penowanyanquis lived his days surrounded by animals. The elements mirrored back the images of these creatures. Unpredictable and wily gods appeared in, and communicated through, forest creatures and in celestial form, which the English found endlessly interesting. Roger Williams recorded with incredulity, "I find what I could never hear before, that they have plenty of Gods or divine powers: the Sun, moon, fire, water, snow, earth, the deer, the bear etc. are divine powers." Governor Winthrop noted that Indian deities of particular import appeared in "diverse shapes" and in some cases proffered very specific guidance. Magic saturated the world into which Penowanyanquis was born. In one ancient Nipmuc creation myth, the unassuming turtle saved early man from a tumbling free fall out of the sky. The turtle, after all, boasted the ultimate protection: a shell impervious to element or attack.

Penowanyanquis's generation marked the last of the Woodland American Indians—a remarkable era of stability and development from 1000 BCE to the arrival of the colonists. Because his childhood took place in those pre-contact years, Penowanyanquis knew few threats outside the relatively rare attacks by bears, wolves, and big cats. His tribe's submission to larger bands of indigenous people limited the possibility of tribal incursions. Even so, he likely set off on his vision quest armed. It is easy to imagine the young traveler delighting in the weight and importance of his weapon before being strong enough to wield it effectively, buoyed by his budding autonomy and the feelings of invincibility that accompany it.

At some point during Penowanyanquis's spiritual trek, an animal materialized in front of him. The type of animal has been lost to time, but in that instant, the boy's life changed. In the young child's eyes, the animal either behaved in a remarkable way or proved superb in its form alone, because its singularity revealed to the boy the presence of a deity within. The spirit before him exhilarated and transfixed him.

Penowanyanquis had only heard legends of this god; he had never encountered anything of such magnitude in his life. It was *Muckquachuckquand*, the "Children's God." An English missionary writing about Algonquian spirituality in the 1640s noted that indigenous youth were "mighty zealous in their worship" of "children-gods." Another settler observed how indigenous parents "dedicate[d] their children to the gods." Worried parents had reason to yearn for special protection for their children; at one Narragansett burial site from Penowanyanquis's era, where the deceased were buried in the fetal position, anthropological excavations showed that 35 percent were children younger than nine years old.

Algonquian language reflects the anxiety over young members of the tribes. The Narragansett believe that humans are imbued with two souls: one is transfixed to dream states, and the other is active and like "breath . . . vital"—*Michachunck*. It is the word for this vigorous soul that is intertwined with the word for Penowanyanquis's Children's God, *Muckquachuckquand.* No spark of life flares with more dynamic energy than a child's. The linked words spoke to children's fearless vitality—a quality that brought danger.

No wonder it seemed, as one scholar put it, that "children were not entirely committed to the living." The indigenous word for the whippoorwill bird reflects the perception of male children in the tribes. A peculiar creature, the whippoorwill is difficult to spot, eerily appearing only in the muted light of dawn and dusk and quickly vanishing. The small bird, which provokes dark legends, shares its name with the Mohegan word for boy, *muhkacuks*—perhaps because the two beings appear so fleeting in nature.

The Children's God came to boys to save them. Penowanyanquis later reported that the animal spoke to him, "bid[ding] him when ever he was in distress [to] call upon him." Gods could appear, as this animal had, without a trace—present without approach and gone without departing. Just as a spirit could inhabit an animal, it could also emanate into the human corpus, a transference Penowanyanquis was poised to receive from the Children's God. A seventeenth-century Algonquian man spoke of being subsumed by the embodiment of an array of spirits. He described having "been possessed from the crowne of the head to the soal of the foot with *Pawwawnomas* (imps), not onely in the shape of living creatures, as fowls, fishes, and creeping things, but brass, iron, and stone."

Childhood visions such as the one Penowanyanquis experienced could turn out to be overwhelming, powerful, and empowering. At the age of nine, Black Elk, the nineteenth-century holy man of the Oglala Sioux, recorded a detailed account of a similarly potent vision:

> The fifth Grandfather spoke, the oldest of them all, the Spirit of the Sky. "My boy," he said, "I have sent for you and you have come. My power you shall see!" He stretched his arms and turned into a spotted eagle hovering. "Behold," he said, "all the wings of the air shall come to you."

The Spirit of the Sky in eagle form continued,

"The winds and the stars shall be like relatives. You shall go across the earth with my power." Then the eagle soared above my head and fluttered there: and suddenly the sky was full of friendly wings all coming toward me.

The remarkable scene Black Elk encountered set his life's course as tribal leader.

Youthful visions could also terrify. In one legend, a group of indigenous young men and a boy, who lived far to the north of Penowanyanquis, reported a vision encounter in which part of their group faced a "dreadful black chasm" as the sky "struck on the earth with great violence and a terrible sound." Some boys traversed the chasm, calling to their remaining friends, "Leap! Leap! The sky is on its way down." Rewards awaited; they met the moon, who had "a white face and a pleasing air." They met the moon's brother, the sun. But these gifts came at a horrific cost. Those who made a "feeble attempt" at their jump plummeted into the unknown. Only two of the boys survived this vision.

Spirit intervention reflected the need for balance. A Nipmuc legend involved a vision of a spirit within a crow alighting on a man's hand and delivering a gift of seeds—and a corresponding burden. A tribal elder observed that "crows would always follow the people because [of] this food," taking from the crop they so critically relied on. The spirits offered benefits and liabilities concurrently, and required that people offer tribute for both. At moments of tribal thanksgiving, men beat distinct rhythms of thanks on their drums, at which point men and women lifted arms and feet higher and faster in recognition and honor.

Young Penowanyanquis would never again have to feel unprotected, and his link to the Children's God was one of the last things we know he spoke about before death. But what was the give-and-take of the Children's God toward Penowanyanquis that kept the world in balance? The Children's God hinted at a future threat, but this god had not foretold death as some guardian spirits did.

On the day of Penowanyanquis's birth, his mother likely dosed him with oil extracted from a bear. This oil offered sustenance for the "guardian spirit" that would one day find and protect her child. Algonquian tradition was clear: If the spirit who appeared during a child's vision quest was an animal, the protection was usually only viable as long as the animal survived. If the physical embodiment of Penowanyanquis's Children's God perished, so too would he. A shadow of danger clung to the growing boy.

Penowanyanquis understood that this special spiritual protection was tenuous—perhaps especially so in the upheavals of the post-contact world, including the extreme overhunting of animals. The new arrivals who had crossed the ocean changed everything. Another young Algonquian boy, Weetucks, who lived generations earlier, had a vision portending much of the dark happenings Penowanyanquis came to face. Spirit messengers visited Weetucks, warning of people from "beyond the sea" who "followed a path of greed and violence." The arrival of these men would bring destruction and disrupt "the balance of life." Weetucks spent hours carving dire warnings to his people on the smooth surface of a large rock that still sits in present-day Rhode Island.

Years later, not far from that carved admonition, when a foe raised a weapon against Penowanyanquis, the tribesman found the strength to escape and run. His adversaries stood confused. Not only did they face an unarmed man, they outnumbered him four to one, yet they fumbled their attempted murder as if a grand intercession took place. As though a powerful god had staved off the worst long enough for Penowanyanquis to seek justice.

Roger Williams later vividly recalled the ordinary start to the day on which he heard about the assault on Penowanyanquis. His Thursday morning, July 29, 1638, began with him writing letters at his desk at home in Providence, in the colony that a few years earlier he named "Ilande of the Rodes" and had become Rhode Island. The only recent excitement had taken place the day before, when Narragansett tribesmen stopped by to tell Williams about an encampment of four "almost famished" settlers lost in the woods, not far from the home of the old hermit Blackstone. It took Williams several rounds of back-and-forth messages, conveyed via Narragansett scouts, to convince these men—Arthur Peach and his companions—to accept his offer of refuge in Providence. While the scouts conveyed Peach's acceptance, the wanderers had not actually arrived at Williams's home that day or night.

By Thursday, Williams no longer preoccupied himself with the lost travelers. He had offered his hospitality and had to attend to other pressing matters. Years before, when banished from Massachusetts Bay Colony for his religious beliefs, Williams had turned a regrettable situation into an opportunity by founding his own settlement on his own terms. Williams's success as a trailblazer rested with his positive disposition and penchant for leadership. His soft features, kind eyes, and slightly plump girth suited his tolerant and agreeable nature.

Williams owed a portion of his triumphs to being a self-taught expert in indigenous cultures. He wrote numerous letters, journals, and books on American Indian customs and learned the Narragansett language. As he later noted, reflecting the cultural divide of the era, "God was pleased to give me a painful, patient spirit, to lodge with [tribesmen] in their filthy, smoky holes, even while I lived at Plymouth and Salem, to gain their tongue." His familiarity with the Narragansett allowed him to broker deals and turn crises between settlers and their indigenous neighbors into alliances.

As Williams focused on his correspondence and his wife cared for their son (also named Providence), one surprising member of the household stood out: an indigenous boy, Will. Williams recently had selected Will from a group of tribeswomen and children who had survived the ongoing Pequot War. "I have fixed mine eye," Williams reported, "on this little one with the red about his neck." The red was likely ochre, a natural pigment used for body paint.

As an Algonquian speaker, Williams could have simply used the boy's Pequot name, but that would have presented a challenge for the other English settlers who dealt with their household. Perhaps Williams did not have the heart to be the one to take away that part of the boy's identity, leading him to make this peculiar entreaty of

Governor Winthrop: "Only I request that you would please to give a name to him." Winthrop obliged; before separating the child from his mother, Winthrop named him Will. Not a diminutive for William, the name reflected the Puritan custom of using virtues as appellations, in this case capturing the tenacity the boy would need to survive being stripped from his family and tribe to labor in subjugation.

Williams's need for labor apparently trumped his professed abhorrence of "perpetual slavery," and the historical record does not fully indicate whether Williams perceived the young Pequot boy as a prisoner of war, a servant, or a slave. He later referred to the child as "my servant," a term that may shed light on his thinking. When captured indigenous children were "put to service" in colonial homes during King Philip's War later in the seventeenth century, they usually worked for a finite period that concluded at age twenty-four. Settlers sometimes identified indigenous children as "orphans" to justify this practice of forced labor, even if their parents were alive. Given the blurred lines between indenture and bondage and the artifice at play, some children saw servitude transform into slavery.

It was in the torpid heat of July 1637 near the undulating green hills of Quinnipiac, in present-day Connecticut, that English soldiers took as prisoners of war a Pequot woman of significant prominence, Wincumbone, and two or three of her children. Evidence indicates that this group of children included Will. Wincumbone, whose husband was the sachem Mononotto, had once intervened to save two English girls from death. Now she used her status and her history of benevolence toward the English to make two demands. She stipulated that the "English would not abuse her body" and insisted that "her children . . . not be taken from her."

Governor Winthrop appreciatively described Wincumbone as a "woman of a very modest countenance and behavior." At the urging of the influential military leader Lion Gardener, who argued for Wincumbone's "better" treatment, Winthrop obliged her requests. ("I have taken charge of her" and her children.) He added the small family to his slaveholding ranks. For Winthrop, separating Wincumbone from one of her children by sending Will to Roger Williams would not have violated his promises, at least in his eyes, since Will would be a messenger who could see his mother on errands to Massachusetts Bay. The plight of the indigenous children placed into servitude inspired the nineteenth-century author Catharine Sedgwick's popular novel *Hope Leslie*, which features Winthrop as a character deciding the fates of Mononotto's children, including Oneco, whose situation resembles Will's.

The sachem Mononotto was as exceptional as Will's remarkably savvy mother. One settler described the tribal leader as one of the "biggest" men, perhaps referring as much to his physical stature as his high-ranking position. Mononotto fought during the Pequot War and distinguished himself as a warrior. In battles that left the Pequot largely decimated through acts of genocide, Mononotto not only survived, he fought back against all odds.

Mononotto fought on July 13, 1637, in Sasquanikut, present-day Fairfield, Connecticut, through overnight "hand-to-hand" fighting in a swamp (a battle in which Arthur Peach could well have participated). The English had the Pequot hemmed in from all sides in a battle one historian described as "one of the fiercest of the war." At some point, Mononotto apparently fled, though no evidence ever materialized to confirm his capture or death. When enemy forces killed Mononotto's brother, the famed Pequot leader Sassacus, later that month, Massachusetts Bay leaders accepted "locks" of his hair as proof. Mononotto's ability to evade the forces closing in on him became legendary, even inspiring a colonial governor to take up pen in reverence.

> *Prince Mononotto sees his squadrons fly,*
> *And on our general having fixed his eye,*
> *Rage and revenge his spirits quickening,*
> *He set a mortal arrow in the string.*

As young Will attempted to acclimate to his new life with Roger Williams in Providence, he faced the unimaginable prospect of an existence without his family or tribe. Williams, however, may have

believed he offered the boy a relatively soft landing. He wrote to
Winthrop expressing gratitude for Will, describing himself as "truly
thankful for the boy" and assuring Winthrop that he would "endeavor
his good." It is hard to know, in the context of the era, what Williams's intentions to treat Will well meant. Williams does not record
any violent techniques of repression as used by other colonists, such
as branding, to keep the child in his household.

While serving in the Williams household, Will had the opportunity to learn Narragansett and to become familiar with the tribesmen
and children who lived nearby. He may have helped them with simple
tasks such as tapping maple trees for sap, waiting for the leaves to grow
to "the size of a field mouse's ear" to harvest the treat. He may have
sampled the "soothing" treat straight from the tree.

The child witnessed the Narragansett feasting and playing at leisure, kicking a ball hewn of layered grasses and leather, racing fast as
*ahtukquag* (deer) down a daunting two- or three-mile-long course—
tournaments of games that could go on for days at a time. Will's labors
for the Williams family likely precluded such playtime, though new
friendships were not out of the question. Intermarriage between the
Pequot and the Narragansett meant overlap of language, religion,
and some cultural traditions and made connections between the
boy and the surrounding Narragansett easier to forge.

Will also likely became familiar with a certain amount of English
and with Williams's religious doctrines, which would have been foreign to him at the outset. One colonist observed how enslaved Pequot
children were instructed. "The Indians children, girls and boys, we
have received into our houses, who are long since civilized, and in
subjection to us, painful and handy in their business, and can speak
our language familiarly . . . and begin to understand in their measure,
the grounds of Christian religion." But this enculturation was not
a choice. As Governor Winthrop noted, "Some of them ran away
and were brought again by the Indians our neighbors, and those we
branded on the shoulder." One seventeenth-century indigenous boy,
ten-year-old Jabez, son of Woompsleow of Pakachoag, fled, apparently successfully, in just such a desperate bid for freedom.

As others risked escape, Will remained; beyond the walls of the Williams household, the child faced threats including perpetual slavery and death. A group of settlers connived to trade boys like Will to far-off lands where life would be even more brutish—places from which there was no hope of ever seeing his family again.

This movement argued that "hostile" enslaved Indian people "be shipped out and replaced with Negroes" from Africa, whom they perceived as less threatening. Discussing a future "just war," one settler calculated that "we might easily have . . . [indigenous] children enough to exchange for Moores." Will likely understood the dreadful jeopardy he faced, watching firsthand as settlers killed Pequot men and sent away male youth. Colonial leaders even instituted a fine in the form of a "tribute," which was "levied against the Pequots for the birth of every male child." Women and girls presented little hazard, as indicated by this contemporary directive: "We send the male children to Bermuda . . . the women and maid children are disposed about in the towns."

Settlers took a risk by letting Will remain alive inside the colonies—especially considering his powerful family and a fierce warrior for a father who remained at large. The acceptance of Will's presence in New England speaks to his mother's careful maneuvering as well as Williams's influence as his protector. It also indicates that Will's age—perhaps as young as ten or eleven years old, since the historical record reflects that settlements only tolerated Pequot males who were so-called "young youths." If Will had been any older, he almost certainly would have faced slavery abroad.

In addition to age as a temporary safeguard, another rationale existed for allowing a growing Pequot boy such as Will to remain in the colonies. Settlers abided "Indians children, boyes and girles," who proved themselves "handy in their businesse." As Will became older, he faced the hellish ultimatum colonial leadership presented him: demonstrate his devotion and usefulness to his master, Roger Williams, or risk the slave galley aboard a transatlantic bark. New England involvement in the trade of enslaved African people began in 1638, the same year Will risked his life to prove himself indispensable to Williams.

That Thursday morning after the attack on Penowanyanquis, the industrious Williams remained at his desk "by break of day" when visitors unceremoniously interrupted his work. The four members of the Peach gang would have passed sunflower-filled Narragansett summer gardens on the way to Williams's door, no doubt attempting calm demeanors to cover up their crisis. Will almost certainly stood close at hand taking in the odd charade, attracted by the excitement of travelers rescued from the woods.

With his keen eye for detail, Williams carefully studied the desperate men in the close quarters of his humble, candlelit cottage. Despite Peach's attempt to appear otherwise, he likely seemed to Williams far more shaken than the circumstances warranted. The leader of the fugitives must have been sweating profusely from the August heat, making him appear nearly as harried as he felt. The men had raced through the night to successfully beat Penowanyanquis's Narragansett rescuers and news of the attack. As Williams's household tended to the newcomers, Arthur Peach unexpectedly interrupted his host to offer a word of caution.

The Peach gang had run into the "the old man at Pawtucket," as the solitary Reverend Blackstone was known, and he had told them a dark tale of violence. Peach imparted to Williams the supposed account by Blackstone of marauding tribesmen—an audacious rumor to spread, given the blood on Peach's hands. Will must have listened to the story with interest and growing fear while Williams, a man who tolerated the mysterious minister Blackstone as long as he remained at the fringes of Providence, added the problem to his long list of local issues to address.

Williams even turned the situation to his benefit by giving the travelers some letters to deliver along the way, dripping his red sealing wax onto the edge of each sheet of dusty parchment, the candle's flame attracting mosquitoes. He pressed his seal down firmly, imprinting the form of a stylized, cryptic-looking spider. Williams admired the fable of Solomon and the spider, in which the down-on-his-luck warrior looks to the spider's tenacity to bolster his spirits. The esteemed settler would soon need to rely on his own renowned tenacity in the fight of a lifetime. He gathered the letters together for Peach and warmly bid them Godspeed, not only with extra food but also with a team of expert guides who could keep them on the right path.

Not long after the Providence leader got back to his work, he was interrupted again. This time, an elderly Narragansett man arrived. With Williams's hard-earned diplomatic status with the tribe, Narragansett often stopped at his doorstep for casual visits. This time, the tribesman delivered a shocking tale of violence. He explained how a Nipmuc called Penowanyanquis had been attacked and found in the woods in dire condition, a tale the tribal elder had heard from a scout dispatched from the scene. According to the elder's information, Indians in the woods near Providence tended to the victim, who was fighting for his life.

News of the event had already caused some of the visiting elder's fellow Narragansett to depart quickly from the Providence settlement into the safety of the woods. Those fleeing feared that the coldblooded attempted murder of a tribesman meant a war was about to break out.

Williams wasted no time. The determined colonial leader hurried along the footpath as fast as he could manage into the darkened forest, despite Blackstone's warnings, as delivered by Peach, about the threat of violence to the colonists. Williams brought two companions with him who were also willing to put themselves at risk for the sake of saving an injured man: Drs. John Greene, forty-three years old, and Thomas James, forty-eight years old, both talented physicians. In the nighttime darkness on the narrow path, they could barely see their hands in front of their faces.

Greene, a solid, florid-faced man with broad shoulders and a commanding presence, was a surgeon from Salisbury, England, who overshadowed the brooding, "melancholick" Dr. James. Many hours later, in a state of exhaustion, the party finally reached Penowanyanquis.

Feverish and immobilized by his injuries, he struggled in the gloom of the dark forest. Described by Williams as a "peaceable" man, Dr. Greene must have been overwhelmed at the savage violence Penowanyanquis had suffered.

As Williams approached, the three indigenous men surrounding the victim retreated, having no way of knowing if the arriving settlers had caused the original violence in the first place. Tribal raids on enemies often commenced with a forewarning of an imminent onslaught—a warning shot, a piercing battle cry, the bludgeoning of a single combatant. The Narragansett men wondered if white settlers—the lost band of bedraggled men encountered in the woods, perhaps, or even the very Providence leaders they had come to trust—carried out their own version of the technique and came to ambush them.

Tribesmen not only feared the possibility of physical attack at the hands of the settlers, but also—in an era when perceptions of magic were so commonplace among the tribes—feared the colonists' stunning mastery of conjuring powers. Indigenous observers took note when a sailor magnetized his metal sword by rubbing it against the ship's "loadstone." "They much marveled" at the sorcery as knives pulled toward the cutlass. If the English now determined to strike against the tribesmen, they may have possessed powers even greater than their thunderous snaphances and swords. A tribal leader had spread word that the English controlled the plague and kept it hidden under a storehouse, ready to unleash the power of the dread illness. Indians scattered deeper into the woods.

Of course, Williams's group had reasons to fear for their lives, too, if old Blackstone's warnings were to be believed. In fact, if a rogue band of tribesmen roamed the forest, the settlers had to suspect that this entire tableau was a trap. But they did not waver. Williams professed his group's good faith, assuring the tribesmen that he knew nothing of the assault and had already taken measures to launch a search for the villain. The few circumspect Narragansett who had stayed behind at their own risk in order to guard the victim decided to let the newcomers through.

"*Muckquachuckquand!*" Penowanyanquis cried out to the Children's God over and over again, the anguished words echoing hoarsely in the woods. These words and the moment of despair haunted Williams. Years later, he recounted the scene of the young tribesman mortally wounded in terse, pained language: "I was once with a Native dying . . . [he] called much upon *Muckquachuckquand* . . . [who] had appeared to the dying young man, many years before." Later Williams came to better understand the notion of the Children's God through his study of Algonquian deities.

Penowanyanquis had cherished the protection of the Children's God. He fervently believed the god that had offered a vision of peace and protection to him years before might now save his life, but even that magical presence had limits heightened by the transformation of his people's lives by settlers. As his strength drained from him that night, Penowanyanquis may have recited a traditional Nipmuc prayer of the dying: "O Great Spirit, whose voice I hear in the wind, whose works I see in the forests, the mountains, the waters, the sun, the moon and the stars. Let my ears be sharp to hear Your voice, make me strong . . . when life ends as the setting sun, I may come to you with straight eyes and a clean heart."

Williams and the blended party of tribesmen and settlers did what they could to staunch the bleeding. Greene and James took the lead in trying to save the dying man, perhaps even resorting to the old battlefield trick of inserting an onion into the incised area before attempting to paste the area closed. In the colonial era, physicians would have mistakenly interpreted pus forming as a good sign, signifying "proper wound digestion." Like Williams, Greene spoke Algonquian and likely communicated directly with Penowanyanquis while treating him. Peach's rapier had missed Penowanyanquis's abdominal aorta, which would have caused a quick death. The blade probably inflicted a double-edged wound, worse than the single slice of a knife. Penowanyanquis's injuries produced massive internal bleeding and a dreadfully painful abdominal infection.

As he assisted Greene and James, Williams had time to contemplate the possible perpetrators of the bloodshed. The Wampanoag were natural suspects. The tribe projected bravery and a fierce guardianship over their tribal lands to the south of Plymouth Colony. But other dangerous elements lurked in the area. Because the Pequot War pit the settlers against the Pequot and other smaller tribes, including the Nipmuc, militias of colonists posed another hazard for any stray Nipmuc. Powerful infantrymen carried flintlocks and kept swords at the ready for close combat.

While the fighting had slowed in recent weeks, aggressions remained fiery. Violence of a kind once inconceivable spilled into local communities, touching any man, woman, or child not on the alert. One infamous battlefield exchange known to Williams from the ongoing Pequot War typified the unrestrained dangers and rage that abounded: "Have you fought enough? [the Pequot asked]. We said we knew not yet, [an English lieutenant responded]. Then they asked if we did use to kill women and children? We [the English] said they should see that hereafter. So they were silent a small space, and then they said, 'We are Pequots, and have killed Englishmen, and can kill them as mosquetoes, and we will go to Conectecott and kill men, women, and children.'"

As Williams watched his companions minister to Penowanyanquis, he realized they would need to find a way to bring the injured man back to the small Providence settlement, carrying him as many as ten miles through the dark forest. "We drest him and got him to town next day," Williams wrote, avoiding details of what must have been a dreadful overnight trek. For the moment, he fervently held out hope that they could still save the young man's life.

# 4

# MANHUNT

———⟪⟫———

*"The country must rise and see justice done."*
—*Plymouth Colony governor William Bradford*

Roger Williams mustered his strength while transporting the rapidly fading Penowanyanquis back to Providence. The son of a tailor, Williams dressed in dainty garb, his beloved ivory waistcoat replete with elaborate intertwining pink and mauve florets. Blood soaked his fine clothing, a bleak reminder of reality as Providence's patriarch yearned for a miracle.

In relief of the efforts of Drs. Greene and James, Williams could employ rudimentary medical techniques prevalent in England and colonial New England; with his usual attention to detail Williams had even studied how Narragansett treated the sick and dying. Not that the autodidact Williams thought himself particularly well suited to deal with a medical crisis. When ill, complaining to friends, "I have bene very sick of cold and feaver," he lamented the treatments at his disposal. "I have books that prescribe powders &c but yours is *probatum* [proven effective] in this countrey," he wrote to a colleague of his hopes for superior remedies; he requested "powder (with directions)" if it "might be sent without trouble."

By this point, Greene and James had had enough time to finish packing the infected wound with peat moss, which was known for its antibacterial properties. Even in his critical state, Penowanyanquis interrupted the lifesaving efforts to tell his story. As the young Nipmuc man lay dying, he did the one thing that had the power both to start a war and to stop one. In his own language, fighting through labored breathing, he offered an answer to the unasked question. With his waning strength he recounted the details of his attack by the Peach gang. He told Williams that "four English had slain him."

The Providence leader realized the truth about the four starving, jittery travelers he had dealt with earlier that day at home: they were the same men who had attempted to murder this tribesman. The terror Williams saw in the eyes of the Indians guarding Penowanyanquis when Williams's party first came on them now made sense. As settlers, Williams and his group fell into the same broad category as the band of men who had passed through the woods earlier, men now implicated in the brutal attack. In all probability, Blackstone's purported warning about indigenous violence had been nothing but a convenient fabrication by Peach, a clever stratagem to keep settlers away from the scene of the crime. With the discovery of the victim, and Penowanyanquis's words as confirmation, the Peach gang shifted from commonplace runaway servants to the most hunted men in the New World—with the indefatigable Williams now first among their adversaries.

Williams steeled himself to help track down the four attackers on the loose, burdened with the fact that he had unwittingly set in motion their getaway. He had fed them, revitalized them after five days in the woods, and, perhaps most damaging, provided Narragansett guides to steer them far from the reach of colonial authorities. They could be long gone. In that moment of epiphany, Williams transformed from helpful outsider to unwitting accomplice. On the other hand, his encounter with the fugitives gave him the key to their identities and other details crucial for a manhunt. His resolve only deepened. "I know that every man . . . and son of Adam, is his brother's keeper and avenger," Williams later wrote, describing his zealous determination.

Penowanyanquis, meanwhile, after days of unspeakable pain, succumbed to his injuries. Woodland people who for millennia had known no westerners had lost a beloved member at the hands of settlers. "Mr. James and Mr. . . . Greene endeavored, all they could, [to save] his life; but his wound in the belly, and blood lost, and fever following, cut his life's thread," wrote Williams. Even though the Providence leader recorded details of Penowanyanquis's death, he had not witnessed it—a fact poised to become crucial.

As Williams and his companions grieved the loss of the young life to an act of senseless barbarity, a new and unexpected twist developed. At some point after Penowanyanquis's death, his body inexplicably vanished. Suddenly, the crime did not just lack a perpetrator, it did not even have a verifiable victim. When Williams looked out at the Narragansett who had attended Penowanyanquis, he would have taken in the startling sight of faces traditionally blackened with heavy coal soot, a show of mourning. The soot was so thick on some that when tears were shed they created deep rivulets.

Reminiscent of the earthquake in the days before the attack, the days immediately after Penowanyanquis's death and disappearance saw a new celestial omen, a "great tempest or hiracano" that hit "twice in six hours"; the storm grounded a ship in Charlestown, near Massachusetts Bay Colony, and demolished a windmill. Most threateningly, the ferocious storm raised sea levels near the Narragansett by almost fifteen feet "upright." Tribesmen already stood on edge and battle ready after the murder of their compatriot. As the storm hit, they witnessed for themselves the fury of a god enraged by the slaying of one of his children.

Roger Williams, during dark days of violence, death, and the tempest, embraced his role as the case's first investigator. As an astute, even brilliant polymath, he was as well suited as anyone might have been for the role. In addition, he had the trust of the local tribal leaders. In spite of his personal participation in indigenous enslavement, Williams fervently advocated for the equality he saw between Indians and his own people: "Boast not proud English, of thy birth & blood, thy brother Indian is by birth as good." For Williams, this same principle applied to the value of Penowanyanquis's life.

With no police force of any kind and only a nascent government, the challenges ahead felt daunting. Eight years earlier, a Plymouth man had shot his neighbor in a dispute. In that case, no questions arose about who committed the murder or why. This felt very different, something new to the region—an unsolved crime. The subsequent search for justice fell to those who lived on the land since time unrecorded and to some of our country's founders, representing their latest uncharted journey.

Williams was in as good a position as anyone in colonial New England to comprehend the repercussions of the crime amid the current climate of war. As a trusted ally of the Narragansett, the Providence leader worked tirelessly to prevent them from joining forces with nearby tribes against the colonists. Most recently, in the days surrounding the Peach gang attack, Williams's desperate efforts to prevent complete regional warfare had been at Massachusetts Bay governor Winthrop's sharp urging.

As Winthrop noted in his journal on August 3, 1638, days after Penowanyanquis's murder, "The sachem of the Niantick [the bold Ninigret, a Narragansett ally], had gone to Long Island and rifled some of those Indians, which were tributaries [submitted] to us." The Monauketts "complained to our friends of Connecticut, who wrote to us about it, and sent Capt. Mason, with seven men, to require satisfaction." The events Winthrop described took place that spring, but word was slow reaching him. Winthrop ordered Roger Williams to alert the Narragansett sachem Miantonomo that he must provide the colonists "satisfaction, or otherwise to bid them look for war." With the prospect of battle already alive and well the summer the Peach gang murdered Penowanyanquis, every man, woman, and child in the Plymouth settlements sensed fighting coming to their doorsteps.

Word that the Pequot had lost more battles against settlers pushed the remaining regional tribes, some traditional enemies of each other, toward cooperation as the perceived threat of the colonists grew— the very situation Winthrop noted in his journal. Dominoes could fall rapidly. If the Narragansett saw Penowanyanquis's murder as an act of aggression against their confederates, the Nipmuc, then the fragile armistice patched together by Williams might fall apart. And if the powerful Wampanoag and Narragansett tribes indeed banded together, settlers stood little chance of repelling the assault. The colonists faced the prospect of being overrun, forced to retreat, their backs to the sea.

Williams, a student of language, must have recalled with irony the name given by "ye ring leader" he had hosted in Providence who now marked the tipping point of these crises. The name of this homicidal fugitive struck an inappropriately sweet note: Peach.


The Narragansett would have wanted to notify other tribes—including the Nipmuc—of Penowanyanquis's death. Tribal criers used a drum or signal rock, *cipusq*, held in place by small stones, to alert indigenous people to urgent tidings. When they removed the stones, the giant rock easily tilted up and down. The low, sonorous thudding of the criers' weary hands on the "talking rocks" reverberated far and wide.

There would have been no realistic way to transport Penowanyanquis's body to his homeland. If the Narragansett wanted to return his remains to his tribe, an ancient American Indian cremation rite provides the most likely scenario—and would explain why the body seemingly disappeared into thin air. While waiting for news of the death to reach other tribes, the Narragansett may have built an enormous funeral fire. Smoke and sparks would have spiraled heavenward in brimstone gusts, and even as the heat grew, emanating off the burning wood, the men would have continued to load branches onto the roaring flames until the bottom logs glowed in red-hot embers. It was then that the Narragansett would have placed Penowanyanquis's body into the pyre, with his remaining possessions—the ones that had held no value to the Peach gang, the items made and collected by Penowanyanquis or his tribe. The intense heat of the pyre would have slowly consumed the body, the corporal form gradually broken down into ash and shards of scorched bone.

This custom was Nipmuc, although not a particularly common one. In normal circumstances, Nipmuc buried their dead in "long rows" in the ground by river bends where moving water hugs rolling grassy stretches of land, willow trees languidly overhanging dark water. Nipmuc cherished these places so much they had a word, *pakachoag*, to describe a setting "where the river turns," the meditative beauty honoring deceased loved ones. The Nipmuc's alternative burial custom involved cremating the deceased's bones and possessions and depositing the ashes in "communal pits," which they returned to for centuries if not millennia. Hundreds of years after Penowanyanquis's death, archaeologists unearthed a significant site of such "cremation internments" near the tribal stronghold of the Nipmuc in central Massachusetts.

It is possible that Penowanyanquis's remains rest underneath or near one of the old stone cairns that to this day dot the rural New England landscape. A "supreme medicine man of the Wampanoag Nation," John Peters Sr., or Slow Turtle, cautions against interfering with burial sites. "We don't believe that the spirit ever dies. The spirit always lives . . . But sometimes our spirits are confined to particular graves if they are negative spirits. Sometimes if negative spirits are dug up, they are released—but shouldn't be." Penowanyanquis, a young, affable trader, might not have manifested such a negative spirit, but his violent death carried a legacy of darkness.


Details on Penowanyanquis's family remain obscured, but his place in society suggests that he was old enough to head a family of his own. His intricately constructed *wetu* would have been rounded and up to fifteen feet in diameter, complete with poles supporting bundled cattail and bulrush reeds, which in turn were bound together with strong, pliable walnut bark. The bulrush retained water and kept the home cool in the summer heat. Mats and the skins of animals that had been painstakingly hunted down or snared would have decorated the walls. It was the center of a life taken away.

The tribe had lost many things in Penowanyanquis: his bravery, his intelligence, his adeptness in complicated deals with high-powered Indians and settlers. In the Algonquian custom, the tribe dismantled

A replica indigenous dwelling at the Fruitlands Museum in Harvard, Massachusetts, provides a chance to visualize Penowanyanquis's everyday life.

his *wetu*, consigning any relatives he left behind to resettle with other tribal members. Pain on top of pain. Just a few years earlier, a ferocious bout of smallpox had hit the tribe, and Nipmuc died one after the other. The loss of so many tribesmen and -women wreaked havoc on their close-knit social structure. Penowanyanquis was yet another casualty.

Life would have already become surreal for Penowanyanquis's family. Interactions with English settlers were still very recent in these remote western woodlands and valleys; the historic first contact had taken place only seven years before. Within a decade or two of contact, Nipmuc moved from a stable way of life to a people forced to adapt to the perplexing norms of the Early Modern English. One of Penowanyanquis's clan members, Nanamocomuck, found himself in a baffling situation, dragged into Middlesex County Court in Cambridge to file a debt repayment plan just as a present-day debtor might. Court officials offered "foure moons" to pay half the debt, and a subsequent promissory note described the amount being repaid in "two hunting times." The language provided a glancing acknowledgment of the collision of cultures.

Nanamocomuck faced injustice in the form of unfair dealings at the hands of colonists, but Penowanyanquis was slaughtered. The accused murderers signified the same type of people who, in a few short decades, had moved from begging indigenous people for help to demanding land and goods through unjust, debt-provoking deals, to outright murder.

Tribal elders would have debated their next steps for the revenge and retribution of Penowanyanquis's killing amid ongoing ceremonies. During ancient traditional feasts and important tribal meetings, the Nipmuc danced fireside in a circle. Women shuffled to the beat, two-stepping rhythmically to the sound of drums. Flames burned high in the center as tribesmen rallied each other. Men's faces surely revealed anger as they readied to demand battle and retribution, a reckoning decades in the making.

Leaders of the tribe may have walked slowly among their best fighters, resting a heavy earthenware pipe on each strong shoulder and locking eyes. Tribesmen drank from ceremonial vessels. A small, perfectly symmetrical cherry-wood bowl was one such Nipmuc receptacle, its handle carved into the form of a sharp-eyed, alert mountain lion, ready for attack—the type of predator that the unyielding tribe had defeated countless times.

The warriors prepared, but ultimately the tribe knew it might not be their battle to fight. The Nipmuc had "submitted" themselves to the Narragansett, paid homage to them financially and through ritual tribute. The first attempt at justice fell to the Narragansett and their English allies.


After leaving Roger Williams's homestead in Providence, Arthur Peach directed the indigenous guides provided by Williams to bring them to Aquidnett Island in Narragansett Bay, present-day Newport, Rhode Island. The men snaked their way, single file, along narrow paths, late-summer vegetation encroaching from both sides. The summer heat wore heavy, the distance well over thirty miles, first on foot and then by boat. But compared to their earlier circumstances in the woods, the runaways could feel light-footed and optimistic.

Peach's choice of destination was savvy considering the sour relations between colonial leaders and those of Aquidnett Island. Massachusetts Bay Colony authorities had recently tried, convicted, and banished the infamous Anne Hutchinson for her unconventional beliefs. Religious leaders considered her influence so deleterious that when a young couple "notoriously infected with Mrs. Hutchinson's errors" delivered a baby, settlers reveled in describing the newborn as a "monster" with "no forehead, but over the eyes four horns, hard and sharp . . . instead of toes it had on each foot three claws, like a young fowl, with sharp talons." Most damning for the monster-inducing Hutchinson, the baby's demonic nature came to light "just" as Hutchinson was "cast out of the church." Exiled, Hutchinson relished the chance to strike out on her own, founding the Aquidnett settlement.

While the Peach gang wound their way closer to Aquidnett Island, the provocative Hutchinson considered her next moves from her home on the island. Her followers, disdained by Massachusetts Bay and Plymouth elders alike, lived nearby. All of this sounded promising for fugitives of a different kind, Peach and his men.

Peach may have also gotten wind of a document drawn up in Aquidnett just that year, the Portsmouth Compact, the name a self-aggrandizing nod to the Mayflower Compact. The Portsmouth Compact took the revolutionary ideas of the Mayflower Compact a step further, calling for a "Bodie Politick . . . submit[ing] our persons lives and Estates unto our Lord Jesus Christ the King of Kings." The renegade settlement's founding document conspicuously avoided mention of the king of England. To thumb its nose at the more established colonies, Aquidnett could harbor Peach and his men. But as the gang moved toward the prospective safe haven, a lone soul furtively hurried after them in the quiet depths of the forest.

Peach did not know it, but they were being watched. Williams had sent one of his domestics—all evidence points to the Providence leader's Pequot slave, Will—armed with details of the crime, "pursuing after them," spying on the gang through the interior stretches of Narragansett territory. Young Will raced after the band of murderers. He likely used skills he had acquired living in his Pequot tribe, where boys learned to track, hunt, and snare prey.

As Peach and his men forged ahead, they came across Miantonomo, the revered sachem of the Narragansett, an encounter that represented a potentially insurmountable challenge to their journey. It was Miantonomo for whom Penowanyanquis had been on his trading mission, an irony that would have been lost on the murderers. But there was no mistaking the authority of the sachem. Miantonomo was depicted as thin lipped, sage eyed, hawk nosed, and heavy eared, the lobes of which swung low with adornments. Wrinkles cut deeply into the flesh around the revered chief's eyes and mouth; his skin may have been partially painted in dusty hues. He would have cut a striking figure against the backdrop of the lush vegetation surrounding him.

Miantonomo would have been quick to halt strangers passing through their lands uninvited, even those accompanied by indigenous guides. He would surely not have tolerated the type of nonsense Arthur Peach attempted with others—slick words, long stories, charming advances—but Peach had something up his sleeve that he hoped would work with the leader of the mighty Narragansett: the letters from Roger Williams.

Will, the Pequot slave who had now lived among both the Narragansett and the English, would have watched the astonishing exchange between Miantonomo and the fugitives. Peach's restless, exhausted companions looked on in mounting horror, their escape about to be foiled in one fell swoop. Peach presented Miantonomo with Williams's letters to Aquidnett Island. They all waited in suspense as the sachem looked over the papers, examining Williams's distinctive seal. Grudgingly, the sachem let the men through without further detention. "And so to Aquednick [Island] they past," Williams later recounted. Williams's letters were worth their weight in gold, and Peach was as good as free.

Peach and his men did not realize that they were about to meet an even greater threat than the impressive Miantonomo, in the unlikely person of young Will, their secret shadow. The men probably had paid little heed to the enslaved boy, if they noticed him at all, while visiting the Williams home. By tailing his subjects, Will ensured that news of Penowanyanquis's murder would travel throughout the area. Having had ample opportunities to meet Narragansett neighbors of Williams's homestead, Will now could tip off the Peach gang's unsuspecting Narragansett guides that their charges were the escaped murderers.

Once receiving this information, the guides knew that Arthur Peach and his men presented a great threat. The guides bided their time as they brought the fugitives to their destination. They had a tremendous advantage: they knew the terrain, while the fugitives depended on them.

The Peach gang, footsore and exhausted from their trek, emerged from the vegetation with their Narragansett chaperones and made their way to shore to waiting canoes. The men eagerly filled the narrow boats, delighted to let their guides paddle them to safety. At last they got off their feet while distancing themselves from the scene of the crime. They trusted in their guides' skills to navigate the slender vessels that sat comfortably on the water. Traveling in the last hours of daylight, in the warmth of August, they could almost relax as they put a stretch of ocean water between themselves and their victim. The fugitives approached the rocky shore of the small Aquidnett settlement. Thick trees and underbrush, only marginally cleared, hemmed in the crescent-shaped beach.

Unnerved, they watched as surprised onlookers approached the party of tribesmen and rugged servants. Peach took comfort in the letters from Williams, the crimson wax seal smudged in his sweaty hands. He could once more leverage the Rhode Island patriarch's good name to ensure their safety. Reasons to have faith had multiplied. They had already tricked the preeminent savior of Providence into believing their cover story, and they had deceived the wise, old Miantonomo as well.

Inside the settlement of Aquidnett, the Narragansett lingered. Williams "had sent [the message with Will] to apprehend the men." The tribesmen surreptitiously recruited the support they needed from the locals, who would have also received word of the murder and Williams's directive to detain the gang from Will. It is chilling to consider what these four adults, these desperate murderers on the run for their liberty, would have done to the child had they gotten wind of his mission; Will, an invisible figure in history, who apparently has never been written about, proved himself worthy of every bit of faith placed in him by Williams. Now the Narragansett guides no longer stood outnumbered, as darkness began to descend on the small settlement. Villagers looked on as tribesmen joined with the Aquidnett leaders and surprised the criminals, trapping them.

Peach, Thomas Jackson, Richard Stinnings, and Daniell Crosse, who had left an unarmed indigenous man for dead in the wilderness, found themselves ensnared by the ingenuity and determination of a remarkable indigenous boy and a group of tribal guides. As former governor Bradford remarked, "By subtilty the Indeans tooke them [the Peach gang]." On his return, Will provided his eyewitness account directly to Williams: "The messenger that I sent . . . returned the next day [with details of the Peach gang's capture]." All this had been overseen from afar by Williams, who now needed help to manage the firestorm triggered by their capture.

The Aquidnett settlers and the Narragansett now had the murder weapon. The rapier was a distinctively Irish object, with an elongated design. Swordsmiths designed the weapon to handle well when thrust directly forward in close quarters. To accomplish this in the chaos of a fight without resorting to frantic slicing motions, a fighter required specialized training. Peach had handled the weapon correctly in the first stab and poorly in the later haphazard swings.

The islanders interrogated the fugitives with a "sudden examination," transcribing the responses. The captors gave this written testimony to young Will, who brought it to Williams, who then directed

John Winthrop, Massachusetts Bay
Colony governor, is one of the few early
colonial New En gland governors to leave
behind a portrait with an authenticated
provenance.

the boy to head north with a copy of the document for the leadership
of Massachusetts Bay. Will did this in an astounding fifty-mile trek.
"This native, Will, my servant, shall attend your worship [Governor
Winthrop] for answer," Williams wrote.

Winthrop, educated at the University of Cambridge, was perhaps
the most respected of the colonial leaders. He was a focused, sharp-
eyed man whose angular face and pointed chin made him appear as
shrewd as he was; his dark hair and eyes contrasted with pale coloring.
Plymouth Colony governor Thomas Prence described his counterpart
as having a "wise heart . . . [and] a cool and quiet spirit."

At home, Winthrop was a devoted and involved family man. He
and his wife adored their children and grandchildren and generally
busied themselves with family affairs. Their grown son would exhort
them to "let . . . [his wife and her children] return" home from her
visit with them. "She knows not how to leave you, nor how to part
with my mother . . . I expected them here by the last pinnace," Winthrop Jr. noted with barely masked annoyance.

On arrival, Will would have reunited with his mother, Wincumbone, one of Winthrop's slaves, and his siblings. The wait for Winthrop's response to Williams provided an opportunity—likely both
gratifying and heart-wrenching—to speak his own language and
reconnect with his family.

It was Will's responsibility to decide when to depart, requiring him to keep an eye on the time and the weather. Not knowing when he would next see his family, he must have put off his return as long as possible. When Will made the decision to leave, Governor Winthrop had to accommodate him: "The messinger is readye to depart, so . . . I must ende," Winthrop wrote. Critical communication among the settlements depended on an effective network of couriers.

With settlers and Indians alike on edge throughout the region, Will would guard Winthrop's letter with life and limb as he traveled the long, lonely journey on foot from Boston back to Rhode Island. Soon, Williams would find out that Winthrop was far less helpful than the courageous and clever Will.

An indigenous man from the colonial era as seen through European eyes. Originally believed to depict the sachem Ninigret, scholars now identify this as a fellow Pequot tribesman from the period in which Will lived (no extant image of Will remains).

Earlier in the summer of 1638, not for the first or last time, the residents of Plymouth Colony elected Thomas Prence governor. William Bradford, the outgoing governor, stepped aside just in time for Prence to face the consequences of murder. Prence likely heard the stunning news of Penowanyanquis's killing while at home at Captain's Hill in "Duxburrow," now Duxbury. His second chance as governor already seemed ill-fated. Soon after receiving the gruesome details of the attack, the powerful "hiracano" that the Narragansett observed struck near Prence's home. As the storm raged, Prence could take in a vista that spanned rain-doused meadows, staggered pine groves, whistling beach grass, and the crescent-shaped, pebble-struck beach that met the steely chop of the Atlantic. But the newly minted governor prepared to leave it all behind and move his family into the heart of the small settlement to deal with the murder.

Prence cut an imposing figure, described as looking suited for the position of governor. A contemporary noted that "he had a countenance full of majesty." He dressed for the job with a severe "blacke broadcloth cloake" and a circular, horn-rimmed pince-nez held up to his face when needed, making him appear owl-eyed. When traveling on horseback, he donned a "paire of ["ryding"] briches" and "fringed gloves with gould and silver."

A fellow settler referred to Prence as "a terror to evil doers," a descriptor that stuck and evolved into the lasting moniker "terror to the wicked." The Quakers, for whom Prence had no tolerance and whom he tried to banish from the colony, argued that he was a terror to all who disagreed with him. One enraged Quaker cursed Prence and his descendants, calling for "anguish and pain that will enter thy veins . . . like gnawing worms lodging betwixt thy heart and liver." Prence antagonized Quakers, but settlers craved hardliners during wartime. Though at the outset of Prence's second term as governor, he had reason to anticipate a period of peace. Pequot War battles became less frequent, and the most pressing problem Prence faced in those early days of his tenure involved labor. He needed workers to grow Plymouth into the center of commerce he envisioned. Instead, indentured servants griped about their unpleasant circumstances, local families began purchasing enslaved adults and children, and recent boatloads of newcomers offered up less-than-ideal candidates to fill the Plymouth workforce. If he had his way, Prence would make significant changes to improve the colony's standing, transforming it from a "remote corner of the earth" into a hub of commerce and religious learning.

The trouble was that Massachusetts Bay Colony outpaced Plymouth in terms of both population and economic development, dwarfing the older and smaller settlement's former prominence. Massachusetts Bay spearheaded the ferocious battles of the ongoing Pequot War, a military campaign that some argued was little more than a land grab. As English settlers focused on increasing their geographic reach and enriching themselves, Massachusetts Bay moved to the forefront of these expansion efforts. Massachusetts Bay, which formerly had boosted Plymouth through trade, outstripped Plymouth's fast-eroding place in the pecking order.

The year of the Peach gang attack, 1638, John Harvard endowed the now eponymous center of learning—the fledgling college had been without a name since its 1636 inception. Plymouth was overlooked for this honor of housing New England's first major academic institution. Colonial leaders instead established the new school in the northern settlement of Cambridge, whereupon with "the Lords blessing . . . they began to erect a college." Also in 1638, an Englishwoman brought over America's first printing press, setting up the clunky contraption in Cambridge, rather than in Plymouth. Even when an affluent merchant class infiltrated Plymouth, they settled on the colony's outskirts in Scituate. Rumblings began that the seat of government should be moved as well, away from Plymouth Colony proper.

That Peach's gruesome attack on Penowanyanquis occurred in this landmark year for the colony and its neighbors, when many developing socioeconomic and political movements came to a head, is no coincidence. The decline in the colony's prestige, the chaos of war, and the influx of servants coupled with their diminishing compensation may have, in part, pushed Peach to flee in the first place. The year 1638 proved a watershed moment for the colony. Plymouth's renewal hinged on prosecuting the Peach gang—as did any hope that the war might come to an end.

With Penowanyanquis dead, the same pressing fears took shape for Plymouth settlers and for Prence that rattled Roger Williams. Neighboring tribes might unite and initiate a preemptive attack against the colonists in response to Peach's crime. Already tribal leaders communicated that Penowanyanquis's "friends and kinred were ready to rise in armes, and provoke the rest thereunto."

Tribal alliances and enmities were in flux. The Narragansett marched on the Wampanoag in 1632, but when the Pequot threatened the Narragansett's own lands, the Narragansett gave up their reach into Massasoit's territory. By 1637, the Pequot reversed their bellicose position toward the Narragansett and instead offered to unite with the tribe against the English. The plan came to naught, likely due to Roger Williams's intercession to save the colonies. When Massachusetts Bay soldiers later attacked the isolated Pequot to devastating effect, an act of attempted genocide, the Wampanoag and Narragansett absorbed a somber lesson. The archenemies now had a reason to forge an alliance against the shared threat: the colonists.

The Narragansett, for their part, as representatives told Roger Williams, feared "a general slaughter" of their people as predicted by the Pequot. They suspected that the attack on their "tributary," Penowanyanquis, marked the beginning. With both sides on edge, escalated warfare seemed inevitable. Alarmed colonists believed that neighboring tribes might be drawn into the fray of the Pequot War.

Miantonomo, the sachem of the Narragansett who detained Peach before allowing him to pass through his territory, publicly called for calm. He cracked down on warriors eager to achieve justice through revenge killings. He warned his own people against taking up arms, issuing "express threatenings" against them if something were to happen to one of the colonists. Miantonomo was a straight arrow as a leader—almost literally. In land deeds, tribesmen identified themselves with pictograms, a symbolic depiction not just of a name but of an identity. Miantonomo's symbol was a ramrod-straight arrow, projecting unwavering strength.

Miantonomo's warriors abided by his decrees. But other factors at play confounded his followers and pulled them away from his dictates. Rumors spread that many Pequot fighters, such as Will's father, had survived the recent assaults by the English. These Pequot men remained battle ready as led by the fearsome Ninigret of the Niantic. Ninigret aimed to enlist an intertribal army against the colonists, and word of his latest attacks filtered into Plymouth Colony.

Narragansett and Pequot vied with each other over their competing interests in nearby Long Island Sound. The Pequot belittled the Narragansett by calling them "women-like men." Still, even the Narragansett admired Ninigret's courage. When the colonists took up arms against the Pequot, it initially benefited the Narragansett, but the settlers' attempts to wipe out the Pequot startled everyone. The Narragansett grew more receptive to Ninigret's compelling warning—what the English could do to the Pequot, they could do to other tribes.

Just a few months before Penowanyanquis's murder, Ninigret led an audacious "amphibious assault" on the island-bound Monauketts, who lived under English protection, just as the Narragansett did. Ninigret and his men crossed the twenty nautical miles of ocean in dugout canoes. He led eighty warriors, of which only twenty were Pequot. The Monauketts desperately pointed out to their attackers that they would have to answer to the mighty settlers. In response, Ninigret disparaged the colonists. "English men are liars," he declared. If Ninigret could attack a tribe under colonial protection without consequence, the Narragansett found themselves in a more vulnerable position.

A power vacuum revealed itself. Ninigret hoped to take advantage and drive a wedge between the Narragansett and the English. With Penowanyanquis's murder prompting calls to arms from multiple directions, and with tensions soaring, no one could predict who might take the next step toward bloodshed and revolt. To stave off the last gasps of violence in the barbaric war, factions of tribal leaders and set-

tlers both had sought a peace treaty. Penowanyanquis's death stymied
that momentum and empowered Ninigret's rallying cry, providing
the sachem of the Niantic leverage to recruit additional fighters for
his own campaign to overpower the English settlers. The murder of
the Nipmuc tribesman endangered everyone, placing cross-cultural
harmony in limbo and stoking the fires of war.

The population of Plymouth and Massachusetts Bay had grown in
recent years, but not enough to allow the English to repel a concerted
attack by an indigenous coalition. Nor was retreating back to England
an option for most of the residents if the colonies fell into disarray,
at least not without great risk. Just a few years earlier Arthur Peach's
master, Edward Winslow, had traveled to England on behalf of the

If settlers mishandled Arthur Peach's murder trial, Governor Bradford dreaded
an uprising of the indigenous tribes surrounding Plymouth Colony. The concerns he articulated echo tales of the Powhatan Uprising, an occurrence of
colonial-era violence that took place sixteen years earlier in Virginia Colony,
as illustrated in this engraving.

colony. He had carried tokens from the New World, including "a great king's pipe . . . [that] doth stink exceedingly of Indian tobacco." The mercurial Archbishop Laud was not impressed: he summarily sent Winslow to prison. As Bradford sardonically noted, "This was the end of . . . this business."

Tribal leaders vowed to work for peace behind the scenes, but that did little to dispel the distrust among colonists who remembered such incidents as the 1622 Powhatan Uprising, an indigenous reprisal to barbarous actions of settlers in the Virginia colonies. The aggrieved sachem who led that surprise assault had gone so far as to profess conversion to Christianity to lure settlers into a state of complacency. In all, local tribesmen killed approximately 330 colonists—no prisoners taken, a rare example of an indigenous raid that resulted in such high casualties. Had the battle taken place in Plymouth, that number would have constituted 60 percent of the settlement's population.

Former Plymouth governor Bradford probably had the Powhatan attack in mind when he railed about the danger of hostilities in the aftermath of the Peach gang assault. "The country must rise and see justice done" or risk that outraged indigenous leaders "would raise a war."

# 5

# ESCAPED

---

"A pair of stocks, with a whipping post,
shall forthwith be made."

—*Governor William Coddington,
Aquidnett Island*

Daniell Crosse, Arthur Peach's companion, burst through nettled underbrush. Crosse followed the winding path toward the waiting ocean through thorn-filled vegetation that ripped clothing and skin. Aquidnett settlers, after springing their trap, had restrained the members of the Peach gang—but not well enough to prevent Crosse from breaking away. The last remnants of late-day sun soared over the island settlement. If he could make it back to the birch *mishoon* (canoe) that was pulled up onto the beach below and keep out of sight, he might have a chance.

The nearest tip of land was in sight across the narrow bay, for better or worse. The Narragansett could overtake him on the water if they spotted him, and he could not be sure how long he had to make his escape before his absence was noticed. Crosse also had no way of knowing whether or not his companions would turn on him once they realized he was gone.

Another problem: the people of Aquidnett had experience hunting escaped men. Settlers had busily pursued yet another fugitive indentured servant, who was punched in the face before fleeing Aquidnett Island. A detailed description of this fugitive spread far and wide in hopes of tracking him down. The escapee's master described him as "26 years, of browne black hair, a full face, [with] a black eye." The fugitive with the telltale shiner crossed the bay to temporary freedom and safety.

Crosse made a break for one of the canoes, swiping a vessel that had taken at least seven years to create when a generation of earlier tribesmen had selected the perfect sapling to nurture for the eventual *mishoon*. Gliding onto water, the exhilaration of looming freedom would have mingled with the horror of life as a hunted man, assuming he made it to the other side. Plenty of settlers met their deaths on the water under less turbulent circumstances. When a party of colonists, a married couple and their companion, had embarked on such a journey, the unsteady vessel had upended. "The 2 men holding fast upon the canoe were saved[;] his wife was drowned, he having hold of her let her goes to save him self." Soon after her death, another settler nearly died when he was unable to handle his canoe piled high with possessions. Without warning, the boat "sunk under him, scarce any wave stirring."

One couldn't be blamed for wanting to thrash the paddles to advance as quickly as possible through the rough ocean surf, but the fugitive probably knew enough to pull quietly at his oars, staying low. Against all odds, Crosse remained undetected. Making it across to the mainland, Crosse still had to trek from present-day Newport, Rhode Island, to Piscataqua, present-day Portsmouth, New Hampshire.

On foot, he traversed well over a hundred miles to the north. Crossing the border between Plymouth and Massachusetts Bay—which also meant crossing a tribal boundary from the Wampanoag to the Ponkapoag—Crosse likely passed the ancient Angle Tree landmark that indicated the line. Incredibly, the borderline extended into uncharted territory across the country to the Pacific Ocean, then called the "Spanish Ocean." The Angle Tree, a near-dead, one-limbed white oak, was a gloomy marker, also signaling the entrance into the deep north woods that would lead to Piscataqua territory. The tree may have been one intentionally shaped to indicate the trail, a common act of indigenous espaliering or tree bending. If Crosse had

An indigenous marker tree reveals a glimpse of everyday tribal life.

ventured into this primeval forest at any other time of year, the frigid temperatures would have killed him.

In addition to Crosse's luck to be on the move in the summer, Piscataqua provided an ideal destination. It was precisely the opposite direction of the Peach gang's known attempted endpoint to the south, New Amsterdam, present-day New York. Plus, Piscataqua— even more than Aquidnett—bucked the dictates and authority of other colonies, making it a fugitive's dream. Now the most hunted fugitive in the New World, he counted on turning the settlement to the north into his sanctuary.

If colonial leaders gnashed their teeth at Crosse's escape, they congratulated themselves on securing the rest of the Peach gang. A new problem surfaced. Where should they send Peach and his two coconspirators? A flurry of correspondence volleyed among settlements over the issue, in America's first jurisdictional dispute. Each colonial governor in the area confronted the daunting prospect of overseeing one of the New World's first, and certainly most explosive, murder trials.

Officials at Aquidnett Island, Providence, Massachusetts Bay, and Plymouth all, to some degree, faced an obligation to consider the assignment and to resolve where the men should be prosecuted. The crime had happened in a desolate area beyond the jurisdiction of any of the established colonies (one of the reasons Roger Williams, investigating the scene after the attack, described the spot hemmed in by trees and swamp as "fit for an evil purpose"). Williams made certain to point out to Governor Winthrop that he "went to see the place" for himself. The Providence leader was not about to let any possible clue escape his attention. He also understood the importance of the crime's location, suspecting Peach's premeditation.

Deciding where to send Peach was complicated by the fact that Aquidnett's governor, William Coddington, was not on the island when the drama unfolded. The settlers who were there, however, knew that there was no chance the trial could move forward on the island—the barely populated settlement had recently established itself and lacked the necessary judicial infrastructure. (On top of that fact, of course, they had allowed one of the culprits to escape.) This crossed one jurisdiction off the list.

Governor Winthrop, in replying to Williams's letter, made it clear that Massachusetts Bay was not about to accept jurisdiction. Though boasting the most mature judicial system, Winthrop's colony had the weakest connection to the case. The Peach gang hailed from Plymouth, crossed through Providence, and came to be captured in Aquidnett; ties to Massachusetts Bay were tenuous.

Disappointed by Winthrop's refusal after Will's exertions to bring about the fugitives' capture, Williams had reasons to step up and volunteer Providence. In addition to the fact that Peach and his men had come to his home and deceived him, Williams had been instrumental in their hunt and capture, as well as in caring for and interviewing the victim before his death.

Before leaving England, Williams had taken up employment with the famed jurist Sir Edward Coke. Coke, perhaps the most esteemed legal scholar in England, cemented the common law tradition. Furthermore, Coke reasoned that it was "the jury's power to determine law and fact." The idea caught on. Williams knew precisely the high expectations his mentor had established for a criminal trial.

The founder of Rhode Island would burn with embarrassment if

Coke got word that he had botched the New World's most significant murder trial. As a new settlement, Providence's relatively nascent
infrastructure and small population meant that there were limited
resources and hardly enough citizens to properly carry off a jury trial.
Any verdict could lead to civil strife, and Williams would likely be
blamed for the fallout. Moreover, in 1638 Williams did not yet possess
a charter from the king for his small community. Without the legal
authorization with which the king imbued a full-fledged colony, Williams's hands were tied. He could not proceed with a trial.

The situation gravely worried him. He had just recently entered a
period of relative calm after his banishment from Massachusetts Bay
into the "howling" wilderness beyond the colony. Banishment had
actually been a better option than the possible alternative of a trial,
which might have carried a death sentence. Remarkably, Williams had
not only recovered from being thrown out of Massachusetts Bay, he
had survived and thrived in his own settlement.

Williams had even proved so resourceful and good-natured that
he had endeared himself to the very man who had sent him off to
possibly starve in the woods—Governor Winthrop. Winthrop now
willingly engaged in friendly correspondence. The governor would
later brag that even "though he [Winthrop] was carried with ye stream
for my banishment, yet he personally and tenderly loved me to his last
breath." Their dynamic exemplified how Roger Williams's ability to
ingratiate himself with leaders matched his ability to infuriate them.
Even the king of England, Charles II, would later note that those
people living near Williams "are yet daily disturbed . . . by certain
unreasonable and turbulent spirits of Providence Colony."

Williams concluded one letter to Winthrop about the murder by
praying that he was "beseeching God to bring us by all these bloody
passages to an higher price of the blood of the Son of God." But he
also pleaded for help and advice to avoid the trial falling to Providence. "I humbly crave your judgment," he implored him. "In case
Plymouth refuse, and the islanders send them to us [Providence],
what answers we may give if others unjustly shift them unto us[?]"
Another danger grew with the uncertainty. Given Crosse's escape, the

longer colonial leaders waited to settle the issue, the greater the risk that the remaining prisoners could abscond on the long journey to one of the colonies.

Williams's relief came through when he wrote, "The [Aquidnett] islanders (Mr. Coddington being absent) resolved to send them . . . by us to Plymouth, from whence they came." This scenario rested on Williams's counterpart in Plymouth: Thomas Prence.

Unlike the leaders of the other colonies, Governor Prence possessed legal and political reasons to prosecute the men in Plymouth Colony. The Peach gang members had resided and fled from Plymouth; successfully prosecuting them would deter other servants from trying to break their bonds. Overseeing a trial of this magnitude, Prence also had the opportunity to prove himself capable of commanding a challenging situation. With Massachusetts Bay Colony usurping the Plymouth settlement's prestige and significance in New England, Prence could reassert the languishing colony's place in the New World—and Prence's own place in the world, for that matter.

The governor projected unwavering strength, but he surely heard murmurs of the disregard in which many held him. Messengers delivered alarmed letters north to south, along indigenous trails, between colonial leaders. Williams and Winthrop worried about Prence's ability to manage a courtroom drama the likes of which none of them had ever seen. Winthrop had been unimpressed in general with Plymouth's leadership and infrastructure in the past. During a 1632 visit, Winthrop had to be carried across Plymouth's North River on a settler's back at a point called "Stoney Reache." He hoped to survey the entirety of the colony, but the necessary bridge had not yet been built.

Then there was the fact that Prence and his fellow Plymouth leaders required a fair amount of pressure to consider jurisdiction. Though the other governors pushed for this outcome, the fact that their colleague caved to their geopolitical maneuvering paradoxically made them question whether he could succeed. As Williams noted to Winthrop, "Our friends [in Plymouth] confessed, that they received much quickening from your own hand." Unable to resist, Williams added dismissively, "I find them [Prence and his colony officials] weakly resolved."

Prence's future, political and otherwise, hinged on proving his detractors wrong. When he confronted a challenge, he did not let his "low condition discourage." He would spend "any labor of love or expense" to see his objectives through. Whatever fears Prence had about his ability to mastermind the trial of the century in the early days of a fresh start for his governorship, he kept them to himself.

While Arthur Peach must have been unaware of Prence's personal misgivings, these insecurities opened an unexpected advantage to the accused murderer. If Prence failed to carry out a sound criminal trial in which the settlement's jurors could effectively examine evidence and testimony, Peach and his men had a good chance of dodging punishment. To pull off his undertaking, Prence would need help from Plymouth's leaders, political and military.

Plymouth Colony military commander Myles Standish would be front and center for any legal proceedings in Plymouth. His responsibility was to ensure that the small settlement administered justice, whatever form it took. Standish was in the business of training and drilling his military recruits, especially in light of the possibility of

This early depiction of the larger-than-life Plymouth Colony Captain Myles Standish, circa 1630, provides one of the few contemporary images of a *Mayflower* passenger.

combat against unified tribes. But Standish also had his eye on other menaces.

In some respects, the French and Dutch settlements to the northwest and south posed equally grave threats as the justifiably enraged tribes. When military leaders like Standish used towering pikes in training drills to practice unseating mounted riders, he readied his force for Dutch and French assault, not for attack by indigenous combatants, who moved on foot or in *mishoon*.

Captain Standish understood that the local tribes' fury over Penowanyanquis's murder could provoke a volley of violence against Plymouth for housing the accused. Attackers might consider setting the settlement on fire and then ambushing the men trying to extinguish it, so Standish readied a team of soldiers to guard the men engaged in firefighting. He had carefully thought out the possible forms of assault.

The military commander was still handsome at fifty-four years old, with a neatly groomed beard, steely brown eyes, and reddish hair sweeping over a wide forehead. The career soldier delighted in reading about the ancient glory of war in Homer's *Iliad* and in tales of Julius Caesar; he also enjoyed referencing his "textbook on artillery." Famously short, at about five feet tall, what Standish lacked in height he made up for with his volatile temper. One settler described him as "a little chimney [that] is soon fired," explaining the caricature by noting the mercurial Standish was "a man of very little stature, yet of a very hot and angry temper." When angered, his wrath became "blown up into a flame by hot words" that could have "consumed all."

In the early years of Plymouth Colony, Standish led a military skirmish at Wessaqqusset, a short-lived English settlement. When Standish heard that Wessaqqusset fell under threat from nearby tribes—and that one of the ringleaders was an indigenous man who had previously threatened Standish—he raced to the settlers' aid. Standish brought a light force of eight men. On arriving in the small village, Standish spotted his foe, Wituwamat. The tribe's sachem, Pecksuot, threw down the gauntlet with some choice words, laying into Standish with the insult guaranteed to provoke his fury:

"You are a great captain, yet you are but a little man." Standish—whose head nearly burst during a later incident when referred to as "Captain Shrimp," a quip needling his stature, red hair, and crimson complexion—coolly replied by inviting the tribesmen into a tiny one-room house.

Wituwamat, Pecksuot, and another young man joined Standish and two of his soldiers inside the small structure. Standish gestured for the door of the house to be closed behind them. When the latch clicked shut, hell broke loose. Standish and his men sliced daggers and cutlasses through their opponents. When it was over, Standish opened the door and emerged soaked in blood. His soldiers stood awestruck and terrified at the haunting sight of the strutting captain. Standish's longtime indigenous friend Hobbomock was present and dryly noted, "To-day I see you are big enough to lay Pecksuot on the ground."

The brutal battle helped quiet threats to Plymouth, and Standish seemed to delight in stoking the memory of the battle for years. Fellow colonists celebrated how he protected them, extolling him as being "of as good courage as conduct." One Puritan who knew him well simply referred to him as the "captain, whom I love."

But while many rank-and-file colonists appreciated Standish's ability to execute a quick strike, others worried about the consequences. Colonial leaders early on partnered him with Governor Prence, ordering that "Standish was not allowed to take the Plymouth force into the field alone; Thomas Prence was appointed to accompany him and 'be his counsel and advise in the wars.'" The two figures' strengths—Prence's steady leadership and Standish's bold strategizing—complemented each other.

Six years before the attack on Penowanyanquis, another set of challenging circumstances put the two men to the test when they failed to repel a hostile takeover of Fort Penobscot, Plymouth Colony's profitable trading outpost near present-day Castine, Maine. This debacle came back to haunt the colony and Standish the very year of the Peach gang trial.

Charles de Menou d'Aulnay, the Frenchman who seized Plymouth's Acadian fort, made an impression for his fashions as much as his military prowess. He wore crisply tailored attire and had a majestic head of dark hair that framed his quintessentially Gallic features, large dark eyes that burned brightly over his aquiline nose. He provoked and irritated Standish to no end.

French officers likely framed the overthrow of the fort with great ceremony, to judge from the French siege on another Acadian fort. I "now deliver up the keys of the Fort," the outgoing official declared, and he assured the new commander that he was "hoping to give . . . a visit next spring."

A flustered Edward Winslow, Arthur Peach's master, noted the Puritans' mortification at the hands of "mounsr. d'Aulney [who] under a pretence of color of commerce did violently & injuriously take a possession [of Fort Penobscot] out of the hands & custody of the agent & servant of Edward Winslow Esqr[,] William Bradford[,] Thomas Prence . . . to their great loss, even to the value of five hundred pounds or thereabout." The amount of money signified a small fortune for Plymouth Colony.

Not only did the lost fort deplete Plymouth's trading income, the fort stood on prime real estate near "fruitful valleys adorned and enriched with trees of all sorts" and near waters with "lobsters as bige as little children." The area in its earliest colonial days reflected cross-cultural influences, including some intrepid European actors staging a striking aquatic theatrical performance, "The Theater of Neptune," on wobbly canoes.

D'Aulnay determined to hold the fort at any expense. The Frenchman carved out a lifestyle befitting his position, upholding "high fashion on the frontier," but he did not mind getting his hands dirty to please his king. D'Aulnay's father had been a high-ranking official in King Louis XIII's inner circle, and he learned of the king's demand for beaver pelts firsthand. Just as Louis XIII's capricious desire for the soft pelts had indirectly pulled Penowanyanquis toward his tragic fate, d'Aulnay's entire existence revolved around maintaining the fort's access to the luxurious beaver the French ruler cherished.

D'Aulnay chose 1638 for his next audacious insult. After receiving authority from French officials, he refurbished Fort Penobscot to his liking. The Frenchman christened the revamped structure Fort St. Pierre. The effects of Peach's crime proved more far-reaching than settlers at Plymouth could have imagined.

If the French were so bold as to rename and overhaul Fort Penobscot, they might also try to expand their territorial control. The renewal of provocations by the French signaled an ominous, strategic awareness of Plymouth's woes and temporary vulnerability. The glaring anomalies of 1638—the astounding earthquake, the murder, and the further subjugation of Fort Penobscot—came with added and largely unfamiliar costs. D'Aulnay's actions posed a possible threat that Standish and the settlement had to guard against.

Invasion from another nation's colony was not farfetched. The Dutch presented similarly unnerving threats to Plymouth. When war between England and Holland erupted years later, Standish was seventy years old. Nonetheless, he good-naturedly dusted off his armor and prepared to fight to the death if local Dutch militias came marching toward his colony. The Maquas tribesmen declared themselves willing to put their lives on the line against the English; they stood "ready to assist the Dutch if the English attacked them." With their respective tribal alliances, the Dutch and French could easily manipulate a perilous situation to their advantage.

During the turmoil of 1638, each of these threats had to be assessed, and Prence's colony—the budding nation itself—could not withstand any combination of them. English settlers realized that the Dutch or French, who were waiting in the wings, could do them in—especially in conjunction with a unified tribal force.

The decision to vest jurisdiction in Plymouth Colony meant that the settlers at Aquidnett unburdened themselves of their prisoners. With Aquidnett's governor Coddington still away, the villagers asked a group of tribesmen to transport the accused murderers—sans the escaped Daniell Crosse—back across the bay and on to Plymouth. The men and women of the small island washed their hands of the Peach gang members.

Governor Winthrop directed the extradition from afar. He counseled, "It would be safest to deliver the principal [Arthur Peach], who was . . . known to have killed the party [Penowanyanquis], to the Indian['s] . . . friends." Recognizing the anger Peach's Narragansett guards must have felt toward the prisoners, Winthrop added darkly that the tribesmen should be reminded not to "put him to torture, and to keep the other three to further consideration." In an age in which news traveled slowly and in fragments, Winthrop was not yet aware that Daniell Crosse was on the lam.

Penowanyanquis's Narragansett allies "carried" the Peach gang through the woods that lay between the Providence settlement and Plymouth. They likely passed the still-bloodstained scene of the crime. Arthur Peach and his men must have remained terrified that their guards would be tempted to give in to blood lust and revenge, regardless of the orders of the influential Winthrop. Nobody on the trek felt at ease. The Narragansett surely cringed with disgust not only to be in the presence of the murderers, but also to prepare to protect the abhorrent men from rogue factions of Indians seeking vengeance.

If they reached their destination alive, Peach and his accomplices faced the prospect of returning to an intimidating colonial leader in Governor Prence, the "terror to the wicked." Prence had even less patience for criminals than he had for his ideological foes, the Quakers. In the unrelenting Prence, Peach faced an antagonist out of his nightmares. It was anyone's guess who would triumph at trial.


Not long after the Peach gang departed Aquidnett under armed guard, Governor Coddington returned to the small island. When he had left, his once-peaceful settlement seemed a picturesque if primitive utopia of order, surrounded by the calm blue waters of Narragansett Bay. Coddington was noteworthy for his unflappable manner. Once, when writing to Winthrop, Coddington mentioned with cool equanimity a bloody tribute gift he had recently received from a local sachem, a bag of "30 fingers and thumes." He earned a reputation for himself as an ambitious merchant and government leader. Coddington had been forced into the wilds of the far reaches of Narragansett territory because of his religious beliefs, a small detour in the successful New World life he planned for himself and his family. He intended to develop his island colony into a well-ordered and respectable locus of mercantile activity and progressive thinking. Few things unsettled him.

But upon his return to the island colony, the governor heard about the intrusion of the Peach gang and the escape of Daniell Crosse. He endorsed a directive "that a pair of stocks, with a whipping post, shall forthwith be made, and the charges to be paid out of the treasury." Coddington, mad as hell, was not about to let any future criminal emulate Crosse and escape on his watch. Coddington could only hope that the new ordinance would prevent embarrassing pandemonium of the sort caused by Peach and his men from ever happening again.

Soon enough, Coddington heard the news that Crosse had reached Piscataqua, the only place in the New World that would welcome a murderer with open arms. One Massachusetts Bay official described Piscataqua by noting that the "desperately wicked . . . went from us to them, whereby though our numbers were lessened, yet we accounted ourselves nothing weakened by their removal." God-fearing colonists who ventured there did so armed. One group of visiting Puritans traipsed through a Piscataqua settlement with a Bible pierced to the tip of a battle-ax, hoping to drive home their unwavering religious zeal.

Piscataqua reciprocated the animosity. Between swigs of "kill-devil [rum]," one Piscataqua leader referred to the men of Massachusetts Bay as "rogues," casually remarking that he would be pleased "to see all their throats cut." As acrimony dragged on, Winthrop at one point went so far as to accuse the minister of Piscataqua, Hansard Knolles, of having "most falsely slandered" the leadership of Massachusetts Bay.

Prence demanded Crosse back from Piscataqua, but the defiant settlement flatly refused the extradition request. The Piscataqua men, grumbled Winthrop, were determined to welcome "all such lewd persons as fled from us to them" and "openly withstood [Crosse's] apprehension." But there was little that Prence or Winthrop could do other than lament Piscataqua's defiance.

Just as Prence wanted to build up Plymouth's status through the high-profile trial, Piscataqua leaders used the opportunity to assert their colony's autonomy by refusing to cooperate. Years of back-and-forth bickering and name-calling had deteriorated relations between the colonies to a breaking point, leaving Daniell Crosse untouchable.

The entirety of the Piscataqua Valley, the verdant expanse west of present-day Portsmouth, New Hampshire, was shrouded in darkness. Other than by smell, the forms of nearby men were undetectable. Even with the nighttime sky cross-stitched in dazzling layers of starlight, the woods blocked out any illumination. The forest stood thick and largely impenetrable. One could only navigate the silent copse of trees by sticking to the ancient path leading down to the river's edge, staying clear of the odd eruptions of howling and grunts that broke up the quiet. Roving packs of wolves were to be feared, as well as bears hunting before winter set in. Mountain lions stalked prey. Even wooly-haired, otherworldly wood bison roamed the forests along the eastern shoreline.

The waters of the Piscataqua River seemed calm, but the surface belied the currents that churned beneath. Men piled into sturdy canoes pulled down from higher ground. Broad stretches of bark enfolded the meticulously crafted boats. Thick reeds at the bow and upper edges, roughly stitched, held together the seams of the canoes. The sharp smell of wintergreen emanating from the bark came across clean and brisk as the chilled forest air.

Daniell Crosse, integrated into the economy and culture of the place, must have felt a near-giddy sense of ebullience and good fortune as the men pushed off. The slender boats skimmed the surface of the water. A settler at the bow of each likely used a rushlight holder, an encased iron clip that held a smoldering fat-doused meadow-rush pith, to light the pitch knot torches that dangled off the bowsprits. The knotted rope burst into flame, and the world suddenly came into focus for Crosse as a bright sphere of warm light illuminated water, canoes, and the shadowy trees swaying eerily in the wind.

The light pitched erratically as the boat rocked. The northern settlers and tribesmen became visible. The fishermen of Piscataqua were now Crosse's kin, and he helped ready large nets. The water, black in the distance and iridescent green under the torch, lapped up around the canoe. The birch looked ephemeral in papery layers of gold.

Thousands of shad swirled up under the light, teeming under the surface of the river. Crosse worked heartily to draw them into large woven nets. The forests of New Hampshire were Crosse's haven, quite literally. After stealing the canoe from Aquidnett, Crosse had traveled a staggering distance to get this far north and escape the reach of Plymouth Colony. While his new existence as a fisherman came out of hopeless happenstance, it proved a boon compared to the toil and labor he had endured as an indentured servant—and a godsend compared to the fury of the tribesmen he had eluded the night of his escape. The life he found was unlike anything he could have ever dreamed of. Most miraculous of all, from Crosse's perspective, he was getting away with murder.

# 6

# JURY SELECTION

———— ✵ ————

*"The rich and mighty should not eat up the poor."*
*—Massachusetts Bay Colony governor John Winthrop*

A single page of parchment that would have begun to show its age by
Prence's new term offered guidance on the daunting task of assem-
bling his jury. Some fifteen years earlier, in unyielding strokes of dark
ink and at the height of the famine of 1623, former governor William
Bradford wrote the first entry in Plymouth Colony's *Book of Laws*
on December 27, requiring all criminal trials to be heard by "a jury
upon their oaths."

Written during the throes of starvation, Bradford's far-reaching act
demonstrated emphatic forethought. When Bradford wrote America's
first law on the books, he understood that a trial by jury signified the
primary protection of the colonists' civil liberties. The settlers had
crossed the ocean for this right, among others. Bradford knew that
legal challenges inevitably awaited the small settlement by the sea,
and a jury would provide a way to dispense justice fairly, a necessity
for the bourgeoning society.

Prence, however, faced a problem: surprisingly few people in Plymouth Colony qualified for jury service. First, the era dictated that only
men could be considered. In canvassing this pool of prospective men,
the governor had to exclude indentured servants, who made up about

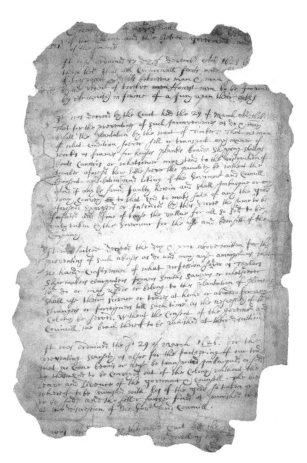

Few people have seen Governor Bradford's original 1623 order mandating the use of jury trials in Plymouth Colony. This document is foundational to American jurisprudence and central to the events that unfolded after Penowanyanquis's murder. It is stored in a fireproof vault at the citadel-styled Plymouth County Registry of Deeds.

17 percent of the population. Only sworn freemen could serve as jurors, but Prence was also precluded by custom from recruiting any of the numerous colony officials, such as Myles Standish, who might exhibit conflicts of interest. Religious leaders also fell outside the scope of potential jurors, as did minors, the infirm, and the elderly. Prence carefully considered those few who were eligible.

Modern-day jury trials in the United States begin with the random selection of jurors, whose inclusion can be challenged by either side. The process attempts to ensure defendants' right to be judged by unbiased peers. Jury selection in colonial Plymouth manifested itself differently. Through a methodical search that was anything but random, the court sought the most knowledgeable settlers outside of colonial leadership and the other excluded classes of people. With the total population of Plymouth Colony topping out at approximately 550 people in 1638, this left alarmingly slim pickings to find thoughtful, principled individuals for jury service. Considering men such as the pompous scofflaw Stephen Hopkins, Prence could reasonably fret how few fit the bill.

Once the bespectacled governor picked up his quill to summon jurors for the trial, he relied on the local constables to winnow through the populace in search of suitable prospects. The constables would scour the population of Plymouth's outlying communities to bring forth eligible jurors. These were officials who filled the medieval role of parish leader and law enforcer, ensuring that "his Majesty's peace be not broken." Petty constables mirrored the ancient role of Saxon tithingmen—the guardians of law and order who looked after each English hamlet. The Normans brought the term and concept of *connectable* with them when they conquered Saxon England.

The practice of constables mustering a jury can be found on a later seventeenth-century colonial summons, ordering "the Constables of Plimouth . . . without delay to warn the inhabitants of your town who by law may act and vote in town meetings that they assemble and meet together at said time as you shall appoint to make choice of" them in order "to serve on a jury of trials." The constable would "warn the persons that shall be so chosen . . . to appear at and attend said court of which you may not fail." The wording of the decree emphasized the unpleasant consequences for those who failed to perform his duty.

One of Prence's decrees went to Constable Anthony Annable, who concentrated on recruiting men from the settlement of Scituate, on the outskirts of the colony. In Scituate, the recently arrived religious leader Reverend John Lothrop held sway. Contemporaries described the unassuming man as one of the "irregular, unconformable fugitive ministers beyond the seas in New England." He had escaped prison in England and made it to the colonies, and his followers implored Puritans still living in England "to direct all . . . friends" to "come over to Citewat [Scituate], where Mr. Lothrop, their pastor, has at length safely arrived." Lothrop took moral transgressions to heart, and the momentous Peach gang trial presented him with a philosophical call to arms.

When Lothrop fled from England under threat of death, he left behind his collection of books. When he repopulated his shelves in Scituate, they reflected broad intellectual interests that went far beyond the one book he did bring, the Bible. The volumes in his small library included works in English, Latin, German, French, Greek, Dutch, Italian, Hebrew, and Spanish. Years later, Lothrop wrote out his will, requesting that his second wife, Ann, dispense with his valuable collection by giving each of his children a book "chosen according to their ages," an echo of his having chosen a single book with which to cross the ocean. He went on: "The rest of my library to be sold to any honest man who can tell how to use it." The latter he noted with cutting mirth and without optimism; few in his community were quite so well educated.

The idea of a popish theistic trinity might have alienated the Puritan Lothrop, but the classical "triumvirate" of Cicero, Plutarch, and Seneca held an irresistible draw. Cicero's call from the ancient world for humanism moved and challenged Puritan men in the New World. This brand of humanism was fueled and defined by the resurgence of "classical learning . . . [Greco-Roman] grammar, rhetoric, poetry, history and moral philosophy." The philosophical movement put the "moral rights of the community" above the individual, a departure from purely Christian traditions. For colonists, the rationale of universally applicable humanist precepts persisted alongside narrower religious beliefs. Many argue that humanism fueled debates about the ethics surrounding Atlantic colonization, provoked Puritan reformation, and encouraged civic-mindedness.

Significantly, as one historian notes, "the humanist education of the [colonial] times looked to the past, to ancient times, for lessons to guide the present." Their wide-ranging libraries stacked prized classical volumes of philosophy resting up against religious tracts—the ideas from both considered in near-equal measure. This practice had been alive and well in Lothrop's Kent, a hotbed of progressive thought. A

Kentish observer recorded that none other than Gaius Julius Caesar remarked that the ancient inhabitants of Kent were even then praised as being above "all others the most full of humanity and gentleness."

Lothrop exemplified the colonial tendency to look backward to the great scholars and thinkers of a bygone era. When he considered Arthur Peach and his vile actions with his congregants, he could look through multiple prisms. Biblical scripture and Puritan ideals undoubtedly guided him, as did the great minds of the ancient Roman Empire. When Peach crossed the Atlantic Ocean and committed murder, New England's puritanical leaders were eager to deal with him—but he might as well have been in the hot, dusty Roman courts, where almost two thousand years earlier courtly philosophers engaged in elevated debates about the fates of such criminals.

Through Lothrop's study of the classics, likely first while still in Kent and then at the University of Cambridge, the reverend learned the art of rhetoric. This was not merely the skill of becoming a polished public orator. Rhetoric entailed adept reasoning, persuasive argument making *and* undoing, and the ability to spot faulty logic. Lothrop became a world-class "orator *optimus*," and he was not unique in those skills among colonists forging policy and politics. Learned individuals with formal education would have been familiar with the tenets of rational reasoning, rhetoric, and humanism. When John Underhill, one of the primary architects of the Pequot War's horrors against women, children, and the elderly, asked at the end of his narrative detailing the appalling events, "Why should you [the soldiers] be so furious . . . should not Christians have more mercy and compassion?," he used a widely understood example of "rhetorical dialogue." The analytical device allows the weighing of multiple sides of an argument.

The most popular ancient texts of the time were those by the Roman Empire–era historian Tacitus. Tacitus urged his Roman followers to adhere to the principles of "prudence and restraint," language echoed when Governor Winthrop tasked Massachusetts Bay Colony settlers with living successfully in the New World by "moderating and restraining them[selves], so that the rich and mighty should not eat up the poor." In 1627, administrators at the University of Cambridge ordered its history professor to desist from teaching Tacitus's precepts—an order endorsed by King Charles I. Tacitus's ideas unsettled the English royal family, who indulged in opulent splendor. In the New England colonies where Tacitus's ideology provided a vibrant clarion call for the Puritans, the views not only went unchecked, they were extolled—every human life had meaning, however often this failed in practice.

Lothrop studied the London preacher Thomas Goodwin's sermons that explored these same ideologies, later procuring a copy of Goodwin's book, *A Child of Light Walking in Darknesse.* Goodwin's teachings could give comfort in approaching as daunting a task as Lothrop's congregants faced in the upcoming trial. The English minister addressed the potential human fallibility of corrupted thought and reasoned that "as the chaff when the wheat is tossed . . . so in these commotions and winnowings of spirit, do our corruptions float in our consciences." A dizzying assortment of notions and biases that could cloud jurors' thought and perception—like those plumes of golden chaff tossed skyward—would need to be set aside for the jurors to succeed.

Colonial leaders took note of the cerebral Lothrop and an impressive contingent of his disciples in Scituate. In recognition of the English county they had left behind, they became known as the "Men of Kent." From this group, Scituate constable Annable ultimately selected Edward Foster, William Hatch, Samuell Hinkley, and Humfrey Turner as prospective jurors. Neighbors saw Turner as a "useful and enterprising man," with a large family, in itself a virtue for a growing community. His wife, Lydia, was pregnant with their seventh child. Foster and Hatch were also known as bedrocks of the small settlement. Lothrop counted on the positive contributions of these congregants, some of whom lived down the narrow sandy lane they had named Kent Street for the place in England they sought to preserve in spirit. Though isolated geographically, the prospective Lothrop jurors represented men on the forefront of new ways of thinking, an elite cohort Prence needed for the case of his lifetime.

In addition to the Scituate residents, the constables also added the settlers John Winslow, William Pontus, Richard Derbye, John Holmes, John Paybody, Giles Rickett, and Gabriell Fallowell, leaving the Lothrop jurors, who constituted more than a third of the jury at that point, a significant contingent. When called upon, each of these eleven men would take to the wooden courtroom benches carrying the weight of the New World with them. While these settlers gave the general impression of hardscrabble farmers, they reflected a population hell-bent on educational attainment. By 1645, 130 university graduates resided in the New England colonies, a significantly high proportion. In 1655, Harvard president Charles Chauncy did not mince words when he warned of children finding "happiness to live in the vast howling wilderness, without any ministry, or schools, and means of education . . . [which] sacrificed their sons and their daughters unto devils." Constable Annable and his colleagues succeeded in finding jurors who, however humble, similarly valued scholarship.

But Prence, who still agonized over finding a twelfth juror, faced another hurdle in ensuring that these crucial prospects would actually arrive at the trial. Reverend Lothrop was in the process of pulling up stakes from Plymouth Colony. In a time when slight doctrinal differences felt like chasms between religious groups, Plymouth's Meeting House did not match up with Lothrop's ministry. He felt determined to transplant his flock of congregants to a place of even greater liberty, where their community could truly be formed with his imprimatur from the ground up. Lothrop had his sights set on a remote area of Cape Cod, but without Governor Prence's approval, Lothrop faced a treacherous time organizing a relocation.

The departure of Lothrop and his followers would decrease the total population of Plymouth by between approximately 10 to 15 percent, removing some of the most esteemed residents in terms of education and acumen and potentially halting the trial altogether.

"I desire greatly to be released," Lothrop pleaded in the run-up to the trial. Prence did not budge. The two leaders remained at loggerheads. Prence needed a cross section of Lothrop's disciples on his jury; he could not let them slip out of reach.

The residents of Plymouth Colony probably had little firsthand knowledge of criminal jury service. Grizzlier legal methods once notoriously practiced in England, such as trial by ordeal—in which innocence was proved only if the accused survived torture—had been for the most part supplanted by juries. However, English jury trials were often reserved for civil cases to consider technical inheritance or property claims. In criminal matters, a contemporary noted that the use of juries had "penetrated little." They would all be learning on the job.

In some ways, a colonial jury resembled modern ones, as is the case with the custom of a jury stepping out of earshot for deliberations, whether by huddling in the courtroom or retiring to a dedicated chamber. One challenge that still resonates was how to persuade selected jurors to set aside urgent work—mainly subsistence farming, in those days—to attend trial. Jurors contended with missed work, travel, stress, and the psychological horror of passing judgment on a defendant who was part of the same community. Colony leaders resorted to a carrot-and-stick approach to deal with these challenges, just as English rulers did, sometimes offering lifetime dispensation from jury duty as a reward for fealty to the crown.

Jurors who "default[ed] in appearance without reasonable excuse made" were fined a prohibitive forty shillings. Meanwhile, those who attended expected to be reimbursed for their time. By the early eighteenth century, historical records clarify the exact payment for jurors: "For each verdict as well in criminal as in civil cases whereof two shillings and five pence shall be to the foreman, and one shilling and five pence apiece to the other jurors." That amount reflected a much-needed raise; the previous amount had been "so small that the sum . . . by no means defray[ed] their charges." "Jurors are oftentimes detained at the trial," lamented one aggrieved settler. Jurors also expected the settlement leadership to pay for their "victuals," especially at a time when food was relatively scarce. Although the record for the Peach gang trial does not detail jury payment, jurors likely would have been fed and perhaps compensated for their time.

While Prence struggled to identify a possible twelfth juror and to stop the departure of Lothrop's followers, two other men were selected to attend the "grand inquest"—the criminal trial. Thomas Besbeech and Henry Bourne were likely grand jurors, a term with a different meaning in colonial New England than today. Seventeenth-century grand jurors were "to inquire into, and present, any breach of law within [a] court's jurisdiction." The pair served as watchdogs, obliged to report malfeasance.

Governor Prence needed to ensure that the jurors' deliberations would be beyond reproach. Some years later, a defendant used an allegation of jury fixing in another colonial court to appeal the jury's judgment. Back in England, judges had ways of dealing with renegade jurors. One law declared that "if any jury conceal the offence, the justices may impanel twelve or more; who, if they find the concealment, every one of the first jury shall pay twenty shillings to the King." Prence was determined that no such issues would arise in this case.

Disagreements between the strong-willed men who had risked their lives to settle in Plymouth Colony could mean hell breaking loose. The author of the book *Country Justice*, which circulated in Plymouth at the time, justified such a scenario: "If a jury being together, shall fall out and fight: this is no riot, because they were lawfully assembled." Prence had to anticipate the possibility of fistfights breaking out during jury deliberations, and accept these as a natural by-product of the process. As the judge at trial, he would need to keep his composure, even in the face of riots or mobs.

Even when violence was not erupting, jurors proved loud and disorderly, rivaling fact-finding judges in the number of questions they hurled at wide-eyed, outnumbered witnesses. The practice of jurors as courtroom fact finders carried over into the New World for centuries. Jurors took their duties seriously and demanded answers when they needed more information to arrive at a verdict. Earlier juries of medieval England also did not disappoint when it came to diligently sorting through confounding clues. In a moment worthy of a Sherlock Holmes mystery, one English jury noted earnestly that the presence of a man's dog near a murder victim did not alone signify that the animal's master was the killer; the circumstantial evidence could be considered a "false clue."

Other English jury practices reflected a more divergent historical trajectory before arriving at modern standards. A single holdout could be disregarded or even reprimanded for slowing down the wheels of justice. When juror unanimity was required, creative solutions could be employed. One English legal observer noted, "If the twelve [jurors] differ in their verdict, others are added until there are twelve who agree, on one side or the other." And that was when twelve jurors were used, as they would be for the Peach gang trial. Juries had varying and random odd and even numbers of men, "9, 36, and 40" serving at a time. Parties agreed on the number of jurors.

There was contention over who would serve as jurors and in which legal matters. "Special" juries were common; men recognized for their expertise gathered to weigh matters related to their craft or trade. In London, epicurean disputes were under the sole purview of "juries of cooks and fishmongers." Historically, knights made up at least a percentage of a jury. One legal commentator regretted the decline of knight-laden juries: "You never saw such a jury taken without a knight."

As far as local legal knowledge went, settlers had a body of law called "custumals," English village laws written down and dispensed by town or borough courts. Local land deeds in Plymouth Colony frequently referenced hyper-regional custumals, dictating, for example, parties "be holden according to the manner [of law] of East Greenwitch in the county of Kent." These customary legal provisions were often utilized when writing up property deeds in the colony. They did not apply to criminal matters, offering little guidance for the upcoming court case.

Former governor Bradford documented the charge against Peach as "willful murder." Ranulf de Glanville, a legal analyst writing in the twelfth century, expressed the legal tradition in England on the charge by defining it as "murder which is secretly perpetrated—no one seeing—no one knowing of it, save the person committing it, and his accomplices, so that hue and cry ["a crowd pursuing him"] cannot be presently made after the offenders." While the colonists removed many of the unforgiving aspects of England's legal tradition in creating a legal code of their own, reducing the extensive number of capital offenses sanctioned in England to a handful, there was no crime of passion or manslaughter defense available. For Peach and his confederates, guilty verdicts meant death.

Giles Rickett, a builder empaneled for the Peach gang trial, represented one example in the range of experiences and perspectives each juror brought to court. When Rickett purchased acres of land by the ocean in Plymouth, he paid in shillings and linen. The linen was "homspon wollin cloth," not fine lace. Rickett traded the fabric, the color of oats untouched by vegetable dyes that came in shades of "red, blue, green, yellow, purple." Rough to the touch, his wares compared poorly with the intricately woven more desirable textiles, such as "fustian, Holland, buckram, kersey, linsey-woolsey, lockram."

Rickett carried out various projects for the colony, including surveying the "high ways" and meticulously constructing wolf traps in the woods surrounding Plymouth. Trapping wolves meant completing gruesome tasks, such as digging and concealing wolf pits and coating hooks and chains in tallow to ensnare the hunted animals. Rickett certainly killed any wolves that survived the grisly traps. One of the select men in the colony authorized to bear arms, along with his two sons, he could shoot the animals dead when necessary and then sever the heads for bounty.

Rickett's track record taking on construction projects commissioned by the colony made him an ideal choice to help build the cage where the accused Peach gang members were held before trial. The makeshift prison needed to meet legal specifications of having "competent strength to detain a prisoner" in a location accessible to "several [Plymouth Colony] neighborhoods." In the colonial era, no attempts were made to ensure prisoners' comfort; one seventeenth-century prisoner in Nantucket spent more than a year confined in a pig pen.

No rules prevented Rickett and the other jurors from observing the gang members in their holding cell. Plymouth Colony constable Joshua Pratt likely served as "jailor." By law, the jailor's duty required that he "keep such as shall be committed" any and all prisoners. Pratt or Myles Standish took turns staying close to the men, ensuring that the remaining gang members did not elude justice as Governor Prence and Constable Annable finalized the details of the jury.

To whatever extent the colony required Rickett's skills in maintaining the crude holding pen as the trail loomed, he may have already begun to form an opinion on the disheveled, dispirited prisoners. Those who did interact with Peach and his men became embroiled in verbal exchanges, the temptation to question the gang and tease out details of the murder impossible to resist. One observer noted that settlers "often examined" the accused men, with "evidence prodused." Whatever the prisoners may have said during their days in jail has been left undocumented.

Rickett's interactions with the miserable gang may have prepared him to facilitate the men's convictions. On the other hand, like many of his peers, he had mixed feelings about the increasing interactions with indigenous neighbors. Rickett added a provision to his land deed denying tribal members permission to pass through his property. His position reflected the stance of a colonial hardliner not willing to incorporate the rights of Indians in wartime. Intolerant of tribal customs, Rickett could deny that last right owed a murder victim—justice.

## 7

# THE TRIAL

"Seeke and make peace if possible with all men."

—*Roger Williams, founder of*
*Providence, Rhode Island*

Perched high on the summit of the colony's seaside drumlin, a severed head rose up from a stake. Next to it, the Meeting House struck an incongruously gothic chord compared to the colony's simpler structures. Little sunlight entered past the salt-stung door into the dim interior. The atmosphere matched the occasion on the morning of September 4, 1638, when judgment day had come for Arthur Peach, Richard Stinnings, and Thomas Jackson.

Stifling heat hung over those crowding into the vast first floor. Intermittent narrow openings in the walls served as bellicose embrasures, allowing weapons to be fired if the Meeting House came under attack but providing little fresh air. The weak light left the observers straining to view the defendants as they entered.

As they took in the scene, Peach and his two companions were hemmed in by the curious, the angry, and those secretly sympathetic. The musty gloom cloaked the defendants' gaunt features, shriveled by malnourishment since their escape from the colony. The suspenseful moment, shrouded by shadow, was as fraught with heightened drama as a Florentine chiaroscuro painting, darkness pitted against light.

Peach and his men were fighting not just for their lives but also for their souls. In the seventeenth century, life and death, good and evil, hovered over everything. Colonists strove to identify their own transgressions each day, duty bound to deny "deviltry" at every turn. That day in September, the people of Plymouth Colony needed to determine not just guilt or innocence, but whether Peach and his coconspirators should be consigned to eternal damnation. Dirty, sweating in the heat, scared, they certainly stank like something demonic, a red flag for those in attendance. Peach, standing before them to answer for murder, might actually have known the devil personally, as far as the bystanders were concerned. For the primary defendant, hell must have indeed felt within reach.

The men's situation would have been pitiable if their deeds had not been so abhorrent. Peach stood trial in a foreign land, parted from family, as a member of the lowest social standing, discarded by whatever influential benefactors he once had. As if waking up on the throes of a well-deserved nightmare, Peach was surrounded by people he had wronged over the years: his companions, whom he had coaxed into trouble; the allies of the Nipmuc man he had murdered; Edward Winslow, whose contract he had flouted and trust he had violated by running away; Stephen Hopkins, whose servant he had impregnated in violation of Plymouth laws; and then there was Dorothy Temple herself, whom he had effectively abandoned. Peach kept his ear to the ground, and even with so many enemies he had reason to believe that the scales of justice could tip in his favor. Peach's jury would seat no tribesmen, being made up of individuals who looked like him, white men. Men who had been in quarrels and wars with tribesmen, who had bought and otherwise finagled land from the indigenous people, sometimes only to find them still "trespassing."

Some settlers made clear that they were unconcerned with the evidence of the crime. Jurors, too, might value fellow settlers, servants or not, over the life of a single tribesman. On this front, former Plymouth Colony governor Bradford noted that within the settlement "the rude and ignorant sort murmured [disapprovingly] that any English should be put to death for the Indean." Such rumblings had to worry

Prence for the jurors' safety. Some years later, a colonial juror sitting on a case in which the defendants were tribesmen came under threat of intimidation from "a mob assembled at . . . [his] home." Fearing for their lives, even open-minded jurors might be unable to arrive at a consensus.

Narragansett and Wampanoag, adorned in traditional clothing, clustered near the banished and controversial colonial leader, Roger Williams, who was in attendance, likely sweating in his trim-fitting waistcoat. There were men present, like those who had urged his banishment from Massachusetts Bay, who would have liked to see Williams dead. One settler who nursed a feud with him called him "an ass, a simple dunce, a knave, a liar, a thief, cheater an hypocrite, a drunkard, a traitor, a whore monger with Indian women." Relations were tense at best among many of the colonial leaders and citizens gathered together in close quarters for the trial.

Williams would have most likely taken along his Pequot servant, Will. Not only would Williams choose to leave female servants to support his wife, Mary, with childcare, and prefer to have his experienced messenger Will to deliver communiqués related to the trial, but the boy's immersion in the backstory of the trial also made him a natural companion. Though neither the Peach gang nor the public knew it, without the resourceful boy there might have never been a trial. Will's clandestine operation for Williams made him the perfect candidate to listen for any whispers of threats to Williams or to Plymouth in general, especially those in dialects he grew up hearing or ones he had learned more recently. If Governor Winthrop brought along his own entourage, one or more of Will's siblings may have also been present, providing another chance for a reunion.

Massasoit, a charismatic and commanding man, wore an extravagantly thick band of costly wampum that rattled across his midsection as he made himself comfortable to wait for the trial. Intricate bands of purple and white beads, polished to rounded perfection, spoke to Massasoit's conspicuous wealth and power. Except for the wampum and a heavy black wolf skin across one shoulder, Massasoit stood "all naked." His fur might have been tinged by the scent of pungent, sultry tobacco, sage, sweet grass, and cedar fireside smoke—the four essentials that imbued indigenous life.

In parts of Kent, England, the birthplace of several of the jurors, the townspeople were called to court by the sound of the enormous, ancient moot horn. The low, sonorous tone could be heard far and wide. In the English village of Sandwich, men seated for jury service gathered in an imposing courtroom where Queen Elizabeth I had once been entertained. Its walls boasted oak panels, adorned with royal arms. The Plymouth Colony Meeting House was humble by comparison but far more solemn.

English town criers traditionally called jurors and spectators to court with the rousing refrain "Attend, good men and true," a summons that may have also drawn the Plymouth Colony jurors to court. Edward Foster, William Hatch, John Winslow, William Pontus, Richard Derbye, John Holmes, John Paybody, Humfrey Turner, Samuell Hinkley, Giles Rickett, and Gabriell Fallowell made up eleven of the twelve men needed to serve as jurors. Clues in the historical record suggest that Prence and Reverend Lothrop managed to agree that if the religious leader kept his congregation in the colony until the end of the trial, the governor would support their relocation.

The jurors were an austere group. No sketches, visual or verbal, survive to reveal how the jurors looked or acted as they convened, but their biographies help fill in the blanks. Though all married or widowed, none wore wedding rings, an affectation disdained by Puritans. Their work-worn hands would have rested unadorned on their roughly hewn garments. Juror Pontus may have showed his fifty-three years of age, the skin around his eyes creased. The hardworking farmer likely appreciated getting away from the fields and off his feet, as jurors were among the few in court to enjoy the luxury of sitting on benches. Jurors Hinkley and Hatch would have greeted each other with great familiarity. They were not just neighbors in the settlement of Scituate but also had traveled to the New World on the same ship, *Hercules*. Juror Hatch had special reason to hold his head high; he had recently been put in charge of "exercising the people in arms at

Scituate" to prepare for any future battles. Now Hatch had to brace himself to consider evidence against a veteran soldier.

Arriving among the jurors and the mass of observers, Governor Prence and his court assistants, three abreast, cloaked and armed, entered the imposing building—by law, men with the right to carry weapons brought them to all public meetings. Myles Standish kept his sidearm at the ready as he escorted Prence, likely also hanging his knife around his neck, the battle-tested blade in condition "as sharp as a needle, and ground . . . to an edge." The colony's military captain remained alert to danger. Prence could count on Standish being at his side, whatever happened in the courtroom.

It was Standish who had taken it upon himself to place the severed head of a battle foe off the Meeting House's upper level. The skull was rotted, and its eye sockets were empty. The remains belonged to the defeated tribesman Wituwamat. Standish added a makeshift flag "of linen cloth dyed in the same Indian's blood." The military leader offered a clear warning to all who entered. The English perfected this technique of creating atmospheric horror to intimidate those approaching government edifices. In defeated Ireland, the English lined one walkway so that supplicants "passe[d] through a lane of heddes . . . [provoking] great terror . . . [by witnessing] dedde fathers, brothers." To colonists, the grisly adornments appeared as appropriate reminders of the dangers that threatened, and to Indians, the skull and blood-soaked linen meant that sometimes settlers sanctioned and glorified the killing of a tribesman.

Those who could not fit inside the Meeting House likely waited close by, hoping to overhear testimony that would directly affect the villagers. Each man, woman, and child had endured a state of constant fear as the trial approached. They stood and strained their ears against the swells of summer wind passing through tasseled corn crops, switch grass, and oak trees, a louder refrain than the quiet harbor waters at the bottom of the hill.

The Pequot, still reeling from the recent slaughter of so many of their people at the hands of the colonists, continued to warn other tribes that "the English would fall upon them," too. Former governor Bradford noted in his journal that he suspected that some indigenous people might prepare for battle, "conceiving they should now find the Pequot's words trew." Settlers feared that the threat might provoke indiscriminate retribution from surrounding tribes. As worried as Prence was for the future of Plymouth Colony and for those who lived in the immediate village, he knew that Penowanyanquis's murder placed the frontier settlers in even greater immediate jeopardy. Those Englishmen and -women on the far outskirts of the colony fully realized their "remoteness and vulnerability." Colonists secured their small homes as carefully as they could at night, keeping their children inside. During the day, the murder was the talk of the colony. Roger Williams simply and accurately noted that among the colonists there was a great "hubbub."

The "very austere" Miantonomo, the Narragansett sachem who had detained Peach and his men in the woods near Providence, shared an ominous warning with the English. "Be careful on the highways," he cautioned; "the natives, friends of the slain, had consultation to kill an Englishman in revenge." The sachem promised his people that the colonists "would see justice done," which helped ease tensions and stifled calls for retributory violence. The English hoped that his assurances would prevent the urge for vengeance. They needed to manifest justice to prevent the Narragansett from rising up against the Plymouth settlers. Plymouth colonists must have wondered whether the jurors would indeed be able to condemn Peach and his men to death if the evidence warranted it. Former governor Bradford suspected that "the rude and ignorant sorte" would not.

Governor Prence, the "terror to the wicked," took his place at the imposing raised paneled pulpit also used for religious services. A chest-high wooden barrier adorned with repeating newels enclosed the pulpit on three sides, providing a barrier from any overzealous court attendees. While Prence focused his studies on the Bible and the Hebrew language, he also owned two law books and a copy of *Blunt's*

*Law Dictionary*, useful tools in preparing the biggest case that had come to a colonial court.

Prence would serve as both fact finder and prosecutor, supervising the proceedings and interviewing witnesses and defendants alike. During the early colonial period, the adversarial structure that now includes prosecutors and defense attorneys did not exist. Defendants advocated for themselves in open court against criminal charges. Judge and jurors, meanwhile, were not asked to presume the accused innocent. The accused had few resources, if any, and dealt with harsh, unregulated conditions while jailed, which often poorly impacted their health. The proceedings' inherent conflicts of interest tilted against Peach, while the checkered history of relations with the tribes did not ensure any presumption of rights for the victim. With few resources and little experience, the scene was set for a chaotic ordeal.

Potential problems seemed to await Prence no matter the outcome. He understood the geopolitical ramifications of failing to secure a conviction, but the undercurrent of support for Peach also laid the groundwork for disaster. If Peach were convicted, Prence could face an uprising. In some ways, this made the possibility of a conviction just as dangerous as the lack of one. But visions of armed colonists in revolt had to wait as the governor opened the proceedings.

Seven of the most powerful men in the colony surrounded the governor. These "gentlemen, & assistants of the said Government" included Myles Standish, Prence's predecessor William Bradford, John Alden, and Edward Winslow. The colonial leaders stared down at the defendants from the lectern. Former governor Edward Winslow, Peach's onetime master, must have trained a particularly fiery gaze on Peach.

When Winslow first learned of Penowanyanquis's murder, he had reason to doubt the news. Four years earlier, Winslow had returned to Plymouth Colony after having visited present-day Connecticut. On his return, he saw the colony's settlers in the throes of grief, but immediately their expressions changed to ones of joy and ebullience. Winslow's dear friend Massasoit, the sachem of the mighty Wampanoag, had carried out an elaborate ruse while Winslow was away. The sachem had ordered a trusted messenger to tell Plymouth settlers that Edward Winslow had been murdered; the messenger took them to the very spot where the murder had allegedly taken place, so all would know with certainty "how & where he was killed." Plymouth fell into a profound state of mourning until Winslow returned, alive and well. When settlers later inquired about the hoax, Massasoit good-naturedly explained that "it was their manner to doe so, that they might be more wellcome when they come home." Massasoit determined that his devoted companion should never be taken for granted. No one would forget the peculiar lesson. Now that Winslow came to terms with the fact that Arthur Peach indeed killed the indigenous trader in the woods, the sight of the defendants at trial represented an especially bitter betrayal, a realization that a murderer had lived under his roof with his wife and young children.

A final housekeeping item affected the assembled jury directly. Prence called Richard Derbye forward from the wooden benches where he and the other jurors sat. Prence demanded that Derbye admit owing "the King, &c" twenty-one pounds, a substantial sum. Derbye's admission reflected a financial downturn. One of his most successful land transactions topped out at 150 pounds—a small fortune in itself. A sly businessman, his deeds were filled with creative exceptions, conditions, and handy encumbrances that would carry over and benefit him long after he sold the land at top dollar. A form of cunning colored his dealings with local colonists. At times he crossed a clear moral line, his behavior becoming downright menacing.

Less than a year after the Peach gang trial, Derbye would be back in court on charges of "giveing of an empoysoned potion of drinke" to several settlers, almost killing them. The colony would impose yet another fine, twenty pounds. Derbye, apparently unfazed, took it all in stride. As the settlers duly recorded his financial woes that day, the juror certainly focused his attention on the young accused murderer, Arthur Peach, a type of man not unfamiliar to Derbye—a rogue with a dark streak.

The juror had reason to view Arthur Peach's actions through a complicated lens. Peach was a servant like those Derbye was busy procuring as part of a money-making endeavor, and Peach's behavior, left unpunished, set an extremely poor precedent. Convicting a servant such as Peach in such a sensational trial could make young indentured men think twice about committing troublesome indiscretions; on the other hand, hearing of three servants swinging by the neck from the gallows could scare away the dwindling number of people entering into service in the first place, which would be a blow to Derbye's financial bottom line.

Derbye was an interesting choice for the jury. Nothing indicates that he strove for notable positions in the community, nor that he was highly regarded. His presence on the jury may have reflected a conscious desire to enroll jurors from the colony's rank and file, untainted by class bias, possibly to balance out Lothrop's elite followers such as Hinkley and Hatch.

As jurors with divergent worldviews and experiences huddled together, the issue of who would be their twelfth man seemed to be answered when Richard Sillis stepped forward. At first glance to the crowd of spectators, the unassuming potential juror would have appeared nothing more than a talesman—term for a last-minute juror. In ancient English tradition, the court drew a talesman from the crowd of spectators on the day of trial to hastily fill an empty jury seat—arguably someone less qualified for the solemn responsibility who could be coaxed into a consensus view.

In fact, Sillis was far from a talesman. He was one of Reverend Lothrop's loyal disciples, one of the "Men of Kent." Though Sillis was a recent arrival, Lothrop found him to be a man who could "stand steadfast," if need be, like Lothrop himself. Lothrop took note of Sillis, referring to him as "goodman," a humble term denoting someone who could not be called "master," which was the more respectable prefix. He got to see firsthand Sillis's admirable qualities. The newcomer owned only a "few old books," among them a Bible and a copy of Preston's *God's All Sufficiency*, the latter speaking to the fundamental responsibility of free will; the sermons also argued that only God could provide true fulfillment.

Because he was not yet a freeman, Sillis remained ineligible for empanelment when he walked into the Meeting House. Someone with clout—most likely Lothrop, perhaps with the assistance of Scituate's Constable Annable—went to great lengths to ensure that Sillis made it onto the jury that otherwise would have been short a man. The very day of the trial, Governor Prence swore Sillis in as a freeman in Plymouth Colony. The upgraded status meant that he could vote and provided the prerequisite to jury service. Colonial leaders did not take the decision to make a settler a freeman lightly, a fact suggesting that Sillis's qualities—being part of Lothrop's philosophical cohort paired with having the fresh eyes of a newcomer—were seen as important additions to the jury. With Sillis in the mix, nearly half the jury was made up of Lothrop's followers.

Prence asked each of the jurors to raise his right hand, as was customary in seventeenth-century New England colonies, and swear an oath "to give a true verdict according to law and evidence." If some doubted whether the Plymouth Colony jurors could adhere to a finding based on the evidence, the devoutly religious men had now sworn to God that they would rise to the occasion.

Historically, English jurors who failed to honorably carry out their duty faced catastrophic consequences. Not only did disgraced jurors forever lose the opportunity to take an oath again, no longer being suitably "othesworth," certain jurors could be punished with imprisonment or loss of goods, or even subjected to knowing that their "wives and children should be turned out of doors, and their lands laid waste." Each of the twelve empaneled jurymen was deadly serious about carrying out their responsibilities.

The stakes for jurors such as Giles Rickett, whose background may have predisposed him to disdain Penowanyanquis's rights, could not have been higher. Failing to honor his oath would amount to a perilous deal with the devil and, if found out, generations of familial impoverishment. The forty-one-year-old certainly prepared himself for a day of soul-searching as he sat uncomfortably in the Meeting House in his carefully tended "shooes . . . stockens & hatt."

No records survive of Prence offering preliminary instructions to the empaneled men, although it is a reasonable assumption that he reminded them of the gravity of their task when they took their oath. Though Prence and Plymouth Colony hosted the trial, leaders from the other colonies also contributed to the proceedings. Roger Williams in particular was well suited to give words of guidance to the jurors. When corresponding with Governor Winthrop's son, Williams took the opportunity to offer unsolicited advice on navigating conflicts between indigenous people and settlers. "First kiss truth where you evidently upon your soul see it: 2. advance justice, (though upon a childs eyes) 3 seeke and make peace if possible with all men," he wrote.

Though Prence was congenial and easy to talk to in daily life, he ruled the courtroom as he did the colony—with a strict hand. Even with the governor projecting unflinching authority at the front of the room, his path to a verdict was as uncertain as a verdict's consequences. To prove the identity of the murderers, Prence would have to rely on the dying declaration against white men spoken not only by a tribesman, but a member of the Nipmuc tribe, disdained even by the other tribes because of its smaller size and perceived insignificance. Another problem was that identification was conveyed later not to fellow Nipmuc speakers but to the Narragansett who had found Penowanyanquis in the woods, and then to Roger Williams, whose translations had to be trusted by people who didn't always trust him, all spoken by a grievously injured, possibly delirious man.

If Prence faced the daunting prospect of synthesizing the disparate fragments of a case that transcended the cultural boundaries, Peach had reason to feel optimistic. Even in the most nail-biting moments during the trial ahead, Peach likely assumed a reluctance on the part of the jurors to convict a fellow settler—to convict anyone of anything that carried a death sentence, for that matter. As the famed English jurist Sir John Fortescue had stridently declared, "Truly I would rather that twenty guilty men should escape through pity than that one just man should be unjustly condemned."

In the crosswinds of courtroom conversation, Peach may have heard about the well-respected governor Winthrop's instructions to fellow colonial officials that echoed Fortescue's admonishment from across the sea, urging restraint to colonial leaders when dealing with criminal matters in the settlement. Winthrop advised authorities to remain mindful that, "in the infancy of plantations, justice should be administered with more lenity than in a settled state; because people are more apt then to transgress . . . partly out of oppression."

Winthrop went on to liken the trouble that might come from strict application of the law to men not living in the ordered kingdom of England but in a seemingly lawless wilderness. He argued that "if the strings of a new instrument be wound up unto their height, they will quickly crack." Peach was just the sort of man Winthrop must have envisioned when he made his case for restrained application of the law. Peach had been a decorated soldier, fighting on behalf of Massachusetts Bay. If leaders enforced laws too harshly against soldiers like Peach, these men the colonies depended on so desperately might begin to avoid their military duties.

The mere presence of John Throckmorton in the court, however, had to bring Peach's hopes down to earth. Roger Williams's trusted friend was poised to present damning testimony. Throckmorton had been the only English settler traveling the Narragansett trail around the time of Penowanyanquis's attack, and he had come upon the Peach gang while they sat by their campfire in the desolate woods.

Throckmorton described the encounter in dramatic detail, as if recounting a ghost story to a rapt audience. He came "upon a sudden by them, was glad he had past them, suspecting them." It is unclear what he suspected exactly, or if knowledge that they were accused murderers clouded his memory and impressions. The wary settler had been on horseback in the woods that day and galloped past the gang in haste.

Despite his observations, Throckmorton could not claim to have witnessed any violence. Each of the defendants offered the court an audacious response to the testimony; they "denied that they had met Mr. Throckmorton."

Not long after Throckmorton's testimony, he visited an attorney who lived in present-day Boston and who possessed a small personal library, and paid a fee to borrow a book. The peculiar volume, *The Printed Relation of the Martyrs*, was filled with gruesome woodcut prints, showing in gory detail the fate of the least fortunate Puritans. The book served as a visual reminder of nightmarish persecution, the illustrations the most impressive known to England at the time. Just possessing a copy of the book could have gotten a Puritan maimed or killed back in England, where limitations on a free press marked the front lines of the authoritarian monarchy's oppression.

Throckmorton took the book back to the Providence settlement and gave it to Roger Williams, who had apparently requested it. Williams seemed to want to revisit the deaths depicted in the woodcut images of the volume. The author of *The Printed Relation of the Martyrs* strove to portray the killings of Puritans as *mala in se*, an inherently immoral transgression. Magnifying the religious animosity of the time, the woodcut depicted Puritan martyrs as victims and their criminal transgressors as malevolent evildoers—a black-and-white conflict. Perhaps the book manifested for both Williams and Throckmorton a view of martyrdom broader than one applicable to just Puritans, one that included Arthur Peach's innocent victim.

Peach's testimony brazenly refuting Throckmorton showed that he was not backing away from the courtroom showdown with his accusers, a sign of self-confidence befitting a man Governor Winthrop described as being of "good parentage and fair conditioned." The defendant would not be a pushover. In fact, Peach's most ambitious defense began before the trial itself; he hoped to appeal his case directly to the king of England, who was the final authority in colonial matters. Peach likely pressed this same defense again in court.

It was not unheard of for the king to become involved in a dispute. A member of Penowanyanquis's tribe who had fled to England and found himself in debtors' prison successfully petitioned none other than King Charles II. The tribesman requested that his land in the colonies be sold off to cover his debt; the king responded by giving the Nipmuc petitioner a letter ordering just that.

While colonial leaders hashed out the legal minutiae of Peach's gambit, Governor Winthrop dismissed the possibility of the appeal to the crown and reassured Prence with an "answer of encouragement." He advised "to proceed notwithstanding, seeing no appeal." "They could not be tried in England," Winthrop argued to his overwhelmed colleague. As Winthrop predicted, nothing came of Peach's plan to reach out to the king, but an unearthed chapter from Peach's initial voyage to the New World demonstrates that the idea had not been outlandish.

When Peach added his name to the *Plain Joan* ledger for passage from Gravesend, England, to the Virginia colonies in the spring of 1635, he joined the humble company of other hopeful young men. The passenger list of Peach's ship—eighty-four able-bodied men and boys, some as young as fourteen—reflects a group with similarly memorable and colorful family names such as Stamp, Raddish, and Viper. Time tended to whittle down and simplify ancient European surnames as they passed through generations and languages. The name of the most prestigious man on the ship is absent from the widely circulated passenger list, a stunning omission.

A careful review of King Charles I's records shows a small entry that dashing Lieutenant Robert Evelyn also boarded the bark for the New World. Evelyn was on his way to join forces with his uncle, Captain Thomas Yong. Yong, a grand explorer with Catholic leanings, had been busy scouting the Delaware River. Some alleged that he was not merely privately a Catholic, but that he also tried to spread Catholicism in the New World, an affront to the crown.

Yong had demanded that his "men" in London and Gravesend "be sent for either by a messenger or a warrant . . . so they may bee commanded to obey him [Robert Evelyn]." This group included Yong's "principal seamen," who were required to defer to him and Evelyn once they reached the colonies. Within this large group, Evelyn was just one member of Yong's team of elite adventurers to help him explore the uncharted territory across the ocean. Peach likely comprised part of this covert team of men, perhaps as a skilled soldier or seaman.

Evelyn carried with him on the *Plain Joan* an extraordinary letter from King Charles I, granting a rare entitlement. "The King expects that he will give every assistance to the bearer, Lieut. Robt. Evelin, who is on his return in the *Plain Joan*, to Capt. Yong in America, upon 'special and very important service.'" The monarch's lavish support for the adventurers hinted at the fact that the king was one of the few who knew that Yong's and Evelyn's planned mission went far beyond colonization and exploration attempts along the Delaware River. The adventurers sought the holy grail of the New World, the uncharted Northwest Passage to the Pacific Ocean. That body of water would change history by opening new trading routes. The king's desire to secure the Northwest Passage explains his blanket protection for Evelyn and his men. Why should King Charles I content himself with the British Empire and the expanding Atlantic colonies when greater wealth awaited beyond?

The English ruler further declared that Evelyn and his men had "already given satisfaction to his Majestie, in swearing their allegiance, and that, therefore, they are not more to be questioned in that point." The king's orders continued: "Mr. Yong and his nephew [Robert Evelyn], and their company, shall freely pass and go out of his dominions, without any of their questions, lets, arrests, stops, pressing, interruptions, or hindrances in any kind whatsoever." Evelyn, with Peach in his company, would have avoided the usual aggressive scrutiny and questioning by portside "searchers," who normally demanded exhaustive oaths of fealty to Charles I and his Protestant Church of England. If Evelyn, or Peach for that matter, had Catholic leanings, the searchers remained in the dark.

The vast majority of Irish people at the time practiced Catholicism, professing Protestantism only when necessary. Some members of the

Peach clan living in Ireland in the seventeenth century, such as Robert Peach the elder and the younger, who were noted as debtors in 1641, identified as "British Protestant," disavowing Catholicism. But this may have been an expediency to access the British court system in seventeenth-century Ireland. Whether or not the description accurately referenced a true religious belief is another matter. By contrast, when Robert "Pe[a]ch," a probable relative, was baptized on July 5, 1647, in Cork, Ireland, he took his blessing at Holy Trinity, a Catholic church.

Peach was in all likelihood the only other Catholic on board the ship, implicating him in this remarkable Catholic spy ring. Peach's English shipboard companions, on the other hand, were Protestant. Two secret Catholics aboard the *Plain Joan* sailing with no connection to the other would be the height of coincidence. Peach was almost unquestionably one of Yong's "company," traveling with Evelyn and embroiled in the lieutenant's high-stakes plans.

The travelers were not out of danger, though. Catholics in the New World faced the constant threat of being exposed and being confronted with the consequences of their faith. In the first years of the seventeenth century in Jamestown Colony, authorities executed a settler for being a Catholic spy; several other men were apparently buried in secret with Catholic objects of worship. One corpse unearthed later had been interred with a silver reliquary filled with bone chips possibly from a saint and a small vial, which might have held blood or holy water.

Massachusetts Bay Colony leaders were dead set against Catholics. They "ordered that no Jesuit or spiritual or ecclesiastical person, (as they are termed,) ordained by the authority of the pope of the see of Rome, shall come within this jurisdiction, on pain of banishment; if returning, shall suffer death, except in cases of shipwreck." Unless a Catholic's bark was thrown up against the rocky coast of New England, in other words, he was better off avoiding the settlements or risk being put to death.

Once in the Virginia colonies, the well-connected Evelyn and Yong were in a position to introduce Peach to Samuel Maverick, a pioneering settler of Massachusetts Bay Colony who had "episcopal-minded" Catholic sympathies. Evidence points to Maverick bringing Peach with him when he set sail out of the Virginia settlements to New England in 1636 on his newly purchased, forty-ton cedarwood pinnace, built in Barbados.

No matter that Peach would be crowded in by fourteen cows and eighty goats; thousands of men would have jumped at the opportunity. Settlers described Virginia as hell on earth. One man wrote about the conditions in the settlements the same month Peach arrived. He described "the misfortunes that swallow us . . . lament[ing] the tumults and broils, wrongs and oppressions, which yearly increase the infelicities of the colony." Another man bemoaned how "people cry out day and night . . . and would not care to lose any limb to be in England again." Peach headed to New England. The trip would take little time. "With a fair wind . . . in four and twenty hours you may send or go by sea to New England [from] . . . Virginia," reported a contemporary source. And even better, Samuel Maverick apparently had a plan in mind for Peach—placement as a servant with a powerful and "smooth tongued cunning fellow" by the name of Edward Winslow in Plymouth Colony. Peach's circuitous path to Plymouth came together.

The social connections that not long before had brought Peach into the orbit of colonial power leaders like Evelyn and Samuel Maverick, leading to his indenture with Winslow, constituted a form of currency, which he tried to cash in for his life when facing murder charges. Powerful men could intervene and hold sway with fellow colonial leaders when soldiers broke laws and faced punishment. Such proved the case with the fellow Pequot War veteran Aaron Stark, who lived in present-day Connecticut.

When colonial leaders discovered that Stark had had a sexual encounter with a woman, they were quick to have "the letter R burnt uppon his cheeke," for having "ravished" her. Authorities also ordered him to marry the young woman. But they did not put the "former Scottish mercenary" to death, as they might have done. Captain John Mason, who had achieved infamy in the Pequot War, stepped in to shield his valuable, battle-tested soldier from the worst. It did not behoove the settlement to lose a useful combatant during a time of war. Peach, like Stark, was a skilled soldier. Researchers have revealed that 30 to 50 percent of Pequot War veterans fought in Europe's Thirty Years' War, meaning that there is a good chance Peach gained prized military skills before sailing for the New World. However, as Peach had committed a graver crime than Stark, none of Peach's associates and contingent of explorer-spies are on record as stepping forward to intervene on his behalf.

Maverick, who likely helped Peach make the trip to New England, faced mounting legal problems of his own. Adversaries suspected his Catholic leanings, and whatever access he had to English royalty, he and his peers could not risk covert missions or shaky political footing through involvement in such a public legal matter. Furthermore, at the time of the trial, Maverick noted that Yong and his associates were fully occupied "carrying their canoes some few times" upriver, bivouacking nearly to Quebec. Yong and Evelyn were unavailable to assist Peach as they continued to hunt for the Northwest Passage in the remote wilds of present-day Canada.

The Irish defendant's insistence that the king of England provide him a lifeline would have bewildered and intrigued the commonsense jurors. The daily life of a juror such as Edward Foster, a farmer, was filled with very different concerns, although he was also vulnerable to repercussions from the trial.

On any other day, Foster likely would have been tending his crops or hunting, maybe taking aim at the slender blackbirds that nimbly perched on early green stalks of rustling corn. The birds cocked their heads, their golden eyes alert to his presence, onyx-sheened wings ready for flight. For every shot Foster took, hundreds of black birds would rush skyward. The flutter of wings above rang out along with the sounds of his musket.

Foster spent his days searching for quarry through dense rows of corn he had hand-seeded alone, not having a son old enough to help him. There was no pleasure in killing a small bird that was not worth eating. The problem was the corn; he needed it to survive. The birds would not leave it alone, eating away his crops. The tribesmen nearby used a different technique, setting up "little watch-houses" in the rippling green fields to shelter their older children, who were at the ready to jump out in the early daybreak hours and scare the millions of *chogan euck* (blackbirds) away from their staple crop. But even if he had had a son old enough to do it, Foster would not have risked a precious child to such work.

He had already lost one son, Timothy, named for Foster's father. The young boy passed away before his first birthday, triggering the singular grief of such a loss. But just recently, as the corn began to break the soil, his next son was born. Again Foster named him Timothy, determined to provide a namesake for his aging father. Already this boy languished with the illnesses that circulated through the colony. Soon enough religious leaders prayed "for ye healing of a bloody cough among [the settlers'] children."

The worried settler must have feared that death stalked him. Praying and working represented his only ballast against tragedy. Foster learned from the Indians, who lived close by, how to work the soil and grow the corn his family needed. He diligently planted several shad fish deep in the soil throughout his *morgens*, or acres, of land on Scituate's Second Cliff. He knew that without the fish, the unfertilized corn would not grow.

For Foster, despair competed with optimism. His marriage to Lettice, a strong woman, proved a good one. Lettice's uncle, Timothy Hatherly, known as the "father of Scituate," had financed much of the growth of the small settlement, part of Plymouth Colony, where they lived. The wedding marked a noteworthy occasion, with the colony's renowned military captain, Myles Standish, officiating at the civil ceremony. The young couple built their bare-bones clapboard house next to the languorous "Satuit" Brook, facing Kent Street, the main thoroughfare. The residents had followed Cato's cardinal rules for colonization: "Secure . . . pure air, a fresh navigable river and a rich country." From this simple dirt road running parallel to the shore, they could listen to the sound of the breaking ocean surf as they fell asleep at night.

If Foster was distracted at times as the jury listened to the ominous tale told by Throckmorton and the denials by Peach, his thoughts must have drifted to his son and the harvesting that would soon start. The salt-marsh grass needed to be taken up. His feet and hands would pay the price, his boots constantly getting sucked downward into the mucky, dark sand, dotted with sharp-edged clams and mussels that lay below the marsh grass. The cumbersome stalks of grass resisted being cut, easily tumbling from his hands to the ground as he tried to collect the hay, and cut at his fingers, leaving him wet and briny and smelling brackish.

The farmer-*qua*-juror had built a staddle, the large, flat stand on which the sea grass would dry in the sun. The precarious dome of hay towered over him. It provided food for cattle and, in the family's hand-to-mouth existence where nothing could be wasted, material for insulation and roof thatch. The newer homes in Scituate, like Foster's, were thatched with fresh-hewn hay. The hay on the "old comers'" homes filled with mildew and moss, a faint green tinge coloring the entirety of the roofs. The distinctive hue, no doubt reminding Foster of the cottages back in Kent, let the world know that its inhabitants endured and survived as the first early settlers.

When news first reached Scituate of the attack in the wilderness, Foster and the other members of Reverend Lothrop's congregation knew that their spiritual leader would have much to say about the seismic event, and its moral and political implications. Foster also knew that he might have to fight if the Pequot War battles drew closer to Plymouth. Returning to England remained out of the question—of that he was certain. Whatever nostalgia Foster maintained for his hamlet of Fittenden in Kent, he knew that officials there terrorized those with Puritan leanings.

Foster was better off in the New England colonies, praying the fatal attack would be handled by a jury instead of soldiers and warriors. If all went well, he might even put his blistered hands to work again away from the land—as a lawyer. When he had occasion to

write up a land deed, his refined penmanship became the most conspicuous aspect of the document. If widespread violence rocked his
small community, if government broke down, the dream of one day
practicing law again would end. Given the circumstances of the killing, it was hard to envision any outcome that was not disastrous.

The murdered tribesman had been attacked after leaving Aptucxet,
where according to William Bradford, the young man had been
"a-trading"—no trivial detail. The complicated use of the valuable
Aptucxet trading post land raised thorny issues for colonists and
tribesmen alike. The assault on Penowanyanquis near that very spot,
of all places, further destabilized an already precarious situation.

The colonies survived on a trade relationship between settlers,
regional tribes, and the English in the Old World. The killing of a
tribesman on trading land would serve as a deterrent to future commerce. The colonists took pains to get the careful arrangements that
protected their claims on land and their access to trade in writing, but
after this fatal attack the recorded deals would be rendered worthless
if the indigenous leaders' trust in them faltered.

It was easy to imagine Penowanyanquis near the trading post,
laden with beaver furs as rounded and wide as a solid oak tree. It was
also easy to imagine the subsequent attack, the tribesman's arms and
hands empty and bloodied as he clawed at the air. The dark scenes
racing through the settlers' minds formed a grim tableau of the death
and misery of a single man—but also bespoke a threat that cut to the
very essence of the colonists' tenuous way of life. In what way did
Foster really possess the land he plowed in Scituate? Would enraged
tribesmen who had their capacity to hunt curtailed and their kinsman
murdered demand their land back?

Foster was now at the center of a still-escalating drama. He would
worry about his son, the war drawing in, and the much-needed harvesting another day.


Jurors, onlookers, authorities, and the two anxious codefendants all
listened and watched as Peach defended himself and responded to

questions that Prence and the others lobbed at him. The low oak ceiling absorbed much of the sound, making it harder for spectators toward the back to take in Peach's exact words, the rise-and-fall cadence of his Irish brogue. The historical record is silent on much of what Peach said at trial and on whether Thomas Jackson and Richard Stinnings attempted to help him advance any strategic arguments. The two men either left their defense in Peach's hands, in keeping with their deference to the armed ringleader during their murderous actions, or their arguments simply went unrecorded.

We do know that when a man named William Schooler, accused of murdering a young woman in nearby Massachusetts Bay Colony in the same period, faced forceful interrogation at trial, he offered an assortment of creative defenses to undermine the evidence against him. An observer noted the details of Schooler's audacious testimony. In response to questions about blood on his hat, he replied that it was that of "a pigeon, which he killed." What of "the scratch on the left side of his nose . . . being of the breadth of a small [finger] nail?" "A bramble," Schooler replied flatly. No, he later amended, it must have been "his piece"—his snaphance or pistol—that scratched his nose. "But that could not be on the left side," the court reasoned. There was no such thing as a left-handed man. How did Schooler explain the young woman's dead body discovered in a pond? He testified that "soon after he left her, he met with a bear and he thought that the bear might kill her." The inventive defenses that stretched the bounds of credibility left the court to ponder whether a pigeon, bramble, bear, or man had caused the bloodshed.

While Schooler admitted to having "lived a vicious life, and now lived like an atheist . . . and had been a common adulterer," he vehemently denied the murder allegation. Peach likely took a similar approach with his testimony, perhaps admitting to fleeing the colony, his servitude, and debts without permission, while refuting the murder charge. If so, Peach's tone may have been imploring, a stab at sincerity, an attempt to speak plainly. But Peach's encounter with Roger Williams had already revealed his inescapable propensity toward bold artifice, complicated stories, and meandering tales.

The absence of Penowanyanquis's body amounted to the center-piece of his defense. He seized on this detail and must have echoed it as a refrain throughout his testimony: "No man could witness that he saw him [Penowanyanquis] dead." Indeed, as the primary witness, Peach likely swore to having seen the tribesman alive.

As a defense based on the evidence, the technicality that no one had seen Penowanyanquis's body could override both the clear facts of the case and basic common sense. The last time he had been seen by any of the individuals gathering for the trial, including Roger Williams, the victim had been very much alive, if mortally wounded. As a nineteenth-century historian later noted, "Here were three men tried for murder, and none of the witnesses could swear the wounded man was dead." For Peach, the strange twist provided a promising turn of fortune.

Williams and Dr. Thomas James stood up in the Meeting House in piqued frustration. They had tried desperately to save Penowanyanquis's life, and their memories of the frightful night remained vivid. Each man gravely swore to God that Penowanyanquis's "wound was mortal." Dr. James, whom a contemporary described as a "good servant in the cause of humanity," gave impassioned testimony on this point "upon oath, before the jurie in oppen courte." He stated that without doubt Penowanyanquis had suffered grievous wounds, noting "that he could not live . . . and so he dyed shortly after." While Penowanyanquis's dead body was not seen, there was no doubt to the men who had witnessed him after the attack that, in the clarity of hindsight, he could not possibly have survived.

Escaping conviction because of this detail would undermine the spirit of the law in the first place—a callous possible outcome, given the cultural rites that surrounded Penowanyanquis's disappearance. But the Peach gang nevertheless remained intent on hinging their fate, until the very end, on the absence of the body. It was almost as if Peach ludicrously hoped the once strong, youthful Penowanyanquis would stroll into the Plymouth settlement and set the matter straight.

Peach himself may not have fully understood how compelling a defense he stumbled upon. New World settlers had established a legal proviso that was iron-clad, forged on God's scriptural teachings. Without a full confession, a murderer could not be convicted unless there was not one but two witnesses to the crime. In Peach's case, the witnesses were his codefendants. Not one of the men turned on the others, and though John Throckmorton and the hermit William Blackstone encountered the gang shortly after the assault, no one could testify to firsthand knowledge of the actual crime. It was an impasse of epic proportion.

Two surprise witnesses among the throng of courtroom observers, though having no official role in the proceedings, announced their intentions to prove that Peach was wrong about the victim. The two indigenous men had traveled a great distance to testify. Plymouth Colony leaders accepted "native testimony in all cases," treating it "as [if] it were the testimony of an Englishman, whether the Indian had sworn an oath on the Bible or not," a notion that would later be codified into law.

In an act of courage, the two Narragansett men faced down the intimidating Peach gang mere feet away from them, setting aside their own personal fears that they would be attacked. As Governor Winthrop of Massachusetts Bay Colony noted, "With much difficulty, [the tribesmen] were procured to come to trial, (for they still feared that the English were conspiring to kill all the Indians)." These men—friends of Penowanyanquis, perhaps—had risked their lives to offer their critical testimony.

They rebuked the Peach gang's defense. Every person at the Meeting House that day understood that "all the question [at trial] was about the death of the Indian, for no man could witness that he saw him dead." The two Narragansett witnesses "made oath" before the court, vowing "that if he [Penowanyanquis] were not dead of that wound, then they would suffer death." The two indigenous men's announcement provided an extraordinary pact made with each other and the court—a singular promise that in all likelihood stands in the annals of the law as historically unique. Their vow to give up their own lives and be put to death if Penowanyanquis were discovered alive represented the ultimate sacrifice, one forged in the depths of friendship, love, honor, duty, and selflessness.

Williams likely stood by as they gave their testimony, interpreting Narragansett into English for the court. If the young Pequot boy, Will, sat nearby, he could have only been transfixed by yet another moment of life-and-death drama. These men, like Will, put themselves at risk for justice.

The witnesses' lives hung in the balance of the trial in multiple ways—by traveling there into a potential hornet's nest of hostile settlers; by publicly staking their lives on Penowanyanquis's death, if somehow evidence surfaced that contradicted them; and by showing their faces to these defendants, who, if they escaped conviction or were freed in any kind of last-minute intervention by the king of England, could hunt them down in revenge. One way or the other, lives would be lost because of this trial, whether of settlers, indigenous men, or both.

If the Narragansett men offered a specific explanation for the disappearance of Penowanyanquis's body, it is lost to history. While clues point to ritual cremation, a Nipmuc legend provides a more spiritual scenario. The ancient story details a miraculous intervention enacted by two towering cedar trees, outstretched limbs taking hold of the body of a Nipmuc man who "was near death." "A large Cedar Tree to the left . . . and another one just to his right . . . stretched out a branch toward the Man. They reached under his arms. They began to slowly lift him. His body was very heavy. Not from his weight, but from his sadness. The Cedar Trees strained a little, but they continued on. Soon his body was rising." To this day Nipmuc storytellers urge listeners, "In the Sacred Cedar Forest, be still and listen . . . you can hear the Trees cry and release the sadness and sorrow of the broken-hearted Nipmuc Man's tears that went so deep unto their roots, so long ago." The witnesses may have spoken of Penowanyanquis's body enveloped in the strong, protective branches and soft fluttering leaves of the trees that clustered around him in his final moments. Anything was possible in forests alive with spirits.

The jurors' analysis would have to juxtapose English medical testimony with the blood oaths of the brave tribesmen. The fates of the Peach gang members were on a collision course with the cultural amalgam forming in front of them. In a time without forensic evidence, Dr. James's crucial testimony established the severity of Penowanyanquis's wounds, but the heartfelt testimony of the Indian witnesses could also sway the court. Only the verdict would answer whether their words counted as proof of death.

The last piece of testimony offered that day came from none other than the murder victim himself. On his deathbed, Penowanyanquis had made clear that "four English had slain him." As Williams described the victim struggling to tell his story, "he had related the truth." Testimony offered by a person unable to attend court, to this day, is typically excluded from consideration; it is considered hearsay, as it cannot be fully questioned and challenged. But dying declarations fell under an ancient exception to hearsay rules, considered spoken with sincere motives and given full weight. The defendants' fates turned—incredibly, given the context of white men tried for an indigenous man's murder—on the oaths of two tribesmen and the victim's own words.

After Penowanyanquis's haunting accusation from the grave, Prence handed the case to the jury. If he offered final instructions, he may have used the noble admonishment Queen Elizabeth's legal adviser provided jurors. "Good men . . . you have heard what these men say against the prisoner, you have also heard what the prisoner can say for himselfe, have an eye to your oathe, and to your dutie, and doe that which God shall put in your mindes to the discharge of your consciences."

The jurors parted from Prence and Standish and their fellow officials, the Narragansett who had risked their lives, and the languishing Peach gang. They faced the daunting task of assessing the credibility of the testimony and evidence offered at trial. Whatever bravado Peach had shown on the battlefield and had mustered in his dealings with colonial and tribal leaders alike, he now faced death not in a moment of glory, but in the agonizingly quiet moments of deliberation.

Little did the jurors know that a surprise legal conference that had taken place days earlier and miles away, in Providence, intended to alter their proceedings and save Arthur Peach's life.

# 8

# OUTSIDE INFLUENCE

"True one wounded him,
but all lay in wait 2 days and assisted."

—*Massasoit, sachem of the Wampanoag*

Massasoit, the great sachem of the Wampanoag tribe, would have traveled a long distance to reach the wooded Providence settlement. Rhode Island's leader could not be certain why Massasoit had come, but there were plenty of meaningful ways Roger Williams had earned the sachem's attention. Not only was Williams the only major colonial leader who had bothered to learn one of the Algonquian languages, but, like any good diplomat, he also studied the culture of the indigenous people around him to understand the significance of the words he was hearing and using.

In addition, Williams had forged a critical relationship with the sachem two years earlier. Exiled from Massachusetts Bay Colony "on foot and alone in the dead of winter," Williams had relied on Massasoit for shelter and companionship when he became ill traversing the desolate forests south of Plymouth Colony. He owed his survival to the sachem. This personal relationship surely factored into Massasoit turning to Williams at another pivotal moment in their lives.

Massasoit came with one thing in mind: he needed an ally to champion his agenda. As they sat near Williams's stone hearth, Williams would have offered his footsore guest food and drink. Mary Williams may have slow-cooked stew on the fire. The hearty dish would simmer with a selection of local ingredients such as wild onions, corn, and starchy, diced white cattail stalk—the same type of razor-sharp shoots that had sliced at Penowanyanquis's ankles the day he fled his murderers. Mary was able to learn about local foods from nearby Narragansett women, who cooked ground "white flint cornmeal" cakes and turtle and seafood dishes in sizzling bear grease on hot stones. At the same time, she treasured a relic of another time and place, her decidedly English tea kettle.

The sachem forcefully uttered his planned declaration to Williams: "The 4 men [the Peach gang] were all guiltier." He parsed out the concept of shared guilt and conspiracy. Williams, always ready for a thoughtful debate, pondered the statement. Then the erudite Englishman replied in crisp Algonquian and pushed back against Massasoit's argument. Williams was guarded and concise. "But one" alone had attacked the victim, he argued.

Only a single man had struck Penowanyanquis, intending to kill him. One of the other three reportedly swiped at the Nipmuc man after Peach did, but missed. For Williams, this was largely an exercise in rhetoric. He, above anyone else, was intent to see all members of the Peach gang tried and punished. He sounded out Massasoit's intentions.

The sachem took note of the rejoinder. In his Algonquian dialect, Massasoit responded carefully: "True one wounded him, but all lay in wait 2 days and assisted." Massasoit was determined that if one were found guilty, all should be found guilty. None should escape justice. It was Williams's turn to deliberate on a reply as they sat in his darkened house. Smoke from fire and pipe wafted in the quiet gloom while the ubiquitous mosquitoes provoked frequent swatting.

Will, the captured Pequot boy, so lost to history, would have had a front-row seat to such moments. He had survived the seminal Pequot War as the son of the tribe's celebrated chief; he served the indefatigable founder of Providence (although not by choice); he had come face-to-face with Governor John Winthrop of the Massachusetts Bay Colony and the Narragansett sachem Miantonomo while on the trail of the Peach gang; and now he could observe this powwow of sorts between his master and another epoch-making figure, Massasoit, in their tense but respectful exchange.

Williams's sagacious friend had raised the legal rationale for trying and convicting the gang members collectively. Williams could not argue against that. Peach's minions had helped carry out a nefarious plan, even assisting, rather than deterring, Peach in the desperate final moments when Penowanyanquis's life could have been spared. Then Massasoit turned his own argument upside down.

He told Williams, "In conclusion . . . the principal must not dye for he was Mr. Winslow's man."

Massasoit's stratagem came into view. He wanted to see the three less culpable men killed for the crime and Arthur Peach spared, and he wanted it known that he understood full well that legally and morally all were guilty. He had a reason for angling to save the life of the guiltiest of the men, and it was based on his culture and his status as tribal leader. The sachem had silently waited for this very moment since the day Edward Winslow had hurried through the woods to save his life. Winslow had resurrected Massasoit from his deathbed; the sachem now stood ready to use his political clout to save Peach's life and, from his perspective, repay Winslow for helping him in his time of need.

It was in the height of Massasoit's glory days, years earlier, when his friendship with Edward Winslow began. Standing on the hilltop above Plymouth Colony, Massasoit had taken in the fragile, lightly populated settlement and the majestic ocean beyond. He commanded it all. The sachem was tall and trim and flanked by sixty armed warriors willing to fight to the death for their leader.

It had been the unassuming Winslow who had been nudged forward and urged to parley with the imposing leader. He trudged up the hill, offering peace and enticing gifts of weapons and jewelry, and endeared himself to Massasoit with his humble courage.

Likewise, Winslow found himself impressed with Massasoit, describing him as "a very lusty [strapping] man, in his best years, an able body, grave of countenance, and spare of speech." He further noted that in Massasoit's "attire little or nothing differing from the rest of his followers, only in a great chain of white bone beads about his neck, and at it behind his neck hangs a little bag of tobacco, which he drank [smoked] and gave us to drink [smoke]." Winslow went on admiringly,

> His face was painted with a sad red . . . and oiled both head and face, that he looked greasily. All his followers likewise, were in their faces, in part or in whole painted, some black, some red, some yellow, and some white, some with crosses, and other antic works; some had skins on them, and some naked, all strong, tall, all men of appearance . . . He had in his bosom hanging in a string, a great long knife.

Soon after, Winslow had been paired with the rabble-rousing *Mayflower* passenger Stephen Hopkins to visit and decamp with Massasoit to continue establishing peaceful relations. His fellow settlers saw Winslow as a virtuous man, emphasized by the fact that he sealed his letters with the symbol of a "pelican in piety" pressed into the hot, crimson wax. The seal alluded to the bird's mythical ability to resurrect its young with its own blood, a Christian reference that spoke to Winslow. Devoutly religious and thoughtful, Winslow proved a counterweight to Hopkins's boisterousness.

Massasoit welcomed the men into his own family bed, where he thoughtfully crooned to them in the warmth of smoky light. The visitors lay awake, listening to the Wampanoag taking turns singing themselves to sleep. Members of the tribe were snug next to them, each adorned with deer and bearskins, enchanting coats of shimmering scales, and turkey feathers "knit together," mirroring the woodland creatures that were nestling down for the night.

Pious Winslow and libertine Hopkins, an ill-suited pair with vastly differing sensibilities, later agreed on two things, complaining that they "were worse weary of our lodging than of our journey," and that they disliked the "barbarous singing." The beauty was lost on them. But Winslow took away an important detail from one of his many observations of the tribes near Plymouth Colony. He remarked on an uncanny indigenous practice of "blind devotion," in which "almost all the riches they have . . . kettles, skins, hatchets, beads, knives, &c., . . . are cast by the priests into a great fire . . . consumed to ashes." The ritual provoked a perplexing idea: the indigenous people did not aim to permanently own their possessions, much like the land the tribesmen hunted on and migrated through. Perpetual ownership was a wholly unknown, even irrelevant concept.

At the height of King Philip's War, decades later, a Nipmuc tribesman, James Printer, drove home the chilling terror the settlers confronted during the steady stream of raids against them. Printer wrote, "Know by this paper, that the Indians that thou hast provoked to wrath and anger, will war this twenty one years if you will; there are many Indians yet, we come three hundred at this time. You must consider the Indians lost nothing but their life; you must lose your fair

Jean Leon Gerome Ferris depicts the 1620 signing of the Mayflower Compact. Captain Myles Standish and Governor Edward Winslow, Arthur Peach's master, were signatories to the historic document. Standish, in armor, sits to the left. Winslow stands centered behind the chest.

houses and cattle." Printer, trained by a trade printer in the settlement of Cambridge, posted the letter on a bridge crossing the Charles River. The Nipmuc tribesman attacked and taunted the colonists where they felt it most—threatening the sanctity of their treasured possessions, the "fair" homes they spent so much time adorning and admiring.

Indigenous people in Winslow's day already understood this lesson too well. It was the colonists who were not yet self-aware enough to see their weakness. The settlers still needed to learn a lesson from their indigenous neighbors: putting material possessions before people was a dangerous practice, one that might unleash the wrath of the gods.

Not long after Winslow's and Hopkins's visit to Massasoit, the young leader of the Wampanoag fell sick. He deteriorated rapidly. Winslow hastened to provide assistance, traveling to Massasoit on some of the same pathways Penowanyanquis later traversed. Before Winslow could arrive, Corbitant, the power-hungry, lower-ranking sachem who decried Massasoit's involvement with the English, raced to his side. There is no evidence that Corbitant assisted Massasoit, but he took the opportunity to deride the settlers to the incapacitated leader. He pointed out their absence in his time of need.

Winslow arrived without a moment to lose, forestalling the deterioration of the Wampanoag-English alliance. Winslow's presence undermined Corbitant's argument. On entering Massasoit's *wetu*, Winslow found Massasoit nearly blinded and bedridden by illness. The Englishman was startled by a "hellish noise" made by the men surrounding the sachem. The sachem's tribesmen were using vocal "charms" against illness, plaintive calls that were meant to protect their loved one. A "quire" of men passionately responded to a shaman's desperate "musical invocation." Winslow later observed that the din was so terrific "it distempered us that were well, and therefore unlike to ease him that was sick."

"*Keen* Winsnow? [Are you Winslow?]," Massasoit asked.

He pronounced Winslow's name with a heavy accent, leaving off the *l* in his name. "They cannot pronounce the letter *l*, but ordinarily *n* in place thereof," Winslow later wrote in his journal.

"*Ahhe*, [Yes]," Winslow answered.

"*Matta neen wonckanet namen*, Winsnow! [O Winslow, I shall never see you again!]," Massasoit cried out to his friend, his eyesight darkening.

Winslow jumped into action. He had brought a "confection [compound]" with him, perhaps having used his sturdy bronze mortar and pestle to macerate an assortment of local medicinal herbs. He used the tip of a knife to pry Massasoit's clenched teeth apart, and placed a trace amount of the thick paste on the sick man's dry tongue. The great sachem perked up. Winslow asked after his sleep. He had not had any in two days. He could open his mouth, but it was "exceedingly furred" and his tongue "swelled." Winslow crouched down by Massasoit's failing body and "scraped his tongue," carefully working to clear the man's swollen, tender mouth.

Winslow paused in his nursing efforts and prepared a letter. He would need better supplies to help the sachem regain his health. "By two of the clock in the morning," Massasoit's fleet messenger was ready to depart with the missive. Winslow directed the settlers at the Plymouth Colony trading outpost "Patuxcet," the very same Aptucxet trading post that Penowanyanquis visited in his final days, to provide "chickens to make him broth, and for other things, which I knew were good for him." Winslow had also brought a bottle of tonic, but it had broken during a "mishap" en route. He needed the men at the trading post to send a new one.

The messenger departed, and Winslow made Massasoit a restorative grog in the interim. Winslow waited for dawn and went outside to root around in the undergrowth near Massasoit's home. He reappeared with small strawberry leaves and then went back for sassafras root, identifying the slender tree by its floppy three-pronged leaves. It wasn't much. It seems Winslow himself was unimpressed with his own knowledge of local remedies. The Englishman, sleep deprived and still irked at the bumbling trouble with the broken bottle of medicine, acknowledged that he was "unacquainted in such businesses."

Winslow did what he could to make a "good relish" out of the root and leaves he had found. After boiling the mixture, he used his handkerchief to strain it. Perhaps surprisingly, Massasoit "liked it very well." The sassafras acted as a diaphoretic, provoking Massasoit to break out in a heavy sweat. The sachem's spirits lifted, and his symptoms disappeared.

In short order, Massasoit miraculously regained his vision and health. He requested that Winslow shoot a duck for him. Plucky, ruddy-cheeked Winslow vowed to oblige. Quickly killing one, he cooked it into a broth. Massasoit refused to let him skim the rich fat off the surface of the soup and he became sick all over again. At this point, the messenger reappeared with chickens in hand. Massasoit would save them for another day. The enterprising Winslow had already delivered him from certain death, and Massasoit remained forever grateful, and he would wait for just the right moment to repay the favor. He waited fifteen years.

As Massasoit sat hearthside anticipating Roger Williams's reply, he likely handled his pipe pensively and smoked. The object had great meaning. An indigenous pipe could reflect a harmonious state: the stem representing man, the bowl bespeaking femininity, and the smoke passing through the two, spirit. Massasoit's pipe was sleek and black like onyx. Perched on its bowl was the form of a mountain lion, the vigilant animal facing him as he drew in smoke. Massasoit had stared down such fierce enemies before, both animal and spiritual; he had confronted death with Winslow's aid. Now, a lifetime later, Massasoit understood that he would have to rely on legal reasoning to argue his case.

Early on, when he attempted to bribe colonial leadership to let him kill a foe, Massasoit learned from Plymouth Colony governor William Bradford that "it was not the manner of the English to sell men's lives at a price." Likewise, the great sachem knew that nothing he could offer the English would influence them to spare Arthur Peach's life. Reason was his only effective weapon.

Massasoit's demand appeared confounding and perplexing. Williams had not foreseen this request to help Peach elude justice and had to reply carefully. Here Massasoit, one of the most powerful men in New England, set out a plan of action to solve the crisis caused by the Peach gang. The sachem made clear that his disdain for the Nipmuc tribe was part of the driving force behind trying to save Peach. Penowanyanquis was "by birth a Neepmuck man: and as not worthy an other man should die for him." The sachem's greater motivation remained ever present—Massasoit believed that Winslow cared deeply for his former servant, Arthur Peach. Roger Williams, however, knew that Winslow would be more than happy to see Peach swing from the gallows. Williams replied tactfully with what he "thought

Cyrus Edwin Dallin's statue of Massasoit Ousamequin of the Wampanoag, a powerful depiction of the sachem who tried to influence Arthur Peach's trial.

fit." He cited the one presence Massasoit would be unable to refute in negotiation with a devout Christian: *vox coeli,* a voice from heaven. "He that doth violence to the blood of any person let him flee to the pit, let none deliver him," Williams argued, evoking religious texts.

This was no simple rhetorical device on Williams's part. In this same era, a notable English political pundit made a compelling argument based not just on arguments shared with him by God, via *vox coeli,* to bolster his points; he also cited various members of the deceased English royal family, who conveniently echoed his assertions from the afterlife.

Massasoit could not counter Williams's purported assertions from God, which spoke to the settler's core beliefs, but his trip to Williams's home had been productive. He had planted an intellectual seed with one of New England's most influential men. Arthur Peach should walk away from the murder unscathed, his life spared—and this belief was asserted by none other than one of the highest-ranking sachems in the land.

## 9

# THE VERDICT

"Felonious murthering & robbing
of the said Penowanyanquis"

—*Plymouth Colony Records*

Even if jurors managed to set aside the specter of threats haunting them and focus on the harrowing testimony, they still faced the prospect of being influenced by the many preconceived notions, biases, and sympathies about the identity of the murder victim, a tribesman, and that of the defendant, an unattached servant from Ireland.

Just as indigenous people wondered about settlers and their customs, many settlers professed confused and troubled ideas about their tribal neighbors. Colonists worried, for example, that "Indians might use magic against them." The mysterious gods the indigenous people called upon, such as Penowanyanquis's Children's God, were worrisome in their foreignness and their possible powers. Many colonists harbored deep fears of magic and the supernatural. Roger Williams, a reliable voice of reason, did not question the possibility that the Pequot had a witch who empowered their tribe. The "witch amongst them will sink the pinnaces," Williams wrote of the threatening adversary, "by diving under water and making holes." Edward Winslow fretted over tribal spiritualists who could see and direct fearsome snakes and sharp-eyed eagles. Whether jurors were captivated by the tribes or fearful of them, their views and biases might color their consideration of Penowanyanquis as the victim of a fatal crime.

Peach also faced prejudice. In addition to the crimes of escaping servitude and committing murder, Peach's singlehood presented a fundamental violation of the strict social norms of Plymouth Colony's burgeoning yet fragile society. By virtue of Peach's servitude, he had been prohibited from marrying. But when Peach left his service behind, he became unattached from the family structure that otherwise bound settlers and servants to each other in a socially sanctioned way. Peach counted as a threat, fiscally and socially, the moment he fled Edward Winslow's home. He ultimately committed far more grievous crimes, but his single status tainted him in a subtler way, an unenviable circumstance for a criminal defendant hoping for sympathy.

Singlehood qualified as a transgression that for all intents and purposes was outlawed in New England. Two years earlier, Massachusetts Bay Colony had ominously ordered its settlements "to dispose of all single persons." Plymouth Colony had directed that "no one shall live within the government of Plymouth without the leave and liking of the Governor and two of the Assistants." A 1638 Plymouth directive further ordered commissioners in the colony's "offshoot" communities to close ranks and offer land grants contingent on the "qualities" of the petitioner. Singlehood counted, in almost all cases, as an insurmountable hurdle to becoming a Plymouth Colony settler. With intolerance for unmarried individuals only growing since Plymouth's founding, Peach came just in time to catch this rising tide. Years later, Plymouth leaders barely contained their venom when they groused about the "great inconvenience [that] hath arisen by single persons in this colony being for themselves and not betaking themselves to live in well governed families."

Occasionally circumstance necessitated the presence of these "single persons" in the settlement. The shortage of marriageable young women in the New England colonies accounted for this. In order to live alone, a single person had to obtain permission from Plymouth leadership. John Tisdale, a recent arrival like Peach, intended to do just that. Colony records reflect that "upon good report made of him, & his good carriage, [he] is allowed to keep house and plant for himself," at least as long as his behavior remained satisfactory.

Tisdale embarked on the experiment of living alone in a settlement where the concept of family rose above almost all else. Tellingly, not long after arriving in the colony as a single man, Tisdale was physically attacked—by none other than Dorothy Temple's master, Stephen Hopkins, who "dangerously wounded" him. The nature of the dispute remains unclear, but Hopkins assaulted Tisdale so violently that the latter won damages for his significant physical injuries. An unmarried newcomer, sanctioned or not, was unwelcome.

Even the local military hero Myles Standish faced the ignominy of singlehood in Plymouth Colony once he lost his wife soon after arriving on the *Mayflower*. If singlehood was a sore point for Standish, it influenced a matter of life and death for Peach. Arthur Peach's standing in the colony stigmatized him in a different way than his actions that summer day in the woods outside Plymouth. Though from an ancient family and boasting an honorable record in the Pequot War, Peach was prohibited from marrying his lover, Dorothy Temple, which left him unattached and vulnerable. A runaway servant, he had forfeited his only protected status in Plymouth Colony. But Peach would have to surmount another obstacle as daunting as being a single, impoverished, escaped servant accused of murder—his nationality.

The most damning part of his identity was the descriptor used repeatedly by contemporaries to identify him: Irishman. Peach and Dorothy Temple were likely among the first Irish settlers living in the New England colonies. Every time Peach opened his mouth to defend himself, his brogue reasserted his foreignness. One Englishman, trying to describe the otherworldly wailing of the indigenous people he encountered, could only think to describe its strangeness by imputing the "howlings" with an "Irish-like" quality. Roger Williams, culturally sensitive compared to his peers, employed the derogatory expression "wild Irish," a phrase used to describe the unruly. Peach's status as an Irishman could play against him or be viewed with sympathy by the jurors, many of whom had experienced prejudice in their own lives.

Prence's predecessor as governor, William Bradford, made a careful study of Peach's character and actions that could help the complex preparations for the case against him. Bradford expressed no concerns about the defendant's origin. He described Peach as "being now out of means . . . and falling to idle courses and company." Peach's failing was a moral one; he was feckless. Bradford's comment on "idle . . . company" may also have been a dig at the corrupting influence of Stephen Hopkins's tavern, where Peach had spent so much of his time. Peach was "a lusty and a desperate young man" who had been brought low by temptation and derailed by his inability to work hard.

If there was a Puritan standard, Peach's actions were anathema to it. Bradford had no question of who should pay the biggest price for the murder. Peach was "ring leader," and evidence suggested that the other members of the gang grew nervous when Peach told them of his murderous plan. If Massasoit wanted to see Peach elude justice and the rest of his gang punished, Bradford had the opposite view: he wanted Peach to pay for his crimes above anyone else. Bradford feared that others agreed with Massasoit's hope of mercy for Peach.

As the first case of its kind, the trial tested the souls of each man on the jury, an unplanned test of whether colonial America's fledgling legal system could withstand its deepest challenge. Were jurors from a close-knit colony—little more than an outpost in a dauntingly vast wilderness—capable of fairly judging Arthur Peach, the unattached Irishman, for the murder of a tribesman? Then again, jurors knew Peach from around the settlement and from their drinking days at the Hopkins tavern. Peach was an outsider who was also one of them.

One of the jurors in particular, John Winslow, the younger brother of former governor Edward Winslow, had a personal interest in seeing justice done. Though no portrait survives, it is possible that John shared the Winslow family's defining features, dark searching eyes offset by wavy chestnut-brown locks of hair. John would have had firsthand contact with the accused murderer during the time he spent at his brother's expansive home, Careswell, where Peach served as an indentured servant.

John had carefully watched his older brother's social maneuvering and rise to power. Edward adroitly dealt with Puritan and indigenous leaders alike, including his pivotal dealings with Massasoit. John's dreams for life in the settlements were more modest, but he still aimed for success. He escaped the challenges that came with being a younger son in England, where he had no standing to claim an inheritance. From day one, as the eldest son and the namesake of his father, Edward upstaged John in almost everything he did. Edward traveled to the New World first, on the *Mayflower*. John followed the next year on the same bark that brought future Plymouth governor Thomas Prence over from England. Once in the New England colonies, Edward maximized every opportunity that came his way, by 1638 serving two terms as governor and erecting the stunning Careswell estate in Marshfield on the bucolic outskirts of Plymouth Colony, where he oversaw an array of servants.

John bided his time, hoping to make his mark in Plymouth, where he lived with his wife, Mary, and their many children. His stalwart, trustworthy character promised success in time. When the colony needed to assess the significant expense of the watch that kept guard over the settlement, leaders called on John to serve on the committee studying the issue. He heard firsthand the worrisome details about their general security.

While some of his neighbors may have taken their safety for granted, John learned from Myles Standish that the small settlement by the harbor persisted under constant threat. They existed at the mercy of the nearby tribes who tolerated their presence during peacetime when trading thrived. If anything altered that fragile symbiotic relationship, John had Standish's word that all hell could break loose—bloodshed the likes of which most had never witnessed. John was convinced that the expense of the watch was warranted.

When Arthur Peach absconded from the Careswell estate, John may have been one of the first to know—though he likely gave the matter little thought. Peach had earned a reputation for being notoriously indolent and "loath to work." His clandestine departure represented yet another act of shiftless misconduct. Most of the families John knew faced similar headaches with their servants. Laborers often complained about being overworked with little prospect of bettering their position at completion of their servitude, but none of that could have foretold Peach's shocking actions while on the run near the banished Roger Williams's settlement.

After all, Massachusetts Bay Colony governor Winthrop had recently noted with pride how easy it was to entice and keep servants in the New England colonies. Winthrop drew a flattering comparison to the struggling southern settlements, writing that many "were amazed to see men of all conditions, rich and poor, servants and others, offering themselves so readily for New England, when, for furnishing for other [southern] plantations, they were forced to send about their stalls [decoys], and when they had gotten any, they were forced to keep them as prisoners to keep them from running away." In other words, the southern colonists were tricking servants into coming to the New World and then subjecting them to forced labor. Even before the despicable violence that came from it, Peach's escape served as an embarrassment to Winslow and tarnished Plymouth Colony.

It also reflected poorly on another settlement fixture, the troublemaking Stephen Hopkins. Earlier that summer, juror John Winslow and his other brother, Kenelme Winslow, a recently arrived fellow colonist, served as witnesses in court against Hopkins. The tavern owner had been charged and fined for selling wine at "excessive rates," wine Arthur Peach likely enjoyed while spending afternoons commiserating with his future coconspirators.

While John may have relished leveling an accusation against Hopkins in open court, issuing a conviction that carried a death sentence was another matter. Three men's lives were at stake. Whatever John knew about Peach personally from the defendant's days at Careswell may have softened the juror's heart toward the young soldier accused of murder. John's attitudes about servitude, forced labor, and even slavery, as he took on the role of juror at the Peach gang trial, are difficult to tease out. The fate of one laborer in John's household stands out and possibly sheds light on his thinking.

At the end of his life, John carefully wrote out a will to settle his vast estate. In the relatively brief document, he highlighted his interest in a young child living in his home, identifying her as "my Negro girle Jane." It is possible that the girl came from the island of Nevis in the Caribbean Sea; John noted also having in his possession "a hogshead of sugar [that] came from Nevis." He stipulated in his will that she "shall be free . . . after she hath served twenty yeares from the date hereof." However, at the end of the document he added a provision that possibly blocked Jane's opportunities for freedom indefinitely, perhaps leaving her in a state of perpetual slavery. "She [Jane] shall service my wife during her life and after my wifes decease she shall be disposed of according to the discression of my overseers hereafter named or any two of them."

The legal instrument John drafted simultaneously confirmed Jane's lack of autonomy and enshrined his desire for her future freedom. John wanted to leave a legacy of merciful deeds, but instead he failed to resist the temptations of control and power. The paradox of Winslow's treatment of Jane manifested itself in the two primary figures he had to weigh from the jury's seats: a member of a race seen as less-than by the colonists on the one hand, and a servant with limited rights on the other.

The fourteen men who sat and listened to the impassioned testimony removed themselves from the spectators, defendants, and colony leaders. The Meeting House had two floors; the trial took place on the first floor around the pulpit. The jurors climbed the stairs to the second floor, which consisted of a large, mostly empty space, offering privacy for deliberations. The only objects on that level were the cannons, which were carefully positioned by slatted windows that opened out onto the threatening world around them. With no chairs, the men leaned up against these armaments—reminders of the dangers lurking, of how much hung in the balance. The jurors readied themselves for the debate of a lifetime.

An intangible, almost mystical element infused the jurors' undertaking. As one English judge observed of jurors, "A witness swears to but what he hath heard or seen; generally or more largely to what hath fallen under his senses. But a juryman swears to what he can infer and conclude from the testimony of such witnesses by the act and force of his understanding." If the witnesses employed their senses, the jurors used their minds, hearts, and souls.

The Peach case did not present an assured victory for either side. Without a body, real room for doubt existed. Without an eyewitness to the attack, the jurors had to consider the possibility that the Peach gang simply could not be convicted, no matter their personal impressions of the wretched-looking prisoners and the array of evidence. During the colonial era, nearly half of defendants were acquitted; of those who faced a preliminary grand jury, many were not indicted. This meant that approximately two-thirds of accused criminals avoided conviction. Settlers did not like sentencing fellow settlers.

But even if jurors came to a consensus on Peach, they had to consider whether all the defendants would be punished the same. After all, it was only Peach whose rapier connected with deadly force. Governor Winthrop, adamantly convinced of Peach's guilt, felt that the other members of the Peach gang should only be given mere "consideration" for their role in the killing. But then again, Peach's companions had "let him alone to do as he would." If Peach were guilty and his companions failed to stop his lethal crime, were they complicit and guilty to the same degree as Peach?

Another fundamental hurdle had to be overcome before conviction could even be considered. Each juror had to weigh his conscience before attempting a verdict. Reverend Lothrop had taught and inspired his followers on the jury to embrace humanist principles. Convicting the Peach gang for the murder of an indigenous man would be a public declaration on the equitable application of law to all men. A guilty verdict would reflect a progressive mind-set, breaking free from a narrow, deeply held Puritan construct.

Condemnation of the Peach gang would symbolize the humanist reformation efforts the Puritans and the so-called Men of Kent wanted to see within the Church of England. While tolerance for such revolutionary ideas came at a cost and carried dangers, that early September day in 1638 the jurors simply needed to follow the evidence, regardless of the victim's identity—no easy task against the stark backdrop of the Pequot War.

Meanwhile, Reverend Lothrop himself must have been present at the trial facilitated by his disciple, Constable Annable, sitting in the lower level of the Meeting House with the crowd awaiting the verdict. Even if Lothrop guessed the way the Men of Kent, who made up almost half of the jury, might lean, the question remained as to how much influence they could have on the rest of the deciders. So much indicated that the old way of seeing the world would sway the minds and hearts; new ideas took time to embrace. Colonial New England, in the eyes of many, was not the place to give birth to them.

Prence and Williams waited in the gallery of the Meeting House, too, as the minutes slowly passed by. Williams took in the sight of the Narragansett tribesmen, whose rage would likely boil to the surface if the jury acquitted the Peach gang, and Massasoit, who may have felt insulted if his attempt to protect Peach failed. Standish, for his part, had to focus on Peach and his men. They could become increasingly desperate as the verdict neared, and Standish had to be ready to prevent a last-minute dash for freedom. With his turbulent temper and impatience, an agonizing wait did not suit the military captain.

Still, Standish appreciated that law and order moved at its own pace. During the early days of the settlement, a tribesman arrived with a threatening message for the Plymouth Colony villagers. Standish advised not harming him, observing that it was "against the law of arms amongst them as us in Europe to lay violent hands on any such [messenger]." Having previously served as a juror himself, Standish knew that his peers needed time to hash through the thicket of facts and laws.

From his days lost in the woods, to his attack on Penowanyanquis, his escape during the manhunt, and the subsequent long trek to

Plymouth Colony, where he lived in a cage with limited food, the trial would have found Arthur Peach and his fellow defendants in a state of physical and mental exhaustion. Peach must have appeared pallid, even sickly, as the jurors deliberated.

Despite their physical deprivation, Peach and his companions, Jackson and Stinnings, could remind themselves of Daniell Crosse's successful escape and his apparent impunity granted by the residents of Piscataqua. Peach had reason to hope that Plymouth jurors might flaunt the law, too, as was their right. Peach could also cling to the discretion to kill granted to him during the Pequot War. Military leaders directed soldiers to annihilate entire villages; from Peach's perspective, he merely had killed one more tribesman after the sanctioned killing of so many others. The old tales of Stephen Hopkins, the master of Peach's sweetheart, who had been sentenced to death for mutiny in Bermuda, only to be pardoned before clawing his way to the top of the pecking order in Plymouth Colony, provided another reason for optimism.

Hopkins, like all the Plymouth settlers, would not have missed the trial. Nor would his servant, Dorothy Temple, whose humble clothing still entailed multiple complicated pieces: skirts, apron, bodice, separate sleeves that tied into a bodice, and shoulder "wings" to cover the area where the sleeves met the bodice, all of which Dorothy managed to use to hide her swollen, pregnant body—at least from settlement leaders. One colony official later noted that Dorothy's condition went unnoticed during the trial, but her secret must have been an open one among many in the small village. As Dorothy searched out a glimpse of Peach, she may have worn a coif, a small cloth cap that covered her long, pulled-back hair and framed her pained face.

The distraction of the sensational trial gave Dorothy a chance to slip away from her chores, and to see the father of her unborn child. Pregnant and alone in the colony, her future must have appeared hopeless. If Dorothy and Peach spotted each other that day, any record of her reaction remains lost. Anger and recrimination could reasonably have mingled with an involuntary tenderness. Before the murder, Peach had abandoned her, however the ex-servant had rationalized it. Now, because of his brutal crime, her innocent child's future also hung in the balance. Dorothy herself was tainted by her sexual indiscretion, the pregnancy glaring proof of her illicit actions. An unwed mother had, by definition, committed a serious criminal act. Dorothy's pregnancy meant trouble awaited her.

Indigenous women outside the Meeting House who heard rumors of the circumstances of the scorned Dorothy Temple would have had complicated ideas about the young pregnant servant. Tradition-ally, tribes tolerated sexual experimentation among their youths. But tribe members learned enough about the English to understand that colonial leaders would view Dorothy's actions with anger, as would those tribal authorities who accepted proselytized Christian teach-ings. One young seventeenth-century Indian woman, Sarah, had to face down a similar sexual transgression. Her Christianized sachem looked at her behavior with disdain when she welcomed her lover's advances. "By his intisements [he] obtained her consent & lay with her," he chastised. Engaging in sexual activities came at a high price to both privacy and dignity.

While Dorothy's pregnancy provoked widespread derision, some felt sympathy. One concerned settler wrote to Governor Winthrop about another wayward colonial mother with measured compassion for her unfortunate circumstance: "He had done the mayd a great deal of rong, & for my part I think had they been wise as they should, she may make as good a man's wife as [any]." During the seventeenth cen-tury, a quarter of Englishwomen were pregnant when they married. Regardless of any quiet supporters, Dorothy now had little chance to become a man's wife. The only meaningful opportunity for advance-ment available to a colonial woman fell out of her reach. The trial, on which the fate of the colony hinged, overshadowed this private and poignant drama, but for Dorothy, her future also depended on the jurors' verdict.

One of the jurors charged with hearing Peach's case, John Holmes, would soon find himself even more directly ensnared in Dorothy's personal tragedy. As Holmes stood among the other jurors on the upper floor of the Meeting House, he likely kept his sharpened sword at his side, a concerted attempt to rise to the solemnity of the occasion like those peers with higher social status. He had stumbled and tripped into the role of respectable colonist, and tended to be his own worst enemy in business dealings.

Thankful to be in Plymouth Colony, the recent arrival worked to earn positions of responsibility and the trust of settlement leaders. Holmes knew Stephen Hopkins's tavern well, but in the years before the trial he increasingly directed his efforts toward starting a family and settling down. In 1636, he married a young woman named Sarah, and she gave birth to their first son, John, his namesake, the same year.

In 1637, eager to support his household and successfully farm his land, Holmes took a gamble to bring over an indentured servant, William Spooner, from Colchester, England. A new master assumed large expenses—the flip side of the struggles faced by servants—with Holmes promising to maintain Spooner for the term of his six-year contract. With his aged father failing, Holmes may have had a hunch that he was on the cusp of an inheritance that would cover the costs. Eight months later, his father passed away in Colchester. But his inheritance proved to be a literal afterthought—a handwritten notation scrawled into the margin of the will. He received five pounds, a "corslet," a pike, and all his father's armor.

The items could come in handy in the New World. Holmes's father had been the "gaoler" for the prison at Colchester Castle, a dank, subterranean, barred cell. Holmes became familiar with the place when observing his father at work. Now with the tools of the trade combined with his hands-on experience, Holmes could vie for the position of court messenger, a role that entailed similar work—jailing, maintaining the stocks, and hanging murderers. While Holmes happily plotted his future, some members of his family frowned at what they perceived as his scheming.

Holmes's sister, Susan, remembered him in her will, too, leaving him five pounds per year to be paid half at "Michaelmas and at the our Lady Day." But she was quick to provide a stipulation, reflecting distrust of her brother. "If the said John Holmes my brother shall any way sue, molest, or trouble my said nephew his son, for any matter or thing whatsoever touching or concerning my estates . . . [he] shall be deprived of all benefit of this my will." Clearly, Susan worried that her brother would connive against his own son to usurp his inheritance. The ugly fear reflected the way John Holmes came to be known to history—"the black sheep of some good family."

Holmes focused on business, deciding to transfer Spooner's indenture to earn—and, in the long term, save—money. Holmes unloaded the responsibility for providing the suits of clothes, bushels of "Indian wheat," and "muskett, bandiliers and sword fitt for service" he had promised Spooner. This was a relief, but by 1638 Holmes regretted the loss of Spooner and searched for another servant. First, he had to contend with the distraction of the court, not yet in the messenger position he hoped to secure, but as one of those drafted by Governor Prence and his constables to decide the fate of the Peach gang.

Holmes likely had little, if any, interaction with Peach before the trial, but he did notice Dorothy, whether or not he realized her connection to the defendant. Holmes had an affinity for the female servant. Perhaps because his own family perceived him as trouble, he gave outcasts such as Dorothy a second chance.

Massasoit took in the scene around him. The sachem waited for the verdict he had made clear he fully anticipated: not guilty. He felt certain that his dear friend Edward Winslow would want an acquittal for his hired man. Massasoit the Wampanoag also had to keep a keen eye on the Narragansett present; he could not trust them and had to be prepared to protect himself if need be.

The fourteen men on the second floor of the Meeting House stared each other down over the enormous metal cannons, as if on a battlefield, the evidence both ammunition and shrapnel. Following the practices of juries at the time, they'd challenge each other with words and ideas, provoking heated discussion while trying to avoid physical altercations. They needed to come to a consensus. The upper floor offered room to pace and move around, helping to relieve the immense pressure on them. If competing camps of thought emerged, those best suited to the role of mediators among them could step forward and sort through the murky mix of law, testimony, belief, and bias.

The introspective Sillis may have been the one to shepherd his fellow jurors toward a unanimous verdict, making the man who believed in free will over brash impulses and religious fulfillment above material conquest arguably one of the jury's most important members. Edward Foster and Sillis, influenced by Lothrop's rhetorical argumentation, were as likely as any to take these leadership roles. They owed that much to the people waiting in the Meeting House below: tribespeople, settlers, servants, landholders, soldiers, and the religiously devout.

As the day drew to a close, they came to their decision. Another seventeenth-century Plymouth Colony jury described such a consensus finding: "We, of the jury, one and all . . . doe jointly and width one consent agree upon a verdict."

The throng of onlookers and colony leaders, as well as Peach and his companions, in a state of tortured suspense, would have been able to hear a change overhead, the murmur of voices now quieting and the occasional creaking of strained floorboards. Though Standish and the other spectators had been poised for violence, given the possibility that jurors' deliberations might devolve into an all-out brawl, no arguments or fights were reported. Governor Prence surely breathed a sigh of relief as the weight of the New World began to ease from his shoulders. The doubts of other colonial leaders—and his own misgivings—that he could pull off this trial ebbed at long last; the peaceful realization of a verdict would be an achievement in itself. They would soon know the jurors' decision along with the rest of the colony and tribes far and wide—men, women, and children who waited on tenterhooks.

The footsteps above would have shaken the first-floor rafters. Over the heads of Arthur Peach and the waiting spectators below, heady motes of dust must have slowly swirled through the remaining shafts of sunlight that quiet September afternoon. The sight recalled the formulation of those corruptions of consciousness Reverend Lothrop and his congregants had studied—like so much chaff or dust eddying through the air and falling by the wayside. Whether they knew it or not, the jurors, including Lothrop's acolytes, were helping form a consensus for a new world order around ideas many thought untenable.

At the front of the Meeting House, high on his pulpit, Prence thundered his order for the jurors to announce the verdict on the charges of "felonious murthering & robbing of the said Penowanyanquis."

The twelve jurors overcame an array of prejudices and the inability to officially confirm Penowanyanquis's death. In a spectacular moment of cross-cultural appreciation and respect, the jurors asserted that the words of the two Narragansett tribesmen fulfilled the two-witness requirement for a finding of murder. They also found that the denials of the ragged men wandering the woods of Pawtucket compared poorly to Penowanyanquis's solemn reckoning that reached the court as though from the grave. The jurors came to a historic conclusion, a groundbreaking judicial decision for colonial history. Their judgment extended to all four defendants, including Daniell Crosse *in absentia*.

When Prence looked over at the three defendants in front of him, the jurors who had depended on him for guidance, the crowd of Plymouth citizens surrounding him carrying the hopes of a colony, the colonial leaders who trusted him despite their misgivings, and the tribal representatives counting on a foreign people, he entered into the record the jury's remarkable, audacious, historic finding that not only set the standard for cross-cultural justice but also sidestepped the threat drawing in on them.

*"Guilty."*

# 10

# DEATH AND SALVATION

*Neenawun tabuttantamooonk newutche wame
mehtugquash kah uppeshauanash wunnegin quinnuppohke.*
(We give thanks for all of the trees and
beautiful flowers surrounding us.)

—*A verse of Nipmuc prayer*

The last days of summer in New England often feature hot blue skies, a full measure of the season before a gradual chill starts to take hold. It may have been on such a day that the jury issued its verdict: "Upon the forementioned evidence, [the Peach gang] were cast by the jurie, & condemned." Before the execution could be carried out, the jurors took care of another legal matter, instituting another fine against Stephen Hopkins for selling spirits at "excessive rates." The timing was conspicuous. Unable to punish Hopkins for hosting Arthur Peach, whose escape plans likely originated at the tavern, the jurors fined him instead.

Whatever stories spread about Richard Sillis's influence on the jury, the community likely remembered it. Almost exactly ten years later, when the colony faced an ugly dispute between two settlers, colonial leaders made the decision to nominate three men to fill the highly unusual roles of arbitrators. The arbitrators' decision would have the binding effect of law. Sillis was chosen as one of those counted on for astute judgment.

Plymouth Colony constable Joshua Pratt, who had the grim task of hangman, most likely brought Peach, Jackson, and Stinnings to the gallows in a rickety, rough-hewn tumbrel. This type of farming cart had transported prisoners to the scaffolds as far back as the thirteenth century. A seventeenth-century death sentence often meant execution immediately following the verdict, and there was no expectation that a man in shock would walk even the short distance to the place of his death.

Within earshot of the seaside, the executioner fitted the three convicts with nooses. Of the large and diverse crowd of spectators, none left a record of any objections at the proceedings. Pratt completed his final tasks at the gallows (or gibbet, as the hangman's structure was called), steadying the ladder each man would climb. Any worries over settlers forming a mob revolt because of a conviction could be put aside.

Governor Winthrop, certainly present for the executions, determined that the jurors arrived at their historic decision based primarily on the remarkable vow made by the two Narragansett witnesses. As Winthrop recorded, it was "upon this [the pledge made by the two indigenous men] they three [the Peach gang] were condemned." The governor, however, could glean additional insight into the jurors' deliberations by considering the dusty volumes tucked away in his substantial library back home in Massachusetts Bay. One particular book enabled Winthrop to delve into the ideas that shaped the jurors' mind-set.

The book, William Lambarde's *A Perambulation of Kent: Containing the Description, Histories, and Customs of that Shire*, published in 1576, held a sentimental place in Winthrop's heart. His father, Adam, had inscribed his impassioned thoughts in the form of a Latin ode. The work itself provided a solid account of legal reasoning born in the "freest of English counties," progressive Kent. The elder Winthrop praised the author as a "student of the common laws . . . wise, learned and religious." He admired the author's ability to maintain religious faith alongside scholarship.

Reverend Lothrop embodied the forward-thinking Kentish ideas Lambarde had written about. Through his congregants, he played a quiet role in the most important legal decision the men of Plymouth

Colony had faced. The stage was set for the nation's jury trials to permit laymen to contemplate laws and facts, free from physical dispute and from consideration of the outward standing and qualities of the defendant or, in the case of murder, the victim.

Captain Myles Standish, standing at the windswept gallows, likely dressed smartly for the grim occasion in his "rust-brown doublet with shoulder caps, braid stripes down the sleeves, and buttoned tie fastenings, with white cuffs." The battle-tested Standish had no trouble bracing himself for the sight of death. Though known more for his brawn than any bookish ideas, he also had transported fairly revolutionary ideas of liberty to the New England colony. That the empowered people of the settlement had ordered the executions, rather than a single authority, represented many of these larger ideals.

Ironically, none other than the authoritarian queen of England contributed to this ideology of freedom. In 1578, Queen Elizabeth I proclaimed her rationale for sending Englishmen to fight in the Low Countries, or the Netherlands, against Spanish forces, an ongoing series of conflicts that Standish would later join. The queen inadvertently articulated a conceptual foundation for the New World's democracy. Issuing her proclamation from the imposing, multi-turreted Richmond Palace on the banks of the River Thames, the queen declared that when "tyrannous . . . forces . . . oppress," and alternative attempts had been exhausted, there was no choice but to call for soldiers "to procure . . . safety [for the "natural people"] . . . to enjoy their ancient liberties" as well as their "manner of government to live in peace." Just as Lothrop's and Winthrop's words at times reflected the reasoning of Tacitus, the most commonly read author in the New England colonies, so too did Queen Elizabeth I repurpose the "ancient liberties" Tacitus identified as inalienable.

As the *Mayflower* bobbed in the waters off Cape Cod years later, in 1620, the settlers onboard drafted the Mayflower Compact. The document outlined settlers' inherent right to "frame . . . just & equal laws, ordinances, acts, constitutions, & offices." The settlers, too, relied on their unassailable "ancient liberties" to form a government that would avoid the dreaded tyranny Tacitus warned against. The English colonists were determined to avoid the oppression possible when a single person with unlimited power dominates an entire populace. And Standish, who signed the compact, may well have thought about the queen's rationales he had heard echoed by others.

The Tacitus-like language of Queen Elizabeth I's declaration retains a familiar ring. Not only did it embolden Standish and the drafters of the Mayflower Compact and flourish in juries whose power could surpass the authority of a single judge, it later evolved into language in America's Declaration of Independence. American revolutionaries demanded "Life, Liberty and the pursuit of Happiness" and a government that could "effect their Safety." Their lives on the line, they further asserted that it was "their right . . . their duty, to throw off such Government . . . [that threatens] the establishment of an absolute Tyranny." When the drafters cited their reasons for declaring independence from England, they noted among the abuses "depriving us in many cases, of the benefit of Trial by Jury."

Jury trials projected a crucial safeguard against the horror of tyranny. While juries had a strong tradition in England, the protection of a jury had been replaced with authoritarian measures when expedient to those in power. The Boston lawyer and revolutionary Josiah Quincy II, who would risk death rather than live under tyranny, willed his teenage son his copy of Tacitus's writings, so that the boy would know the "spirit of liberty." Quincy understood that civil liberties became meaningless unless preserved in all circumstances.

Not only could jurors push back on the application of law, their duties mandated that they do just that, especially in the New World. Massachusetts Bay cultivated this judicial safety net. As John Adams later noted, "A general verdict . . . assuredly determine[d] . . . the law"; it was not just a juror's "right but his duty in that case to find the verdict according to his own best understanding, judgment, and conscience, tho in direct opposition to the direction of the court." Jurors could challenge the highest laws in the land without repercussion with a unanimous decision. During pivotal stretches of history, when individuals outside the monarchy and landed class lacked power, they forged unprecedented clout in the courtroom.

Even the king's formidable chancellors lost their sway when compared to the empowered citizens of the jury. "The jury are chancellors," Roger Williams's esteemed former employer Sir Edward Coke clarified. Kings realized that jurors vied with monarchies and lawmakers to make law—and were winning.

Incredibly, English jurors with their growing power and their sanctioned closed-door deliberations had usurped king and judge, and even the rabble-rousers' cries for vengeance. When juries made law in the colonies, they wrested control from centralized authorities and empowered local communities—a foundational principle for the fledgling nation. Average individuals, otherwise disenfranchised, became surrogate lawmakers. They became world changers.

The jury in Plymouth Colony achieved justice for a stranger—indeed, for a tribesman whose only surviving name meant, essentially, "stranger." If democratic notions functioned for the judiciary, a government for and of the people also became possible. With "the eyes of the world upon" them, the jurors in the Peach trial became a harbinger of a period in the late seventeenth century that would become known as the "heroic age of the English jury."

In a landmark case from that period in England, jurors refused to convict religious leaders on trumped-up charges, avoiding outright tyranny. Those jurors became known as "saviors" of the "sacred bulwark of the nation." Though largely overlooked today, the Plymouth jurors' remarkable stand for justice in 1638, in the face of raging bias and fraught loyalties, played a part in enabling later juries to rise against all odds as a democratic cornerstone.

Arthur Peach and his accomplices had no time to ruminate on the rationale for the jury's decision or for its place in the history of the fledgling nation's democratic infrastructure. A final matter remained. Governor Prence pressed the Peach gang for monetary restitution to help make the Nipmuc whole. Penowanyanquis's family and tribe already faced a time of widespread losses; a large number of clan members had died of illnesses spread by settlers. The tribe had also lost much land to unscrupulous trades. Now they contended with the loss of one of their best traders, a young man who not only had gained the trust of a more powerful tribe but also had known how to navigate the mystifying world of the colonists.

Restitution represented a common practice. For example, when the settler Thomas Heyward stole from the tribesman Wannapooke, he was ordered to make restitution in the form of valuable Indian corn. Peach and his companions dashed any hopes on this front. The men stated "that they, nor any of them, had any lands or tenements, goods or cattle, at the time of the said felony committed that they know of." The declaration refuted the image Peach had projected back in the days of drinking at Hopkins's tavern: the ensnared indentured servant who really was a soldier and adventurer, a man from an affluent, landed family ready to return to glory, able to boast relationships with important colonists such as Samuel Maverick and Robert Evelyn. Peach, at this point, had no stakes to claim income, land, or inheritance, and the Nipmuc received nothing for their loss.

Though Peach's exact last words are now forgotten, Governor Winthrop noted that the three men finally "did all confess" in their last moments. Peach admitted that "they all complotted," or conspired; "they did it to get his [Penowanyanquis's] wampum." Regardless of their overdue confession at the gallows, there was no way to take back what Peach had done or bring back the life he had stolen.

There is no record that any of the convicted men uttered words of regret as they prepared to die. We might listen to the voice of another New England servant later sentenced to death, a young man named Julian, who wrote a tract shortly before his execution for murder in the early eighteenth century. Julian admitted to having "abused God's patience," and he implored his fellow servants to "be obedient to your masters; don't run away from them, nor get drunk, for if you do it will bring you to ruin as it has done me."

Whatever emotions the embittered Arthur Peach experienced in his final moments probably did not resemble Julian's desperate pleas for compliance. But Winthrop described Peach and one of his accomplices as having died "very penitently," perhaps with a show of contrition. If this was true, it was most likely a by-product of resignation at the sight of the noose. Peach, after all, felt slighted by the unfulfilled promises and unfair personal restrictions of his servitude. The soldier who had "done very good service against the Pequot" tried to hide the fear he must have felt in the face of death. Winthrop's reference to penitence also may have been a technical one. A convict who donned a white shirt and uncovered his head and feet before death was said to have shown penance, leaving the world almost as he had entered it.

Colony leadership recorded the last moments of Arthur Peach, Thomas Jackson, and Richard Stinnings at the "place of execution" where they were "hanged by the neck until their bodies were dead." It likely took a fair amount of time to complete the grisly act—perhaps one reason why indigenous people considered hanging a particularly inhumane form of killing. William Bradford noted the somber mood of the moment in a passage he titled "Crime among the Saints," describing the events of Penowanyanquis's murder and the three executions as "a matter of much sadness to them [the old comers] here."

Standish may have overseen the disposal of the men's bodies, since he almost certainly advised colony leadership on proper burial practices for soldiers, even a disgraced one such as Peach. It was a matter of law in Plymouth "that when any of this military company shall dye or depart this life, the company, upon warning, shall come together with their arms, and inter his corpse as a soldier." This sacrament may have had significant meaning for Standish, who had served in prolonged and bloody fighting in the Netherlands. He would have witnessed the horror of countless soldiers slaughtered and left unburied in the chaos of war, gruesome memories reawakened by reading the opening lines of his treasured copy of Homer's *Iliad*: "Destroying wrath that . . . hurled down . . . many a valiant ghost of a warrior, but *them* left as pickings for dog packs and carrion crows." Given Peach's transgressions, Standish may not have minded seeing the murderer and his men left for "pickings." A disgraced member of the English forces against the Pequot, Peach would not receive the military honors Standish valued for his soldiers.

The location of the Peach gang's graves is unknown. Over time, the land running from the hilltop Meeting House down to the ocean gradually filled with bodies, and the ever-growing cemetery encroached on the settlement. Colonists tended to bury transgressors, men like Arthur Peach and his companions, in unconsecrated ground on the outskirts of burial areas for those they considered "rogues and excommunicates."

If Dorothy Temple passed by Peach's grave in the weeks and months following his death, the barren spot would certainly have offered little to comfort her. After she gave birth to a son at the Hopkins tavern, likely in the tiny cold-storage pantry called a "buttery," Hopkins turned his back on her and the infant, forcing them from his home. Plymouth leaders intervened, ordering Hopkins to "keep her and her childe" sheltered or face being "committed to ward for his contempt." The court demanded that "hee shall either receive his servant Dorothy Temple, or else provide for her elsewhere at his owne charge." The unyielding order brought about a remarkable twist of fate. None other than the Peach gang juror John Holmes purchased Dorothy's remaining two-year indenture, for the bargain price of "three pounds sterling." A few years earlier, a Plymouth Colony resident had paid another Peach gang juror, John Winslow, ten English pounds for the two-year remainder of an indentured servant's contract.

Holmes and his wife welcomed the woman "begotten with child . . . by Arthur Peach," the very same man he had helped sentence to death. The Holmes family lived in close quarters, perhaps accommodating mother and child in their extra trundle bed. Whether self-interest or benevolence motivated Holmes's decision to take in Dorothy, it is safe to say settlers reproached him and scorned her. Court records commonly referred to an unmarried mother as a "slut with child," this in a time when the word "whore" was an interchangeable reference for the devil. The following month, the arrangement apparently began to take a toll, and Holmes fell apart. Colony leaders reprimanded him "for sitting up all night drinking inordinately."

Holmes's internal turmoil worsened when his worlds collided in his official capacity as newly appointed court messenger, work that entailed executing the court's often harsh criminal sentences. After having lived with Dorothy and her baby for several months, he attempted the unbearable task of carrying out her castigation. Fulfilling the court's mandate, Holmes flogged the mother (who was almost certainly still nursing) for "uncleanes and bringing forth a male bastard," a punishment that had been delayed by childbirth. In dry prose, colony officials lodged the last recorded details of the tragic saga. "Fainting in the execution of the first [whipping], the other [whipping] was not executed." This final footnote in the scandalous drama concluded, Plymouth settlers eagerly turned their attention toward the future and the prospect of peace.

The Peach gang jurors' verdict, and the subsequent executions of Peach and his men, quelled the hellish atrocities of the Pequot War. The equitable application of colonial law in the Peach case represented a resounding answer to the English minister Peter Bulkeley's compelling invocation to pilgrims departing to the New England: "The eyes of the world are upon us . . . but heaven, and earth, angels, and men, that are witnesses of our profession, will cry shame upon us, if we walk contrary to the covenant which we have professed and promised to walk in." The jurors in this case seemed to hear his admonishment from across the sea.

Their verdict neutralized the rampant fear and misgivings between settlers and indigenous tribes, at least temporarily. On September 21, 1638, a little more than two weeks after the Peach gang faced trial by jury, conviction, and execution, colonial and indigenous leaders gathered to sign the Treaty of Hartford, officially ending the Pequot War.


Beyond the formal treaty concluding military hostilities, the year 1638 transformed the New England colonies in other significant ways. As exhibited by the jurors in the Peach gang's trial, belief in reformation and humanism took hold. These revolutionary ideas developed with nearly inconceivable consequences.

In 1638, England demanded the return of the Massachusetts Bay Colony charter; the colony declined, shockingly without consequence. Not coincidentally, that very same year, the emboldened colony formed the Massachusetts Artillery Company to train an elite band of soldiers for future military encounters. After its founding two years earlier in 1636, Harvard College at last opened its doors to students, a symbol of the way enlightenment became an entrenched cultural fixture in New England. While the turmoil, unrest, and explosive developments that unfolded that year can be witnessed in the events of the Peach gang murder, it was, in part, the verdict itself that embodied the seminal year.

The ideas reflected by the verdict reached farther than the settlers could have imagined. Four years later, when demands for progressive reforms went unanswered in the Old World, the English civil war broke out. Incredibly, the British monarchy ended, and the English populace lived in upheaval for more than a decade, the so-called interregnum. The birth of New England, fraught with horror, blood, and powerful new ways of thinking, had found vitality in a dusky Plymouth Colony courtroom. Life in the colonies moved forward at an unrestrained gallop, with intrusion from the Old World temporarily eliminated.

Fighting between the English Puritan Parliament and those who supported King Charles I brought some men from the colonies to the one place they thought they had forever left behind. Harvard's first class graduated in time for the outbreak of the English civil war in 1642, leaving them free to join the fight. Some members of the colonial New England Artillery Company returned to England, eager to fight for their beliefs in Puritan and humanist ideals. The new humanist reverend of the Scituate settlement, Christopher Blackwood, a University of Cambridge–educated man who had replaced Reverend Lothrop, joined the fighting as well. The minister was willing to put his life on the line for his beliefs at the outbreak of war, putting down his Bible and picking up his snaphance. Others remained and demonstrated their Puritan zeal by "wait[ing] in the wilderness, to come upon the back of God's enemies with deadly fastings and prayers, murderers that will kill point-blank from one end of the world to the other." The far-flung colonies, trifling outposts of the kingdom no longer, had a hand in the monarchy's undoing.

The ideas that Roger Williams's mentor Sir Edward Coke advanced regarding juries as a vehicle for liberty and equality, as one historian puts it, "helped inspire the revolution which . . . toppled Charles I." These were the precepts on which America would be founded, but they were ones the country would forget time and again until called on to reforge their singular American ideals—like the jurors of 1638 in Plymouth.

Three years after the start of the English civil war, this short-lived period of enlightenment peaked when a Plymouth Colony leader called for toleration of all faiths, "Turk, Jew, Papist, Arian." While many "applauded it as their Diana," this tolerance was not attained. As tribes across New England knew too well, equality remained a paradigm rather than a reality. When settlers limited the beneficiaries of these tantalizing new freedoms, they chipped away at their fragile democratic institutions and their foundational ideas.

Our democratic structures have been tested in continuous refrain. The workings of our republic endure not because of our unflinching adherence to principle. We often take principles for granted. Our experiment persists in part because every American settler fled political systems marred by limited freedoms and shortchanged dreams and joined in the fight for democracy. When tested, Americans engage liberty, however imperfectly, by vote, by utterance of free words, by challenge to leadership, and by jury.

# Epilogue: Aftershocks

While the trial of the Peach gang quieted much of the unrest provoked by Penowanyanquis's murder, the killing cast a long shadow. Governor Coddington bemoaned Daniell Crosse's escape from Aquidnett Island. He summoned up funds and demanded a prison for his small settlement, but years later it still had yet to be built. When Aquidnett residents accused a fellow colonist of criminal behavior in 1640, they again let the suspect slip through their fingers. An exasperated Coddington noted that "wanting a prison he mayd an escape."

Twenty years after Crosse's audacious maritime getaway, Coddington finally got his prison. Settlement leaders felt so optimistic about this new edifice, they declared it "the prison for the whole colony." It remained a prison for hundreds of years before becoming the Newport, Rhode Island, police headquarters. In 1986, the building reopened its doors as the Jailhouse Inn. On their website, innkeepers point to the long-standing local belief that the jail, in all its iterations, was "never considered a particularly strong place," the site of frequent escapes over the centuries. Throughout his lifetime, Coddington must have found the matter of the prison endlessly vexing.

The ultimate fate of Daniell Crosse, who so daringly escaped across the water from Aquidnett Island to Piscataqua, is lost to history. No surviving records suggest that colony officials recaptured him. The records of New Hampshire's Portsmouth Athenaeum reveal two men with the surname Crosse, who dutifully paid their Piscataqua taxes in 1727. If this later generation of Crosses descended from Daniell, they inherited more than just the distinctively spelled name from the man who had somehow navigated such rough waters while concealing himself. The men listed their occupation as mariners.

One last epilogue of sorts exists for the man who had coaxed Crosse into so much trouble, the man at the center of it all who altered so many lives with one twist of his rapier: Arthur Peach. It was an eerie case of history repeating itself, as if the old New England omens that tantalized and confounded Peach contained a larger, unending, ill-fated prophecy—this time one that played out in the country from which Peach and Prence and Williams had fled, England.

A twenty-three-year-old soldier decided to lie in wait by a lonely path, surrounded by woods and thicket, bent on theft and murder. When he spotted his two victims, he attacked—stealing from one he would leave for dead and killing the other. He fled. But one victim, against all odds, survived to identify her attacker and recount the details of the horrifying crime.

The soldier was tried, convicted, and hanged. The year was 1941—a little more than three hundred years after the Peach gang trial. The twentieth-century murderer's name was Arthur Peach.

The year after the earlier Peach's trial, a young attorney out of Boston who owned a grim book called *The Printed Relation of the Martyrs*, which he once lent to John Throckmorton, was censured for his aggressive representation of his client. Thomas Lechford overstepped the boundaries of an essential legal institution, and Massachusetts Bay Colony governor Winthrop intervened to safeguard his sacrosanct jury. With the memory of the Peach gang jurors so fresh in his mind, Winthrop ordered Lechford to desist from going "to the jury & plead[ing] with them out of court." Winthrop resolved to ensure the "integrity of the jury trial system." No one would tamper with a jury on his watch.

Arthur Peach owed his deliverance from the hellish Virginia colonies to Samuel Maverick—and likely his placement with former governor Edward Winslow, too. Maverick, also associated with the shadowy Thomas Yong and Robert Evelyn, who may have secured Peach's passage from England under the auspices of covert operations, not only played a pivotal role in offering Peach a new life in Plymouth Colony, he also helped settle Massachusetts Bay.

Maverick's many descendants thrived, but one in particular became especially noteworthy. The nineteenth-century Samuel Maverick of Texas owned a significant amount of property in the state. It was this Maverick who brought the family name to the attention of future generations, doing away with the practice of cattle branding, which he found inhumane and unnecessary. Branding helped with identification, but with Maverick's vast land holdings, his cattle had few chances to wander onto land he did not own. This unconventional, forward-thinking man, who in some ways mirrored his ancestor's tendency to forge his own path, inspired the transformation of the Maverick surname into a common noun and adjective. When we use the word "maverick," we harken back not just to the nineteenth-century Maverick but to the seventeenth-century one as well.

The name of the old hermit whom Peach ran into in the woods, William Blackstone, endures in New England. The National Park Service notes that Blackstone River—and consequently Blackstone River Valley, which extends from Massachusetts to Rhode Island—is named after him. The river played an important role in the Industrial Revolution.

It is unknown whether Blackstone had children with the American Indian woman who lived with him against her will for so many years in his home on Study Hill. If so, a branch of American Indian Blackstone descendants could join the ranks of those relatives who descended from his later-in-life marriage to a female settler. Black-stone and his significantly younger wife welcomed a son the year he turned sixty-five. One of the son's descendants became a wealthy industrialist. Observers can only wonder at the very different fates of any offspring who went unrecognized.

Directly to the west of Blackstone River, within Rhode Island, lies the Nipmuc River. While dams have constricted the Blackstone's high-running waters, the Nipmuc runs free and unobstructed. If you follow the Nipmuc almost directly north into the state of Massachu-setts, you arrive at the ancient Nipmuc stronghold in Grafton, where the present-day seat of Nipmuc Nation can be found, fiercely guided by Chief Cheryll Toney Holley. It is called Hassanamessit Reserva-tion and represents the only continuously owned Nipmuc property in Massachusetts.

On the rugged northerly coastline of present-day Maine, Charles de Menou d'Aulney, Myles Standish's foe who had stolen away Plym-outh's valuable fort, died by drowning when his canoe overturned more than a decade after the Peach gang trial. D'Aulnay's refined and fashionable waterlogged clothes, which likely included a felted beaver hat, weighed him down. Legends recount that his indigenous guide, a man d'Aulnay once mistreated, orchestrated his demise. If true, cruelty toward an American Indian once again played a role in a fatal comeuppance.

Roger Williams's role as mediator between local indigenous people and his fellow English did not end with the events of the Peach gang trial. He found himself at the center of regional geopolitical maneu-vering for the rest of his life. He gamely presented his services as "moderator" free of charge. He offered, he said, "gratise, my time and paines." When sachems transferred land from their tribe to the En-glish, Williams asserted himself in the morally precarious position of both beneficiary and fiduciary. He returned to these same men repeatedly to redraft land deeds with fresh assurances that the indigenous men indeed conveyed the land of their own free will. This exercise ended up being counterproductive in terms of protecting Indian positions, with the highly technical language of the deeds, "fee simple" land grants, tainting the conveyances rather than enhancing them.

When King Philip's War arrived at his doorstep later in the seventeenth century, the elderly Williams, ever the pacifist, stepped forward to speak with the indigenous people. His home and the remains of the colony of Providence smoldered nearby. "This house of mine now burning before mine eyes hath lodged kindly some thousands of you these ten years," he said. To the end, Williams perceived his outreach to the neighboring tribesmen as an evolved act of mercy. The tribes saw things differently. Their lives were intertwined with the land they lived on, and the English had taken it from them.

The physician John Greene, who tended to the dying Penowanyanquis, was one of the sons of a landed English gentleman. In England, primogeniture laws precluded an inheritance for him, and he dreamed of creating an estate in the New World instead. Four years after the Nipmuc's death, Greene bought approximately seven hundred acres in present-day Warwick, Rhode Island, from the sachem Miantonomo.

His son, John Greene Jr., built a modest saltbox house on the land. With a brick chimney, weathered shingled roof hammered together with rustic, "low-grade bog ore" nails, and a semicircular oyster shell driveway by the front door, it resembled a quintessential Cape Cod cottage. A more substantial house was to come. Unlike his father, Greene Jr. did not bother learning Algonquian. He ate with dainty spoons embellished with strawberry knops, and he may not have fully registered the spiraling crisis that beckoned a new war later in the seventeenth century.

Today, the waterfront swath of land, smaller by a third, remains in private hands and still evokes estate living. Archeologists still carefully unearth remnants left there by the American Indians who once lived on and farmed the property.

With the verdict handed down and peace finally established, the ascendant Reverend Lothrop finally had the leverage he needed to extract his congregation with the support of Plymouth Colony and start his own community—following the model of other visionaries such as Roger Williams. Writing forcefully to Governor Prence days after the hangings, Lothrop declared, "Now we stand steadfast in our resolution to remove our tents and pitch elsewhere." Having been the hidden philosophical lynchpin behind the historic jury, Lothrop earned his graceful exit. Ever the diplomat, Lothrop assured Prence that, once settled in his new home, he would remain in a state of "humble thankfulness in the perpetual memory of your exceeding kindness." Lothrop was not one to burn bridges. And there was some-one else who added his name alongside Lothrop's signature at the end of the lengthy exit letter to Prence: Anthony Annable, the resourceful Scituate constable who had helped fill the jury spots with the Men of Kent. Annable, like so many others of the congregation, followed Lothrop into a new experiment.

Lothrop sold his beloved Scituate home on the cliff to none other than the last-minute jury addition Richard Sillis. The preacher and many of his followers packed up their few possessions, along with the crops they had so carefully cultivated in Scituate, and set out, pilgrims once again on foot and horse. They finally reached Cape Cod, a new land that seemed to possess unparalleled beauty and peace. Lothrop's unwavering fortitude, faith, and, not least of all, classical education served him well there; his gentle form of grit and strict sense of empa-thy forged a truly all-American redemption story.

Lothrop had been to hell and back, but at last he found his free-dom: a "church without a bishop . . . and a state without a king." A New World order that almost no one believed possible had begun. As one historian remarked on the Puritans' unlikely success, "The traditions of a thousand years were continuously hampering their progress," yet somehow Lothrop and his acolytes overcame the long odds.

The Men of Kent who joined Lothrop in settling the town of Scituate and who honored Penowanyanquis through their verdict brought with them to the New World an exceptional combination of iron-willed fortitude and an appreciation for scholarship, humanism, and religious faith. Today the Men of Kent cemetery in Scituate memorializes this trailblazing group of early settlers.

Lothrop's descendants went on to serve our nation in numerous ways. Among Lothrop's progeny are four American presidents: Ulysses S. Grant, Franklin Delano Roosevelt, George H. W. Bush, and George W. Bush. One Lothrop offspring played a significant role in the Ohio Underground Railroad, and his house is now protected as a historical site. A historian tallied the remarkable number of abolitionists who emerged from the Lothrop clan over the centuries.

Lothrop's copy of Thomas Goodwin's *A Child of Light Walking in Darknesse*—such a strong influence on him and his followers who guided the jury—was ultimately bequeathed to his granddaughter and passed down over generations. The volume has survived almost four hundred years and can be found at Cape Cod's Sturgis Library in Barnstable, Massachusetts. At a time when few women owned books, other than the Bible, it was carefully inscribed, "Rebekah Lothrup— hir book."

The trial witness John Throckmorton, who had been alert to danger on his ride past the Peach gang in 1638, soon faced greater threats closer to home. In 1643, he attempted to settle Throgg's [Throckmorton's] Neck in present-day New York. The endeavor proved short-lived. Governor Winthrop recorded the details of a violent attack soon after the inception of the burgeoning settlement. Those members of Throckmorton's family who were home at the time were killed. Throckmorton survived and moved near his friend Roger Williams in Providence, Rhode Island, buying up land that once belonged to the minister-physician Thomas James.

Sixteenth-century colonial leaders in Virginia and Maryland desperately feared the spread of Catholicism. They dreaded the possible reach of the Spanish monarchy that had its sights on the New World. Spain hoped that the pope would one day control the territory. These concerns bled into early-seventeenth-century life in the region, clouding Peach's time in Virginia with secrecy and concern that his possibly forbidden religious beliefs would be uncovered. But despite the dark intrigue that marked the earliest days of settlement life in the area, the Virginia colonies remained intact. Attempts to impose anti-Catholic laws soon gave way to "practical toleration" of Catholics.

There is no extant evidence from the historical record to shed light on Will's life after the Peach gang trial. Colonial leaders and then historians carefully preserved Roger Williams's writings, but any texts dispersing his assets are missing. Such a document might have explained what happened to Will in his later years. Nevertheless, we do know that the young Pequot boy's remarkable acts of bravery impressed Roger Williams. Williams's detailed record of the child's involvement in the gang's capture suggests his admiration.

Today, there are people who trace their heritage to the Pequot tribe and to Providence. Perhaps Will's descendants are among them.

Some New Englanders perpetuate the mistaken belief that American Indian populations in the area were primarily decimated by war and disease due to events that took place generations ago. While the ferocious fighting of King Philip's War forever changed life in New England, it wasn't the death toll that did the most lasting damage—rather, it was the bad blood caused by the merciless fighting, raids, and unjust land acquisition that undermined the once commingled existence of English settlers and indigenous people.

Nipmuc men and women began to live apart from those they had once seen as neighbors, as English settlers enacted a multitude of laws preventing indigenous people from living and working with colonists. Settlers and their descendants controlled property, legal institutions, and government; the Nipmuc people had no means of recourse for the grievances. But American Indians did not simply disappear after King Philip's War. In 1840, of all "colored" people living in Worcester, Massachusetts, the traditional Nipmuc stronghold, more than 20 percent were American Indian. Nipmuc people still populate Massachusetts, including in their homelands.

When Reverend John Eliot purchased Nipmuc land for a pittance in 1651 to set up his "praying town" in Natick, Massachusetts, he began work on a thorough translation of the Bible from English to Algonquian, *Mamusse Wunneetupanatamwe Up-Biblum God*. In the seventeenth century's pastiche of cultures, Lady Armin of England soon held in her hands one of the first copies, a quaint keepsake to thank her for supporting Eliot's proselytization efforts. Never mind that the Nipmuc and other American Indians quickly mastered the English language, had no need for the translation, and languished without their land.

Generations later, the Nipmuc plight has been largely forgotten by the general population, while for those whose people were wronged, the frustrations are ever present, as real today as they were during Penowanyanquis's life. In June 2004, the Office of Federal Acknowledgement (OFA) of the Bureau of Indian Affairs rejected the official status of two groups of Nipmuc petitioners, refusing to recognize the tribe. The OFA based its conclusions on the 1861 Earle Report.

John Milton Earle, a newspaper publisher turned politician, took a stab at assessing the Nipmuc tribe when he served as the Massachusetts Indian commissioner. The OFA relied on Earle's "admittedly deficient" nineteenth-century report and its antiquated terminology, which made use of the grouping "Miscellaneous Indians," negating the ability of those so categorized, or their offspring, to self-identify as Nipmuc. Earle used an offensive standard of racial purity to make the sweeping statement, "There is not one person of unmixed Indian blood [in the Commonwealth]." In a single breath, he denied the

American Indian identity of every such person in the state of Massachusetts, despite the evident dynamic populations interspersed throughout.

In another form of justice, rediscovering Penowanyanquis's story gives voice to the ongoing quest of the Nipmuc, who likewise demand to be seen as more than strangers.

# Acknowledgments

I am delighted to have the chance to thank the many people who helped with this project, offering thoughtful guidance at every turn. From its inception, Samantha Shea, my agent, shepherded this book forward with uniquely insightful guidance and absolutely boundless support. Victoria Wilson at Pantheon, my editor, empowered me with a fervent belief that this remarkable moment in history should be brought to light and with her earnest encouragement. Her shrewd editing elevated this book beyond measure and provided me the opportunity of a lifetime. Marc Jaffee at Pantheon provided kind assistance over the years. Amy Stackhouse enhanced the narrative with her sharp edits.

This book would not have been possible without the ardent and generous support of Nick Basbanes, Kevin Birmingham, Megan Marshall, Gabriella Gage, Megan Kate Nelson, Melissa McWhinney, and Kathleen Dunn. The superb work of Glenn W. LaFantasie, Katherine A. Grandjean, and Larry Spotted Crow Mann informed and inspired this book. Bill Keegan and Kristen Keegan, historical geographers, supported and contextualized this history with their unparalleled map.

I am grateful for the thoughtful assistance provided by Ashley Bissonnette; Professor Kevin McBride; Professor William Simmons; Professor J. Stanley Lemons; Rebecca Griffith of Pilgrim Hall Museum; Robert Kluin and Kate Sheehan at Plimouth Plantation; Registrar John R. Buckley Jr. and John Zigouras of the Plymouth County Registry of Deeds; and Jess Dougherty and Fiona Fitzsimons. Members of the Friends of Pine Hawk, including Linda McElroy, Bob Ferrara, Tim Fohl, Ken Leonard, Sydney Blackwell, and Lynn Horsky, were exceedingly generous with their time. Larry C. Kerpelman, PhD, offered astute edits, feedback, and insights.

I am also appreciative of the generous assistance of staff members at the Tomaquag Museum; Peabody Essex Museum's Phillips Library Reading Room; Pilgrim Hall Museum; Massachusetts Historical Society; New England Genealogical Historical Society; Natick Historical Society and the Natick Public Library; Scituate Historical Society; Scituate archivist Elizabeth Foster (an Edward Foster relation); Plymouth County Registrar of Deeds; Mayflower Society library; Rhode Island Historical Society; New Hampshire Historical Society; Congregational Library and Archives; American Antiquarian Society; Plimoth Plantation; Massachusetts Archives; Honorable John J. Burns Library at Boston College; Rauner Library at Dartmouth College; Worcester Historical Museum; Sturgis Library of Barnstable, Massachusetts; Institute of Native American Studies; Project Mishoon; Kate Pourshariati at Montgomery County Community College Audio Visual Library; Heather L. Olson at the Public Archaeology Laboratory, Inc.; and Russell Handsman, David Tall Pine White, Professor Rae Gould, and Chief Cheryll Toney Holley of Nipmuc Nation. Daisy Hochberg, Dorian Cohen, Alyssa McCarthy, Natalie Edwards, Katherine Sayn-Wittgenstein, Amanda Forsythe, Xiaoyi Huang, Judith Solar, Harold Gordon, and Carol Spack offered their kind guidance.

I owe a tremendous debt of gratitude to my parents, Marsha L. Selley and Ernest G. Wiggins Jr., and to the Wadson, Moore, and Pearl families. Ian Pearl in particular inspired me with his infectious love of history. And I am supremely grateful for my beloved children and husband, Matthew Pearl, who warmly and tirelessly encouraged me. Thank you for your patience and support as I researched these sojourners from another time, a task that happily included woodland walks with our loyal Petey.

While I am profoundly thankful for the help I received with my research along the way, any errors are my own.

# A Note on Research and Sources

Referenced historical figures spoke or wrote all quoted words within this work. I have modernized some spelling and added an occasional punctuation mark for the sake of clarity, while leaving colonial language intact whenever feasible. I based detailed descriptions of climate, topography, ecology, clothing, and cultural norms on research into the relevant historical record.

To honor indigenous voices absent from archival records, I made every effort to incorporate oral history, transcribed and spoken. As the staff of the Mashantucket Pequot Museum and Research Center cautions, for cultures defined by oral histories "the power is in the telling"; retelling oral histories presents "the risk of their being misunderstood." I have attempted to provide meaningful context to mitigate this possibility, and I believe the risks involved in recounting these events are overshadowed by the importance of sharing this history—one that is salvaged from the horrors of the Pequot War.

# Notes

### INTRODUCTION

3 His elders passed: Larry Spotted Crow Mann, *Drumming and Dreaming* (CrowStorm Publishing, 2017), p. 79.

The Nipmuc cautionary: Ibid., p. 67.

The attack on: Larry Kerpelman, notes from March 1, 2018.

4 He landed in: George D. Langdon Jr., *Pilgrim Colony: A History of New Plymouth, 1620–1691* (New Haven, CT: Yale University Press, 1966), p. 44.

Such a war: Roxanne Dunbar-Ortiz, *An Indigenous Peoples' History of the United States* (Boston: Beacon Press, 2014), pp. 49 and 50.

5 One colonist described: Edward Everett Hale Jr., *Note-book Kept by Thomas Lechford, Esq., Lawyer, in Boston, Massachusetts Bay, from June 27, 1638, to July 29, 1641* (Cambridge: John Wilson and Son, 1885), p. xi.

The rulers of: Ibid.

Each man's ears: Ibid., p. xii.

The convicts who: Ibid.

Authorities ordered them: Ibid., pp. xi–xii.

Half the original: Langdon, *Pilgrim Colony*, p. 44.

The settlers who: William Bradford, *Of Plymouth Plantation, 1620–1647*, vol. 1 (Boston: Massachusetts Historical Society, 1912), p. 37.

To make matters: Karen Ordahl Kupperman, *Indians and English: Facing Off in Early America* (Ithaca, NY: Cornell University Press, 2000), p. 36.

The brutal weather: Ibid.

6 Darkness descended quickly: Edward Winslow and Others, *A Relation or Journal of the Proceedings of the English Plantation Settled at*

*Plymouth. Mourt's Relation* (Boston: John Kimball Wiggin, 1865), pp. 77 and 78.

6 With no shelter: Ibid.
At the break: Ibid.
The dog quickly: Ibid.
The settler hurled: Ibid.
The man managed: Ibid.
In the first: Bradford, *Of Plymouth Plantation*, p. 194.
One settler gathering: Ibid., p. 290.
When a critically: Ibid., p. 196.

7 Incredibly, the *Mayflower*: Ibid., p. 194.
Governor Bradford acknowledged: Ibid., p. 196.
Standish had even: Winslow and Others, *A Relation or Journal*. p. 70.
Standish's desire to: Stephen Merrill Allen, *Myles Standish: With an Account of the Exercises of Consecration of the Monument Ground on Captain's Hill, Duxbury, Aug. 17, 1871* (A. Mudge and Son, 1871), p. 12.
While the heartiest: Ramona L. Peters, "Consulting with the Bone Keepers: NAGPRA Consultations and Archaeological Monitoring in the Wampanoag Territory," *Cross-Cultural Collaboration: Native Peoples and Archaeology in the Northeastern United States*, ed. Jordan E. Kerber (Lincoln: University of Nebraska Press, 2006), p. 43, n. 2. I refer to Massasoit Ousameequin as Massasoit, as he is widely known. But as Peters notes, "Massasoit" is the term for a leader of the "greatest esteem among the Wampanoag"—not a name. I credit Peters for this information, which I also reference in a footnote in the "Cast of Characters" section.
Wampanoag families lived: Margaret Ellen Newell, *Brethren by Nature: New England Indians, Colonists, and the Origins of American Slavery* (Ithaca, NY: Cornell University Press, 2015), p. 112.
"A youth in: Bradford, *Of Plymouth Plantation*, p. 179.
They gave "him: Ibid.
Indigenous men and: Ibid.
Enchanted, they sang: Ibid.

8 Unexpectedly, the sojourner: Susan Hardman Moore, *Pilgrims: New World Settlers and the Call of Home* (New Haven, CT: Yale University Press, 2007), p. 45.
The colonial traveler: Ibid.
Baffled, howling with: Ibid.
Colonists even built: Samuel Deane, *History of Scituate, Massachusetts: From Its First Settlement to 1831* (Boston: James Loring, 1831), p. 10.

Tribes had used: From a diorama created by Sarah Annette Rockwell, circa 1960, on exhibit at the Science Museum of Boston.

Settlers hoped to: Deane, *History of Scituate*, p. 10; Sydney V. James Jr., *Three Visitors to Early Plymouth: Letters About the Pilgrim Settlement in New England During Its First Seven Years—John Pory, Isaack de Rasieres, Emmanuel Altham* (Bedford, MA: Applewood Books, 1997), pp. 75 and 76.

In the spring: Ibid.

With their intricate: Ibid.

"Good eating for: James, *Three Visitors to Early Plymouth*, p. 69.

The rapidly expanding: Langdon, *Pilgrim Colony*, p. 37.

Plymouth settlers found: Ibid.

As colonists moved: Ibid.

One optimistic settler: Ibid., p. 38.

Word had spread: John Underhill and Paul Royster, eds., "Newes from America; Or, A New and Experimentall Discoverie of New England; Containing, A Trve Relation of Their War-like Proceedings These Two Yeares Last Past, with a Figure of the Indian Fort, or Palizado" (1638), *Electronic Texts in American Studies* 37, p. 17, digitalcommons.unl.edu /etas/37.

9 One Englishman urged: Dennis Cerrotti, *Hidden Genocide, Hidden People* (Wellesley, MA: Sea Venture Press, 2014), p. 16.

Indeed, King Charles: Newell, *Brethren by Nature*, p. 8.

The king further: Calendar, vol. 1661–1668, #494. Col. Entry book 60, f. 22, "The kings letter to the colony of Massachusetts in the behalf of the Proprietors of the Narragancet Country," p. 10, Gay Collection, Massachusetts Historical Society.

It contained gruesome: Newell, *Brethren by Nature*, p. 150.

A utopian element: William E. Nelson, *The Common Law in Colonial America: The Chesapeake and New England, 1607–1660*, vol. 1 (New York: Oxford University Press, 2008), p. 49.

They craved permanency: Dunbar-Ortiz, *An Indigenous Peoples' History of the United States*, pp. 34 and 35.

During the sixteenth: Ibid.

10 The changes pushed: Ibid.

This transformation in: Ibid.

For all of: Carole Doreski, *Massachusetts Officers and Soldiers in the Seventeenth-Century Conflicts* (Society of Colonial Wars in the Commonwealth of Massachusetts, New England Historic Genealogical Society, 1982), p. vii.

10 This particular settler: *Records of the Colony of New Plymouth, in New England: Deeds, &c., 1620–1651. Book of Indian Records for Their Lands* (New Plymouth Colony, Massachusetts General Court: W. White, 1861), p. 111.

The legal document: Ibid., p. 227.

Back in court: Frederick Freeman, *The Annals of Barnstable County, Including the District of Mashpee* (Boston: Geo. C. Rand and Avery, 1858), p. 258.

11 He improvised language: Drew Lopenzina, *Red Ink: Native Americans Picking Up the Pen in the Colonial Period* (Albany: State University of New York Press, 2012), p. 205.

A Wampanoag commentator: Ibid., p. 151.

When New England: John Winthrop, *Winthrop's Journal, History of New England, 1630–1649*, vol. 1 (New York: Charles Scribner's Sons, 1908), pp. 83 and 84.

Settlements pushed into: Cerrotti, *Hidden Genocide, Hidden People*, p. 87.

Settlers drew parallels: Kupperman, *Indians and English*, p. 30.

12 Josiah Winslow, a: Lock of hair belonging to Josiah Winslow, Massachusetts Historical Society.

He led approximately: James W. Mavor Jr. and Byron E. Dix, *Manitou: The Sacred Landscape of New England's Native Civilization* (Rochester, VT: Inner Traditions International, 1989), p. 96.

When Josiah became: Freeman, *The Annals of Barnstable County*, p. 258.

In 1671, when: Winslow Mss. Collection, 1672 deed note, Pilgrim Hall Museum archives.

He won judgment: Ibid.

Fallowell was beside: Plymouth Colony Records, vol. 4, p. 82, March 7, 1665.

13 In fact, Harry: James Wilson, *The Earth Shall Weep: A History of Native America* (New York, NY: Grove/Atlantic, Inc., 2007), p. 85.

The court ordered: Plymouth Colony Records, vol. 4, p. 82, March 7, 1665.

They carried gifts: "Massachusetts Bay officials return gifts given by the Pequot in the winter of 1634," Battlefields of the Pequot War Interactive Timeline, Mashantucket Pequot Museum and Research Center, pequotwar.org.

In the summer: Ibid.; Dunbar-Ortiz, *An Indigenous Peoples' History of the United States*, p. 62.

It also underscored: Alfred A. Cave, *The Pequot War* (Amherst, MA: University of Massachusetts Press, 1996), pp. 86 and 87.

This displacement of: Dunbar-Ortiz, *An Indigenous Peoples' History of the United States*, p. 8.

The fighting started: Underhill and Royster, eds., "Newes from America," p. 35.

The Battle of: Dunbar-Ortiz, *An Indigenous Peoples' History of the United States*, pp. 62 and 63.

A colonial soldier: Andrea Robertson Cremer, "Possession: Indian Bodies, Cultural Control, and Colonialism in the Pequot War," *Early American Studies* 6, no. 2 (Fall 2008): 295–45, at 329; Cerrotti, *Hidden Genocide, Hidden People*, p. 27.

14 The Pequot War: Ibid.

The four hundred: Bradford, *Of Plymouth Plantation*, p. 189.

The victims died: Ibid.

Roger Williams, founding: "Roger Williams reports that the Pequot are subdued," Pequot War Timeline, November 10, 1637, Mashantucket Pequot Museum and Research Center, pequotwar.org.

Certain camps of: Lopenzina, *Red Ink*, p. 173.

When twelve colonists: For the largely undocumented and likely rudimentary trials of John Billington and William Schooler see Bradford's *Of Plymouth Plantation* and Winthrop's *History of New England*.

Relatively young, skilled: Lynn Betlock, "New England's Great Migration," *New England Ancestors* 4, no. 2 (2003): 22–24, www.greatmigration.org.

Those colonists ultimately: Perry Miller, *The New England Mind: The Seventeenth Century*, vol. 1 (Cambridge, MA: Harvard University Press, 1983), pp. 217–18.

15 Their story, too: Spotted Crow Mann, *Drumming and Dreaming*, p. 67.

## 1. Earthquakes and Omens

17 The formidable stands: John G. Erhardt, *This History of Rehoboth, Seekonk, East Providence, Pawtucket & Barrington*, vol. I: *Seacuncke, 1500s to 1645*, TX 1-226-547 (Seekonk, MA: 1982), p. 72.

They stopped in: Ibid., image IV.

Elongated and worn: Ibid.

Peach and his: Ross A. Muscato, "Tales from the Swamp: From Ape-Like Creatures to Glowing Lights, Hockomock Has Kept Its Secrets for Centuries," *Boston Globe*, October 30, 2005.

17 To this day: Ibid.

18 The men's choice: "Tribal Territories of Southern New England about 1600," image, commons.wikimedia.org.

The location fell: Thomas Williams Bicknell, *Sowams: With Ancient Records of Sowams and Parts Adjacent—Illustrated* (New Haven, CT: Associated Publishers of American Records, 1908), p. 151.

Earlier in the: Christy K. Robinson, "The Great New England Quake of 1638," September 7, 2011, marybarrettdyer.blogspot.com /2011/09.

First, Peach noticed: Ibid.

In describing the: Ibid.

The Providence patriarch: Erhardt, *This History of Rehoboth*, p. 67.

The aftershocks rumbled: Robinson, "The Great New England Quake of 1638."

20 The expansive stretches: Author interview with Jess Dougherty, docent, Careswell Estate, Marshfield, MA, August 3, 2018.

The ambitious settler: Margaret Ellen Newell, *Brethren by Nature: New England Indians, Colonists, and the Origins of American Slavery* (Ithaca, NY: Cornell University Press, 2015), p. 55.

The vast size: Ibid.

The distinctions among: Ibid., p. 49.

Tribal spiritual leaders: Karen Ordahl Kupperman, *Indians and English: Facing Off in Early America* (Ithaca, NY: Cornell University Press, 2000), p. 32.

21 When he later: Michael L. Fickes, " 'They Could Not Endure That Yoke': The Captivity of Pequot Women and Children After the War of 1637," *New England Quarterly* 73, no. 1 (March 2000): 58–81, at 78.

The colony declared: Lawrence W. Towner, *A Good Master Well Served: Master and Servants in Colonial Massachusetts, 1620–1750* (New York: Garland Publishing, Inc., 1998), p. 7.

Arthur Peach faced: Ibid., p. 29.

Just a few: Patricia Scott Deetz, "Servants and Masters in Plymouth Colony," chart 3, indicating the sharp decline of indentured servitude terms beginning in 1642, Plymouth Colony Archive Project, www .histarch.illinois.edu/plymouth/Galle1.html.

It was precisely: Newell, *Brethren by Nature*, p. 56.

22 Hopkins's small wattle-and-daub: Caleb Johnson, *Here Shall I Die Ashore: Stephen Hopkins: Bermuda Castaway, Jamestown Survivor, and Mayflower Pilgrim* (Xlibris Corporation, 2007), p. 251.

The bleak abode: Ibid.

23 Hopkins, the court: Ibid., pp. 132–33.

As one enraged: MS Deposition, III 8, Davis Scrapbooks, Pilgrim Hall Museum archives.

The "lusty" Peach: William Bradford, *History of Plymouth Plantation 1620–1647*, vol. 2 (Boston: Massachusetts Historical Society, 1912), p. 264.

Settlers soon learned: Ibid., p. 363.

Dorothy Temple, one: Johnson, *Here Shall I Die Ashore*, p. 153; 17th Century Personal and Household Items collection: Peter Brown's Wooden Beer Tankard. Material: Oak, birch. Made in England or the Baltics, circa 1620. Descended in the family of *Mayflower* passenger Peter Brown. Pilgrim Hall Museum. (This provides an example of a period tankard.)

24 Shakespeare needed a: Robert C. Fulton III, " 'The Tempest' and the Bermuda Pamphlets: Source and Thematic Intention," *Interpretations* 10, no. 1 (1978): 1–10.

He acquainted himself: Robert Ralston Cawley, "Shakspere's Use of the Voyagers in *The Tempest*," *PMLA* 41, no. 3 (September 1926): 688–726, at 690.

The narrative yielded: Ibid.

("Here's my comfort: William Shakespeare, *The Tempest* (Cambridge, MA: Macmillan and Company, 1863), II.2.40–45.

While the counter-authoritarian: Rowland Wymer, " 'The Tempest' and the Origins of Britain," *Critical Survey* 11, no. 1 (1999): 3–14, at 10; Kent Cartwright, *A Companion to Tudor Literature* (West Sussex, UK: John Wiley and Sons, 2010), p. 38.

Contemporaries had plenty: Johnson, *Here Shall I Die Ashore*, p. 45.

Hopkins was sentenced: John Frederick Dorman, *Adventurers of Purse and Person, Virginia, 1607–1624/5: Families G-P* (Clearfield Company, 2018), p. 355.

In a pitiful: Ibid.

25 His sad appeals: Johnson, *Here Shall I Die Ashore*, p. 45.

And while Peach: Parker L. Temple, "The Most Likely View of Abraham, Based on DNA: Dr. L. Parker Temple's Version," www.temple-genealogy.com/nmorigin.htm. (The theory that Dorothy Temple was Irish hinges on the connection I have drawn between her and Abraham Temple of Marblehead, MA. A direct descendent of the New England Temple clan, and likely Dorothy Temple's relation, revealed his DNA haplotype—one that is clustered in greatest concentration in southern Ireland.)

26 These understandings between: William Waller Hening, *The Statutes at Large; Being a Collection of All the Laws of Virginia from the First Session of the Legislature in the Year 1619*, vol. 1 (New York: R. and W. and G. Bartow, 1823), p. 411 (citing law: "Concerning secret Marriages," passed in its 1658 session, revising one passed during the 1643 session).
In an example: William Lee, *John Leigh of Agawam (Ipswich) Massachusetts 1634–1671* (Albany, NY: Joel Munsell and Sons, 1833), p. 69. Digitized by the Internet Archive in 2010 with funding from Allen County Public Library Genealogy Center.
Male servants greatly: Fickes, "'They Could Not Endure That Yoke,'" p. 63.
Only after Peach: Bradford, *History of Plymouth Plantation 1620–1647*, vol. 2, p. 264.
To reach new: Ibid.
Peach must have: Ibid.
Leaving the Careswell: Cynthia Krusell, Marshfield town historian, in response to a Marshfield Historical Society inquiry: "It would have been an old Indian trail that came to be known as the Green Harbor Path. It led up from Plymouth along the shore to the original Winslow House. This road was formally laid out by the Plymouth Colony court in 1637 and quite possibly was the first court-ordered road in the country."
Ten-year-old Josiah: Author interview with Jess Dougherty, docent, Careswell Estate, Marshfield, MA, August 3, 2018. Archeologists excavated the whistle from the "Winslow House." It is held at Plimouth Plantation, though currently unavailable to the public or researchers.
27 Continuing south and: Bradford, *History of Plymouth Plantation 1620–1647*, vol. 2, p. 363.

## 2. MURDER

28 Indigenous infants were: James Axtell, *The Indian Peoples of Eastern America: A Documentary History of the Sexes* (New York: Oxford University Press, 1981), p. 3.
The bare-chested traveler: Kimball Webster, *History of Hudson, New Hampshire: Formerly a Part of Dunstable, Massachusetts, 1673–1733* (Manchester, NH: Granite State Publishing Company, 1913), p. 65.
29 "[I] will kill: William Bradford, *History of Plymouth Plantation 1620–1647*, vol. 2 (Boston: Massachusetts Historical Society, 1912), p. 264.
The indigenous man: Glenn LaFantasie, ed., *The Correspondence of*

*Roger Williams*, 2 vols. (Hanover, NH: Brown University and University Press of New England, 1988), pp. 172 and 176.

This was the*: Siobhan Senier, *Dawnland Voices: An Anthology of Indigenous Writing from New England* (Lincoln: University of Nebraska Press, 2014), p. 391.

Many fellow tribesmen: Ibid.

The "Three Sisters": Ibid.

It was time: Ibid.

30 The 1627 accord: Michael J. Vieira, *A Brief History of Wareham: The Gateway to Cape Cod* (Arcadia Publishing, 2014), p. 23.

Leaders from England: Ibid.

The Wampanoag sachem: Charles C. Mann, "Native Intelligence," *Smithsonian Magazine* (December 2005), www.smithsonianmag.com /history/native-intelligence-109314481.

Allying himself with: Ibid.

Massasoit offered Plymouth: Ibid.

The savvy sachem: Ibid.

Some of the: Alvin Gardner Weeks, *Massasoit of the Wampanoags: With a Brief Commentary on Indian Character; and Sketches of Other Great Chiefs, Tribes and Nations; Also a Chapter on Samoset, Squanto and Hobamock, Three Early Native Friends of the Plymouth Colonists* (Norwood, MA: Plimpton Press, 1919), p. 85.

They were displeased: Ibid.

A few years: Alfred A. Cave, *The Pequot War* (Amherst, MA: University of Massachusetts Press, 1996), p. 58.

In 1633, the: Ibid.

The treaty explicitly: Ibid.

31 While the Pequot: Ibid.

The beaver he: Glenn W. LaFantasie, "Murder of an Indian, 1638," *Rhode Island History* 38, no. 3 (1979): 67.

As Massasoit sold: Weeks, *Massasoit of the Wampanoags*, p. 85.

32 The Aptucxet trading: Sydney V. James Jr., *Three Visitors to Early Plymouth: Letters About the Pilgrim Settlement in New England During Its First Seven Years—John Pory, Isaack de Rasieres, Emmanuel Altham* (Bedford, MA: Applewood Books, 1997), p. 74.

A few settlers: Ibid.

Beaver make their: Dorcas S. Miller, *Track Finder: A Guide to Mammal Tracks of Eastern North America*, 2nd ed. (Birmingham, AL: Adventure KEEN, 2017), p. 16.

32 Their large tails: Ibid.

Seated in canoes: Axtell, *The Indian Peoples of Eastern America*, p. 116.

The pelts taken: Tom Tierney, *Historic Costume: From the Renaissance Through the Nineteenth Century* (Mineola, NY: Dover Publications, 2004), p. 51; 17th Century Personal and Household Items collection: Constance Hopkins' Beaver Hat, 1615–40. Pilgrim Hall Museum.

With hollowed-out burls: Pequot War presenter, Mashantucket Pequot Museum and Research Center, June 24, 2017; 17th Century Personal and Household Items collection: Burl Bowl. Material: Burl maple. Possibly Wampanoag, 1630–1750. Pilgrim Hall Museum. "Bowls such as this one were used for preparing and serving food. Burlwood bowls are exceptionally strong, as they don't crack along the grain."

33 Archaeologists have shed: Kevin McBride, lecture at Mashantucket Pequot Museum and Research Center, June 24, 2017.

Previously, arrow tips: Ibid.

The king had: James Hunt, *Stammering and Stuttering, Their Nature and Treatment* (London: Longman, Green, Longman, and Roberts, 1861), p. 16.

By embracing a: Tierney, *Historic Costume*, p. 51.

In describing the: Nathaniel Bartlett Sylvester, *Historical Sketches of Northern New York and the Adirondack Wilderness: Including Traditions of the Indians, Early Explorers, Pioneer Settlers, Hermit Hunters, &c.* (Adirondack Mountains, NY: W. H. Young, 1877), p. 18.

34 The nearby forests: McBride lecture.

The intentionally interspersed: Roxanne Dunbar-Ortiz, *An Indigenous Peoples' History of the United States* (Boston: Beacon Press, 2014), p. 28.

Indeed, a contemporary: Ibid.

The young trader: Stephen Mrozowski and Heather Law Pezzarossi, *The Archaeology of Hassanamesit Woods: The Sarah Burnee/Sarah Boston Farmstead*, Andrew Fiske Memorial Center for Archaeological Research, University of Massachusetts Boston, Cultural Resource Management Study No. 69 (October 2015), pp. 133 and 162; Dennis A. Connole, *The Indians of the Nipmuck Country in Southern New England, 1630–1750: An Historical Geography* (Jefferson, NC: McFarland and Company, 2007), pp. 18–19.

With each party: Denys Delge, *Bitter Feast: Amerindians and Europeans in Northeastern North America, 1600–64* (Vancouver: UBC Press, 1995), p. 102.

The Nipmuc boasted: Russell G. Handsman and Ann McMullen, *A Key into the Language of Woodsplint Baskets* (Washington, CT: American

Indian Archaeological Institute, 1987), p. 84, fig. 40; baskets observed by the author, September 27, 2016, Natick Historical Society, Bacon Library, Natick, MA.

The designs conveyed: Handsman and McMullen, *A Key into the Language of Woodsplint Baskets*, p. 85, ns. 42 and 100, and fig. 46.

They were a: Carl Waldman, *Encyclopedia of Native American Tribes* (Infobase Publishing, 2014), p. 196.

In the end: John Winthrop, *Winthrop Papers*, vol. 4 (Boston: Massachusetts Historical Society, 1944), p. 49.

35 The beads Penowanyanquis: McBride lecture.

English and indigenous: Barbara Brennessel, *Good Tidings: The History and Ecology of Shellfish Farming in the Northeast* (Hanover, NH: University Press of New England, 2008), p. 49.

Fathoms of wampum: Ibid., p. 48.

Wampum came either: Ibid.

In the mid-1630s: Nick Bunker, *Making Haste from Babylon: The Mayflower Pilgrims and Their World: A New History* (New York: Knopf, 2010), p. 363.

The plague had hit: Peggy M. Baker, *The Pilgrims and the Fur Trade*, Pilgrim Hall Museum, www.pilgrimhallmuseum.org/.

With Black Death: Ibid.

He likely walked: Edward J. Lenik, *Picture Rocks: American Indian Rock Art in the Northeast Woodlands* (Hanover, NH: University Press of New England, 2002), pp. 116–18.

Penowanyanquis could see: Ibid., pp. 116–18 and 155.

Next to it: Ibid., pp. 116–18.

36 Both of these: Ibid.; Mann, "Native Intelligence."

These stone landmarks: Doug Harris, Narragansett Tribal historian, "Narragansett Stone Terminology" handout, provided by Linda McElroy, Friends of the Pine Hawk, May 2017.

This landscape was: Christine M. Delucia, *Memory Lands: King Philip's War and the Place of Violence in the Northeast* (New Haven, CT: Yale University Press, 2018), p. 16.

The trail was: Connole, *The Indians of the Nipmuck Country*, p. 20.

Hundreds of years: Michael Ward, *Ellison "Tarzan" Brown: The Narragansett Indian Who Twice Won the Boston Marathon* (Jefferson, NC: McFarland and Company, Inc., 2006), pp. 11–12. (Within the text are numerous examples of Brown completing races while barefoot.)

Though Penowanyanquis likely: Cheryl Stedtler, Project Mishoon, findings: "The third one [*mishoon*] is a different design, probably older and different wood. We hope to date that this year. Lastly, we identified a stone axehead. Although was in the general area of the dugouts, it was not near them." Note emailed to author on August 3, 2016; Caleb Johnson, "Massasoit Ousemequin," mayflowerhistory.com/massasoit/.

37 The rakish John: LaFantasie, ed., *The Correspondence of Roger Williams*, p. 72.

He knew the: Jeremy Dupertuis Bangs, *The Seventeenth-Century Town Records of Scituate, Massachusetts*, vol. 3 (Boston: New England Historic Genealogical Society, 2002), p. 303.

As a soldier: J. H. Trumbull, *Public Records of the Colony of Connecticut*, vols. 1–3 (Hartford, CT: Brown and Parsons, 1850), p. 10.

He had also: McBride lecture.

The strapping young: Ibid.

A few years: John Winthrop, *Winthrop Papers*, vol. 1 (Boston: Massachusetts Historical Society, 1944), p. 142.

One seasoned traveler: Sydney V. James Jr., *Three Visitors to Early Plymouth: Letters About the Pilgrim Settlement in New England During Its First Seven Years—John Pory, Isaack de Rasieres, Emmanuel Altham* (Bedford, MA: Applewood Books, 1997), p. 75, n. 25.

38 A tinge of: Mrozowski and Pezzarossi, *The Archaeology of Hassanamesit Woods*, describing earthenware or "redware" technique.

39 As outgoing Plymouth: Bradford, *History of Plymouth Plantation 1620–1647*, vol. 2, p. 264.

Rapier readied, Peach: Ibid.

Then he "made: LaFantasie, ed., *The Correspondence of Roger Williams*, p. 172.

One of the: Ibid.

Penowanyanquis bounded out: Ibid.

But "they pursued: Ibid.

Penowanyanquis tumbled down: Ibid.

Once more "they: Ibid.

One last time: Ibid.

He ventured even: Ibid.

The dense vegetation: Robert Miller, "Let the Glorious Season of Skunk Cabbage and Singing Frogs Begin," Newstimes, March 20, 2016, www.newstimes.com/news/article/Robert-Miller-Let-the-glorious-season-of-skunk-6896691.php.

40 He may have: John G. Erhardt, *This History of Rehoboth, Seekonk, East Providence, Pawtucket & Barrington*, vol. 1: *Seacuncke, 1500s to 1645*, TX 1-226-547 (Seekonk, MA: 1982), p. 35.

If he did: Ibid. While the Native American name for this area was Seekonk, settlers renamed part of it Rehoboth—an example of colonists obscuring indigenous place names.

As dusk fell: Dianne Ochiltree, *It's a Firefly Night* (Maplewood, NJ: Blue Apple Books, 2013), endnotes.

Massasoit called the: Leo Bonfanti, *Biographies and Legends of the New England Indians*, New England Historical Series, vol. 1, rev. ed. (Danvers, MA: Old Saltbox Publishing, 1993), p. 43.

Shut out from: William Apess, *On Our Own Ground: The Complete Writings of William Apess, a Pequot* (Amherst, MA: University of Massachusetts Press, 1992), p. 42.

41 Ironically, given Penowanyanquis's: Katherine A. Grandjean, "The Long Wake of the Pequot War," *Early American Studies: An Interdisciplinary Journal* 9, no. 2 (Spring 2011): 379–411.

Many Narragansett took: Ibid.

42 (Local tribesmen referred: Author interview with Professor J. Stanley Lemons, Rhode Island College professor emeritus of history, Providence, RI, December 19, 2017.

43 Their ancient legends: Erhardt, *This History of Rehoboth*, p. 68.

Through the door: Ibid., p. 45.

44 He rode his: John Wilford Blackstone, *Lineage and History of William Blackstone, First Settler of Boston* (Wisconsin: John Wilford Blackstone Jr., 1907), p. 70.

There he fondly: James Truslow Adams, *The Founding of New England* (Boston: Atlantic Monthly Press, 1921), p. 184.

His home in: Ibid.

Indeed, Blackstone had: *Pawtucket Past and Present: Being a Brief Account of the Beginning and Progress of Its Industries and a Résumé of Early History of the City* (Pawtucket, RI: Slater Trust Company, 1917), p. 1.

The young tribeswoman: Margaret Ellen Newell, *Brethren by Nature: New England Indians, Colonists, and the Origins of American Slavery* (Ithaca, NY: Cornell University Press, 2015), pp. 70 and 105.

Blackstone's move to: Ibid., p. 104.

The dark-cloaked: Winthrop, *Winthrop Papers*, vol. 4, p. 49.

45 The injured Nipmuc: Bradford, *History of Plymouth Plantation 1620–1647*, vol. 2, p. 363.

The Narragansett men: Roger Williams, *Publications of the Narragansett Club: The Letters of Roger Williams*, vol. 6 (Providence, RI: Narragansett Club, 1874), p. 112.

Quickly, the Narragansett: Ibid., p. 60.

46 Governor Winthrop documented: Winthrop, *Winthrop Papers*, vol. 4, p. 49.
Only steps ahead: Ibid.

### 3. The Children's God

47 The sacred area: James W. Mavor Jr. and Byron E. Dix, *Manitou: The Sacred Landscape of New England's Native Civilization* (Rochester, VT: Inner Traditions International, 1989), p. 41.
The "Fresh Water: Ibid.; Colin Calloway, ed., *After King Philip's War: Presence and Persistence in Indian New England* (Hanover, NH: University Press of New England, 1997), p. 221, n. 2.
Interestingly, as the: Mavor and Dix, *Manitou*, p. 41.

48 Their territory counted: Ibid., p. 42.
Near Hassanamessit, and: Ibid., pp. 44, 50, and 52.
Indigenous elders taught: Ibid., p. 52.
Within the stone: Ibid., pp. 50 and 51.
Stone cairns built: Ibid., p. 52.
The rise and: Ibid., p. 53.
We know the: Ibid., p. 52.
In 1524, when: Ibid., p. 54.
Indigenous people believed: John Hanson Mitchell, *Trespassing: An Inquiry into the Private Ownership of Land* (Lebanon, NH: University Press of New England, 2015), p. 14.
"Terrible roarings and: Ibid.
Nipmuc feared that: Ibid.
Settlers also took: Ibid.
It sounded to: Ibid.
To this day: Text from sign marking Hassanamessitt land of Nipmuc Nation, abutting Grafton, MA, Massachusetts Bay Colony Tercentenary Commission.

49 A river or: Russell G. Handsman, *A Theoretical Foundation for Indigenous Archaeologies: Towards Archaeological Histories of the Nipmuc Indian Community in the "Lost Century" (1820–1920)*, presented to the EcoTarium, Worcester, MA, 2003, p. 33.
This small settlement: Notes from the Friends of Pine Hawk group, whose work supports Nipmuc cultural preservation, Acton, MA, April 30, 2017. In the area we cleared: natural stone-grinding basin, dozens of stone cairns, an indigenous rock wall. Details provided by Linda McElroy and Bob Ferrara.

Unlike the walls: Ibid.

In the Algonquian: Marcin Kilarski, *Nominal Classification: A History of Its Study from the Classical Period to the Present* (Amsterdam and Philadelphia: John Benjamins Publishing Company, 2013), pp. 110–11.

Instead, the Nipmuc: Ibid.

The Nipmuc tellingly: Ibid.

Indeed, their spirit: Lynn Horsky. Local guide: Sarah Doublet Forest, Littleton Conservation Trust; Mavor and Dix, *Manitou*, p. 90.

From forest glens: Lynn Horsky. Local guide: Sarah Doublet Forest, Littleton Conservation Trust.

Settlers who encountered: Daniel Gookin, *Historical Collections of the Indians in New England*, collections of the Massachusetts Historical Society (Рипол Классик, 1792), p. 149.

50 One of the: Sarah Simon letter, April 4, 1769, MS-1310, 769254.1, Rauner Library, Dartmouth College.

While busy with: Dawn Dove and Holly Ewald, "Indigenous Life in Rhode Island: An Introduction, by Paulla Dove Jennings, as told to Holly Ewald," *Through Our Eyes: An Indigenous View of Mashapaug Pond* (Lulu Publishing, 2012), p. 39; Friends of Pine Hawk website, pinehawk.abschools.org/.

Children in the: Roger Williams, *Publications of the Narragansett Club: Key into the Language of America* (Providence, RI: Providence Press Company Printers, 1866), p. 4; Friends of Pine Hawk website.

Names were relatively: James Alan Marten, *Children in Colonial America* (New York: New York University Press, 2007), p. 35.

As Roger Williams: Williams, *Publications of the Narragansett Club: Key into the Language of America*, p. 5.

Careful scrutiny reveals: James Hammond Trumbull, *Natick Dictionary* (Washington, DC: U.S. Government Printing Office, 1903), p. 122. (Roger Williams's "dog key," in which he noted the distinctions for the translation of the word *dog* over several Algonquian dialects, shows marked similarity, though variation too. "Penowanyanquis" may have been a variant of "Penowe" and carried over in other Algonquian dialects as well.)

One current member: Ramona L. Peters, "Consulting with the Bone Keepers: NAGPRA Consultations and Archaeological Monitoring in the Wampanoag Territory," *Cross-Cultural Collaboration: Native Peoples and Archaeology in the Northeastern United States*, ed. Jordan E. Kerber (Lincoln: University of Nebraska Press, 2006), p. 41.

51 He may have: Williams, *Publications of the Narragansett Club: Key into the Language of America*, p. 82.

(Roger Williams observed: Ibid., pp. 82–83.

He was fit: Ibid., p. 6.

He could effortlessly: Ibid., pp. 62 and 86; "Roger Williams' Compass which is round with screw top, finely engraved, and has a folding sun-vane," Rhode Island Historical Society. Not on display.

He could also: Williams, *Publications of the Narragansett Club: Key into the Language of America*, pp. 62 and 86.

The nighttime "heavenly: Ibid., p. 62.

Unpredictable and wily: Ibid., pp. 20 and 117; Siobhan Senier, *Dawnland Voices: An Anthology of Indigenous Writing from New England* (Lincoln: University of Nebraska Press, 2014), p. 390.

Roger Williams recorded: Dennis Cerrotti, *Hidden Genocide, Hidden People* (Wellesley, MA: Sea Venture Press, 2014), p. 106.

Governor Winthrop noted: Michael L. Fickes, " 'They Could Not Endure That Yoke': The Captivity of Pequot Women and Children After the War of 1637," *New England Quarterly* 73, no. 1 (March 2000): 58–81, at 73.

In one ancient: Harold Gordon, antique dealer, Templeton, MA, carved "Indian box," with "falling man" on the upper right held up by turtles. Native American origin, likely Nipmuc, Pioneer Valley, MA.

52 Penowanyanquis's generation marked: Lucianne Lavin, *Connecticut's Indigenous Peoples: What Archaeology, History, and Oral Traditions Teach Us About Their Communities and Cultures* (New Haven, CT: Yale University Press, June 25, 2013), pp. 143–44 and 272.

In the young: Marten, *Children in Colonial America*, pp. 34–35; Williams, *Publications of the Narragansett Club: Key into the Language of America*, p. 118.

The spirit before: William Scranton Simmons, *Spirit of the New England Tribes: Indian History and Folklore, 1620–1984* (Hanover, NH: University Press of New England, 1986), p. 41.

An English missionary: Gregory H. Nobles, *American Frontiers: Cultural Encounters and Continental Conquest* (New York: Hill and Wang, 1997), p. 29.

Another settler observed: Daniel Neal, *The history of New-England, containing an impartial account of the civil and ecclesiastical affairs of the country, to the year of Our Lord, 1700. To which is added, the present state of New-England. With a new and accurate map of the country. And an appendix containing their present charter, their ecclesiastical discipline, and their municipal-laws. In two volumes* (London: J. Clark, R. Ford, and R. Cruttenden, 1720), p. 37.

Worried parents had: William S. Simmons, *Cautantowwit's House: An Indian Burial Ground on the Island of Conanicut in Narragansett Bay* (Providence, RI: Brown University Press, 1970), p. 62.

It is the: Ibid., p. 54; *nota bene*: "The former [*Cautantowwit's House: An Indian Burial Ground on the Island of Conanicut in Narragansett Bay*] gives some evidence that the words for children's god and the word for one of the two human souls may be connected," email from William S. Simmons, July 26, 2017.

53 No wonder it: Simmons, *Cautantowwit's House*, p. 62.

A peculiar creature: Ibid.

The small bird: Ibid.; Stephanie Fielding, *A Modern Mohegan Dictionary* (2006), p. 124. Prepared for the Council of Elders, reviewed by the Cultural and Community Programs Department. Property of the Mohegan Tribe.

The Children's God: American Folklore Society, *The Journal of American Folk-lore*, vol. 12 (Boston and New York: Houghton, Mifflin and Company, 1899), p. 212.

Penowanyanquis later reported: Williams, *Publications of the Narragansett Club: Key into the Language of America*, p. 150.

Gods could appear: Senier, *Dawnland Voices*, p. 390.

He described having: Alden T. Vaughan, *New England Encounters: Indians and Euroamericans ca. 1600–1850: Essays Drawn from* The New England Quarterly (Boston: Northeastern University Press, 1999), p. 192.

At the age: Black Elk and John G. Neihardt, *Black Elk Speaks: Being the Life Story of a Holy Man of the Oglala Sioux, the Premier Edition* (Albany, NY: SUNY Press, 2008), p. 24.

54 "The winds and: Ibid.

In one legend: Henry Rowe Schoolcraft, *Schoolcraft's Indian Legends* (East Lansing: Michigan State University Press, 1991), p. 144.

Some boys traversed: Ibid.

Rewards awaited; they: Ibid.

They met the: Ibid.

Those who made: Ibid.

Only two of: Ibid.

A Nipmuc legend: Senier, *Dawnland Voices*, p. 390.

54 A tribal elder: Ibid.

The spirits offered: Ibid.; Dove and Ewald, "Indigenous Life in Rhode Island," p. 38.

At moments of: Dove and Ewald, "Indigenous Life in Rhode Island," p. 38.

But what was: Ibid., p. 10.

The Children's God: James Axtell, *The Indian Peoples of Eastern America: A Documentary History of the Sexes* (New York: Oxford University Press, 1981), p. 54.

On the day: Ibid., p. 3.

55 This oil offered: Ibid., p. 5 (referencing Calvin Martin's research).

Algonquian tradition was: Mavor and Dix, *Manitou*, p. 145.

Another young Algonquian: Edward J. Lenik, *Picture Rocks: American Indian Rock Art in the Northeast Woodlands* (Hanover, NH: University Press of New England, 2002), pp. 133 and 134.

Spirit messengers visited: Ibid.

The arrival of: Ibid.

Weetucks spent hours: Ibid.

His Thursday morning: John Winthrop, *Winthrop Papers*, vol. 4 (Boston: Massachusetts Historical Society, 1944), p. 48.

The only recent: Ibid., p. 49.

56 As he later: Mss. Misc. Boxes W. Number 86650, one folder, Roger Williams Papers, American Antiquarian Society; Romeo Elton, *Life of Roger Williams: The Earliest Legislator and True Champion for a Full and Absolute Liberty of Conscience* (London: Albert Cockshaw, 1852), p. 18.

"I have fixed: Margaret Ellen Newell, *Brethren by Nature: New England Indians, Colonists, and the Origins of American Slavery* (Ithaca, NY: Cornell University Press, 2015), p. 37.

Perhaps Williams did: Roger Williams, *Publications of the Narragansett Club: The Letters of Roger Williams*, vol. 6 (Providence, RI: Narragansett Club, 1874), p. 54.

57 Winthrop obliged; before: Winthrop, *Winthrop Papers*, vol. 4, p. 51.

Not a diminutive: Joseph Norwood, "A Boy Named Humiliation: Some Wacky, Cruel, and Bizarre Puritan Names," *Slate*, September 13, 2013.

Williams's need for: Author interview with Professor J. Stanley Lemons, Rhode Island College professor emeritus of history, Providence, RI, December 19, 2017; Williams, *Publications of the Narragansett Club: The Letters of Roger Williams*, vol. 6, p. 54; Newell, *Brethren by Nature*, p. 37.

He later referred: Winthrop, *Winthrop Papers*, vol. 4, p. 51.

When captured indigenous: Christine M. Delucia, *Memory Lands: King Philip's War and the Place of Violence in the Northeast* (New Haven, CT: Yale University Press, 2018), pp. 55 and 56.

Settlers sometimes identified: Ibid., p. 56.

Given the blurred: "The Last Will and Testament of John Winslow," Pilgrim Hall Museum.

It was in: David R. Wagner and Jack Dempsey, *Mystic Fiasco: How the Indians Won the Pequot War* (Scituate, MA: Digital Scanning Inc., 2010), p. 222. Note: When Roger Williams wrote to Winthrop late in the summer of 1637, he noted Will's "mother (who is with you [Winthrop] and two children more)."

Evidence indicates that: Ibid.

Wincumbone, whose husband: C. S. Manegold, *Ten Hills Farm: The Forgotten History of Slavery in the North* (Princeton: Princeton University Press, 2010), p. 42.

Now she used: Ibid.

She stipulated that: John Winthrop, *Winthrop Papers*, vol. 3 (Boston: Massachusetts Historical Society, 1943), p. 457.

Governor Winthrop appreciatively: Manegold, *Ten Hills Farm*, p. 42.

At the urging: Wagner and Dempsey, *Mystic Fiasco*, p. 188.

("I have taken: Manegold, *Ten Hills Farm*, p. 42.

58 The sachem Mononotto: Williams, *Publications of the Narragansett Club: The Letters of Roger Williams*, vol. 6, p. 54.

One settler described: Wagner and Dempsey, *Mystic Fiasco*, p. 105.

Mononotto fought on: "Battlefields of the Pequot War," Mashantucket Pequot Museum and Research Center in collaboration with the American Battlefield Protection Program of the National Park Service, pequotwar.org/.

The English had: Ibid.

When enemy forces: Ibid.

"Prince Mononotto sees: Samuel G. Drake, *The Book of the Indians of North America* (Boston: Josiah Drake at the Antiquarian Bookstore, 1835), p. 109.

Williams, however, may: Manegold, *Ten Hills Farm*, p. 42.

59 He wrote to: Williams, *Publications of the Narragansett Club: The Letters of Roger Williams*, vol. 6, p. 54.

He may have: Dove and Ewald, "Indigenous Life in Rhode Island," p. 37.

The child witnessed: Ibid., pp. 38 and 50.

59 Intermarriage between the: Fickes, "'They Could Not Endure That Yoke,'" p. 76.

"The Indians children: Ibid., p. 73.

As Governor Winthrop: Ibid., p. 75.

One seventeenth-century: Delucia, *Memory Lands*, p. 56.

60 This movement argued: Fickes, "'They Could Not Endure That Yoke,'" pp. 80–81.

Discussing a future: Manegold, *Ten Hills Farm*, p. 49.

Colonial leaders even: Andrea Robertson Cremer, "Possession: Indian Bodies, Cultural Control, and Colonialism in the Pequot War," *Early American Studies* 6, no. 2 (Fall 2008): 295–345, at 337.

Women and girls: Manegold, *Ten Hills Farm*, pp. 41–42.

It also indicates: Fickes, "'They Could Not Endure That Yoke,'" p. 62.

Settlers abided "Indians: Ibid., p. 72.

New England involvement: Manegold, *Ten Hills Farm*, p. 43; Drew Lopenzina, *Red Ink: Native Americans Picking Up the Pen in the Colonial Period* (Albany: State University of New York Press, 2012), p. 107.

61 That Thursday morning: Winthrop, *Winthrop Papers*, vol. 4, p. 49.

The four members: Dove and Ewald, "Indigenous Life in Rhode Island," p. 37.

Despite Peach's attempt: Winthrop, *Winthrop Papers*, vol. 4, p. 49.

As Williams's household: Ibid.

Williams even turned: Mss. Misc. Boxes W. Number 86650, one folder, Roger Williams Papers, American Antiquarian Society. Example of Roger Williams's seal with embedded mosquito.

62 He pressed his: Ibid.; Eric R. Eaton, "Kaufman Field Guide to Insects of North America." "It looks like it has enough legs to be a spider . . . ," June 28, 2016, correspondence.

Williams admired the: Roger Williams, *The Complete Writings of Roger Williams* (Eugene, OR: Wipf and Stock Publishers, 2007), vol. 4, p. 455.

This time, the: Winthrop, *Winthrop Papers*, vol. 4, p. 49.

Greene, a solid: John Winthrop, *Winthrop's Journal, History of New England, 1630–1649*, vol. 1 (New York: Charles Scribner's Sons, 1908), p. 176.

63 Described by Williams: Williams, *Publications of the Narragansett Club: The Letters of Roger Williams*, vol. 6, p. 54.

Indigenous observers took: Karen Ordahl Kupperman, *Indians and English: Facing Off in Early America* (Ithaca, NY: Cornell University Press, 2000), p. 179.

"They much marveled: Ibid.

A tribal leader: Ibid.

Williams professed his: Winthrop, *Winthrop Papers*, vol. 4, p. 49.

"*Muckquachuckquand!*" Penowanyanquis cried: Williams, *Publications of the Narragansett Club: Key into the Language of America*, p. 149.

64 Years later, he: Ibid.

Later Williams came: Ibid.

As his strength: Natick Nipmuc Band, "O Great Spirit" prayer, natick nipmuc.com/index.html#.

Greene and James: Winthrop, *Winthrop Papers*, vol. 4, p. 149; C. K. Murray, M. K. Hinkle, and H. C. Yun, "History of Infections Associated with Combat-Related Injuries," *Journal of Trauma and Acute Care Surgery* 64, 3 supp. (March 2008): S221–31.

In the colonial: Ibid.

Like Williams, Greene: Caroline Frank and Krysta Ryzewski, "Excavating the Quiet History of a Providence Plantation," *Historical Archaeology* 47, no. 2 (2013): 16–44, at 22.

65 Powerful infantrymen carried: Kevin McBride, lecture at Mashantucket Pequot Museum and Research Center, June 24, 2017.

"Have you fought: Cerrotti, *Hidden Genocide, Hidden People*, p. 68.

As Williams watched: Winthrop, *Winthrop Papers*, vol. 4, p. 48.

"We drest him: Ibid., p. 49.

## 4. MANHUNT

66 The son of: Oddly shaped cloth fragment with . . . floral vines and cream accents, stated to belong to Roger Williams, possibly a piece of a waistcoat. Rhode Island Historical Society, not on display; Perry Miller and Thomas H. Johnson, *The Puritans: A Sourcebook of Their Writings* (Courier Corporation, September 22, 2014), p. 214.

When ill, complaining: Letter from Roger Williams, [1647]. Series II. Governor John Winthrop Jr. MSS 413, B2 F20, p. 268. Winthrop Family Papers, Phillips Library Reading Room, Peabody Essex Museum.

"I have books: Ibid.

By this point: Kathy Merrill, "Several Early Physicians," *William and Mary Quarterly* 14, no. 2 (1905): 100. (Transcribed by Kathy Merrill for the USGenWeb Archives Special Collections Project.)

67 He told Williams: Glenn LaFantasie, ed., *The Correspondence of Roger Williams*, 2 vols. (Hanover, NH: Brown University and University Press of New England, 1988), p. 172.

"I know that: Ibid., p. 173.

68 "Mr. James and: Ibid., p. 172.

68 When Williams looked: Roger Williams, *Key into the Language of America* (Bedford, MA: Applewood Books, 1997), p. 201.

The soot was: Ibid.

Reminiscent of the: John Winthrop, *Winthrop Papers*, vol. 1 (Boston: Massachusetts Historical Society, 1944), p. 272.

Most threateningly, the: Ibid.

In spite of: Williams, *Key into the Language of America*, p. 53.

69 As Winthrop noted: Winthrop, *Winthrop Papers*, vol. 1, pp. 320–21.

The events Winthrop: Julie A. Fisher and David J. Silverman, *Ninigret, Sachem of the Niantics and Narragansetts: Diplomacy, War, and the Balance of Power in Seventeenth-Century New England and Indian Country* (Ithaca, NY: Cornell University Press, 2014), p. 44.

Winthrop ordered Roger: Winthrop, *Winthrop Papers*, vol. 1, p. 321.

70 Williams, a student: William Bradford, *History of Plymouth Plantation 1620–1647*, vol. 2 (Boston: Massachusetts Historical Society, 1912), p. 362.

Tribal criers used: Dawn Dove and Holly Ewald, "Indigenous Life in Rhode Island: An Introduction, by Paulla Dove Jennings, as told to Holly Ewald," *Through Our Eyes: An Indigenous View of Mashapaug Pond* (Lulu Publishing, 2012), p. 36; Doug Harris, Narragansett Tribal historian, "Narragansett Stone Terminology" handout, provided by Linda McElroy, Friends of the Pine Hawk, May 2017.

When they removed: Dove and Ewald, "Indigenous Life in Rhode Island," p. 36.

The low, sonorous: Ibid.

In normal circumstances: Duane Hamilton Hurd, "History of Middlesex County, Massachusetts," waymarking.com. (The burial ground was the place where remains found in the area were buried. Several graves were discovered when the church built the wall in its yard, and "a long row" of remains was found when pipes were being laid by the Bailey Hotel, in South Natick.)

71 Nipmuc cherished these: Ellie Oleson, "Nipmuc Artifacts Tell Tale of Their Role in Early Massachusetts," November 21, 2014, www.telegram.com/article/20141121/TOWNNEWS/ (quoting the Auburn Historical Society president, Sari Bitticks).

The Nipmuc's alternative: Russell G. Handsman, *A Theoretical Foundation for Indigenous Archaeologies: Towards Archaeological Histories of the Nipmuc Indian Community in the "Lost Century" (1820–1920)*, presented to the EcoTarium, Worcester, MA, 2003, p. 33.

Hundreds of years: Jennifer Banister, John Daly, and Suzanne Cherau,

*Historic and Archaeological Reconnaissance Survey, Concord River, Diadromous Fish Restoration Project Talbot Mills Dam*, p. 29.

It is possible: Mary E. Gage and James E. Gage, *A Guide to New England Stone Structures: Stone Cairns, Stone Walls, Standing Stones, Chambers, Foundations, Wells, Culverts, Quarries and Other Structures*, 2nd ed. (Amesbury, MA: Powwow River Books, 2016), p. 9.

A "supreme medicine: Brona G. Simon, "Collaboration Between Archaeologists and Native Americans in Massachusetts: Preservation, Archaeology, and Native American Concerns in Balance," *Cross-Cultural Collaboration: Native Peoples and Archaeology in the Northeastern United States*, ed. Jordan E. Kerber (Lincoln: University of Nebraska Press, 2006), p. 44.

"We don't believe: Ibid.

His intricately constructed: Dennis A. Connole, *The Indians of the Nipmuck Country in Southern New England, 1630–1750: An Historical Geography* (Jefferson, NC: McFarland and Company, 2007), p. 18; Dove and Ewald, "Indigenous Life in Rhode Island," p. 11.

The bulrush retained: Dove and Ewald, "Indigenous Life in Rhode Island," p. 37.

Mats and the: Connole, *The Indians of the Nipmuck Country*, p. 18; Dove and Ewald, "Indigenous Life in Rhode Island," p. 11.

In the Algonquian: Roger Williams, *Publications of the Narragansett Club: Key into the Language of America* (Providence, RI: Providence Press Company Printers, 1866), p. 3.

72 Just a few: Michelle H. Johnstone, *The Journey of an Ancient People: A Chronicle of the Nipmuc: 1631–2014* (Worcester, MA: Worcester State University, Spring 2014), p. 9 (citing Carolyn Merchant, "The Colonial Ecological Revolution," *Ecological Revolutions: Nature, Gender, and Science in New England* [Chapel Hill: University of North Carolina Press, 1989, p. 90]).

The loss of: Handsman, *A Theoretical Foundation for Indigenous Archaeologies*, p. 33.

Interactions with English: Johnstone, *The Journey of an Ancient People*, p. 9 (citing D. Hamilton Hurd, "Grafton," *History of Worcester County* [Philadelphia: J. W. Lewis, 1889, p. 935]).

Court officials offered: Connole, *The Indians of the Nipmuck Country*, pp. 53–54.

73 Flames burned high: Observations made by the author during a Nipmuc Nation ceremonial dance on July 31, 2016, at the tribal homeland, Grafton, MA.

73 Leaders of the: Ibid.; Stephen Mrozowski and Heather Law Pezzarossi, *The Archaeology of Hassanamesit Woods: The Sarah Burnee/Sarah Boston Farmstead*, Andrew Fiske Memorial Center for Archaeological Research, University of Massachusetts Boston, Cultural Resource Management Study No. 69 (October 2015), describing earthenware or "redware" technique.

A small, perfectly: Johnstone, *The Journey of an Ancient People*, p. 14.

The Nipmuc had: Connole, *The Indians of the Nipmuck Country*, p. 80.

74 Massachusetts Bay Colony: Richard V. Simpson, *Historic Tales of Colonial Rhode Island: Aquidneck Island and the Founding of the Ocean State* (Charleston, S.C.: History Press, 2012), pp. 10–11.

Religious leaders considered: John Winthrop, *Winthrop Papers*, vol. 4 (Boston: Massachusetts Historical Society, 1944), pp. 266–67.

Most damning for: Ibid., p. 268.

Exiled, Hutchinson relished: Simpson, *Historic Tales of Colonial Rhode Island*, pp. 10–11.

Her followers, disdained: Ibid.

Peach may have: Ibid.

The Portsmouth Compact: Ibid.

The renegade settlement's: Ibid.

75 Williams had sent: Winthrop, *Winthrop Papers*, vol. 4, p. 50.

He likely used: *History & Culture eBook* (Mashantucket, CT: Mashantucket Pequot Museum and Research Center, 2017), p. 33.

Peach presented Miantonomo: Winthrop, *Winthrop Papers*, vol. 4, p. 50.

"And so to: Ibid.

77 Williams "had sent: Ibid., p. 49.

As former governor: Bradford, *History of Plymouth Plantation 1620–1647*, vol. 2, p. 363.

On his return: Winthrop, *Winthrop Papers*, vol. 4, p. 50.

The Aquidnett settlers: Ibid.

The rapier was: R. Ewart Oakeshott, *The Archaeology of Weapons: Arms and Armor from Prehistory to the Age of Chivalry* (Mineola, NY: Dover Publications, Inc., 1996), pp. 25–26.

Swordsmiths designed the: Ibid., p. 26; Colin Burgess and Sabine Gerloff, *The Dirks and Rapiers of Great Britain and Ireland*, vol. 7 (British Isles: C. H. Beck, 1981), p. 113.

To accomplish this: Ibid.

Peach had handled: Ibid.

The islanders interrogated: Winthrop, *Winthrop Papers*, vol. 4, p. 50.

78 "This native, Will: LaFantasie, ed., *The Correspondence of Roger Williams*, p. 173.

Their grown son: Winthrop, *Winthrop Papers*, vol. 4, pp. 117–18.

"She knows not: Ibid.

On arrival, Will: Roger Williams, *Publications of the Narragansett Club: The Letters of Roger Williams*, vol. 6 (Providence, RI: Narragansett Club, 1874), p. 54.

79 When Will made: Letter to his son, John, [1633]. Series I. Governor John Winthrop Jr. MSS 413, B2 F1. Winthrop Family Papers, Phillips Library Reading Room, Peabody Essex Museum.

Soon, Williams would: John Winthrop, *Winthrop Papers*, vol. 5 (Boston: Massachusetts Historical Society, 1947), p. 169; Miller and Johnson, *The Puritans*, p. 89.

An indigenous man: Katherine A. Grandjean, *American Passage: The Communications Frontier in Early New England* (Cambridge, MA: Harvard University Press, 2015), p. 83.

80 A contemporary noted: Roland Greene Usher, *The Pilgrims and Their History* (Boston: Macmillan, 1918), p. 258.

He dressed for: The Inventory of Thomas Prence, Plymouth Colony Archive Project. Plymouth Colony Wills 3:60-70, No. P205. April 23, 1673, references spectacles; 17th Century Personal and Household Items collection: Spectacles with case. Material: Glass, horn, wood, and leather, 1600–1700. Probably made in England. The frames of these armless spectacles are horn, which has been wrapped in leather. The case is pine. Pilgrim Hall Museum. (These provide an example of period spectacles.)

When traveling on: Inventory of Thomas Prence.

A fellow settler: Eugene Aubrey Stratton, *Plymouth Colony: Its History and People, 1620–1691* (Salt Lake City: Ancestry Publishing, 1986), p. 152.

One enraged Quaker: Joseph Banvard, *Plymouth and the Pilgrims, etc., with Plates* (Boston: Gould and Lincoln, 1851), p. 188.

81 If he had: William Brigham, *The Colony of New Plymouth and Its Relations to Massachusetts: A Lecture of a Course by William Brigham* (Massachusetts: Press of J. Wilson, 1869), p. 3.

Massachusetts Bay spearheaded: George D. Langdon Jr., *Pilgrim Colony: A History of New Plymouth, 1620–1691* (New Haven, CT: Yale University Press, 1966), p. 38.

Massachusetts Bay, which: Ibid.

81 The year of: Samuel Eliot Morison, *The Founding of Harvard College* (Cambridge, MA: Harvard University Press, 1995), p. 221.

The Colonial leaders instead: Edward Johnson, *Johnson's Wonder-Working Providence, 1628–1651* (New York: Charles Scribner's Sons, 1910), p. 187.

Also in 1638: Drew Lopenzina, *Red Ink: Native Americans Picking Up the Pen in the Colonial Period* (Albany: State University of New York Press, 2012), p. 107.

That Peach's gruesome: Margaret Ellen Newell, *Brethren by Nature: New England Indians, Colonists, and the Origins of American Slavery* (Ithaca, NY: Cornell University Press, 2015), p. 51.

82 Already tribal leaders: Bradford, *History of Plymouth Plantation 1620–1647*, vol. 2, p. 364.

The Narragansett marched: Daniel K. Davis, *Miles Standish* (New York: Chelsea House Publishers, 2011), pp. 92–94.

The plan came: Dennis Cerrotti, *Hidden Genocide, Hidden People* (Wellesley, MA: Sea Venture Press, 2014), p. 69.

The Narragansett, for: Winthrop, *Winthrop Papers*, vol. 4, p. 49.

83 Ninigret aimed to: Fisher and Silverman, *Ninigret, Sachem of the Niantics*, p. 32.

The Pequot belittled: Ibid.

Still, even the: Ibid.

When the colonists: Ibid.

The Narragansett grew: Ibid.

Just a few: Ibid., p. 44.

Ninigret and his: Ibid.

He led eighty: Ibid.

The Monauketts desperately: Ibid.

"English men are: Ibid.

A power vacuum: Ibid.

Ninigret hoped to: Ibid.

84 Penowanyanquis's death stymied: Ibid.

85 He had carried: Harry M. Ward, *Statism in Plymouth Colony* (Port Washington, NY: National University Publications Kennikat Press, 1973), pp. 58 and 153.

The mercurial Archbishop: Ibid.

As Bradford sardonically: Ibid.

Tribal leaders vowed: David Marley, *Wars of the Americas: A Chronology of Armed Conflict in the New World, 1492 to the Present* (Santa Barbara, CA: ABC-CLIO, 1998), p. 134; Roxanne Dunbar-Ortiz, *An Indigenous*

*Peoples' History of the United States* (Boston: Beacon Press, 2014), pp. 60–61.

The aggrieved sachem: Marley, *Wars of the Americas*, p. 134.

In all, local: Ibid.

"The country must: Bradford, *History of Plymouth Plantation 1620–1647*, vol. 2, p. 364.

5. Escaped

86 If he could: John Winthrop, *Winthrop Papers*, vol. 4 (Boston: Massachusetts Historical Society, 1944), p. 60.

87 The escapee's master: Edward Everett Hale Jr., *Note-book Kept by Thomas Lechford, Esq., Lawyer, in Boston, Massachusetts Bay, from June 27, 1638, to July 29, 1641* (Cambridge: John Wilson and Son, 1885), p. 59.

Crosse made a: Larry Spotted Crow Mann, *Drumming and Dreaming* (CrowStorm Publishing, 2017), pp. 77 and 78.

"The 2 men: Winthrop, *Winthrop Papers*, vol. 4, p. 118.

Without warning, the: Ibid.

Incredibly, the borderline: A. E. Foss, *Resident and Business Directory of Foxborough, Massachusetts, for 1887–88: Containing a Complete Resident, Street and Business Directory, Town Officers, Schools, Societies, Churches, Post Offices, &c., &c. Foxborough, 1890*, pp. 8–9.

The Angle Tree: Ibid.

The tree may: Natalie Zaman, "The Rabbit Tree," *Magical Destinations of the Northeast: Sacred Sites, Occult Oddities & Magical Monuments* (Llewellyn Worldwide, 2016).

The crime had: Glenn LaFantasie, ed., *The Correspondence of Roger Williams*, 2 vols. (Hanover, NH: Brown University and University Press of New England, 1988), p. 172.

89 Williams made certain: Ibid.

Before leaving England: "Williams, Roger,—1683," Yale Indian Papers Project, yipp.yale.edu/bio/bibliography/.

Coke, perhaps the: Bernadette A Meyler, "Substitute Chancellors: The Role of the Jury in the Contest Between Common Law and Equity," 2006, Cornell Law Faculty Publications, Paper 39, 2, scholarship.law.cornell.edu/lsrp_papers/39.

Furthermore, Coke reasoned: Ibid.

Williams knew precisely: Jim Powell, "Edward Coke: Commonal Law Protection for Liberty," November 1, 1997, fee.org/articles/.

90 Moreover, in 1638: Author interview with Professor J. Stanley Lemons, Rhode Island College professor emeritus of history, Providence, RI, December 19, 2017.

He could not: Ibid.

He had just: Jere R. Daniell, *Colonial New Hampshire: A History* (Hanover, NH: University Press of New England, August 2015), p. 39.

The governor would: Mss. Misc. Boxes W. Number 86650, one folder, Roger Williams Papers, American Antiquarian Society.

Even the king: Calendar, vol. 1661–1668, #494. Col. Entry book 60, f. 22, Gay Collection, Massachusetts Historical Society. "The kings letter to the colony of Massachusetts in the behalf of the Proprietors of the Narragancet Country," p. 10.

Williams concluded one: Joseph Barlow Felt, *The Ecclesiastical History of New England: Comprising not only Religious, but also Moral, and Other Relations* (Congregational Library Association, 1855), p. 353.

"I humbly crave: LaFantasie, ed., *The Correspondence of Roger Williams*, p. 172.

"In case Plymouth: Ibid., pp. 172–73.

91 During a 1632: Samuel Deane, *History of Scituate, Massachusetts: From Its First Settlement to 1831* (Boston: James Loring, 1831), p. 13.

He hoped to: Ibid.

As Williams noted: Winthrop, *Winthrop Papers*, vol. 4, p. 60.

92 Unable to resist: Ibid.

When he confronted: Harry M. Ward, *Statism in Plymouth Colony* (Port Washington, NY: National University Publications Kennikat Press, 1973), p. 153.

He would spend: Ibid.

93 When military leaders: Pequot War presenter, Mashantucket Pequot Museum and Research Center, June 24, 2017.

Attackers might consider: Daniel K. Davis, *Miles Standish* (New York: Chelsea House Publishers, 2011), p. 73.

The military commander was: Ibid., p. 8; 17th Century Personal and Household Items collection: Myles Standish Razor & Case. Material: Steel, horn, brass, and pasteboard. Probably made in Toledo, Spain, 1612. Found at the site of the Myles Standish house, Duxbury, MA. Pilgrim Hall Museum.

The career soldier: Tudor Jenks, *Captain Myles Standish* (Massachusetts: Century Company, 1905), p. 227.

Famously short, at: Davis, *Miles Standish*, p. 8.

One settler described: William Hubbard, *A General History of New En-*

*gland* (Cambridge: Hilliard and Metcalf, 1815), p. 111; David Beale, "Captain Myles Standish: Separatist Pilgrim, or Roman Catholic Soldier of Fortune?" (Ankeny, IA: Faith Baptist Theological Seminary, November 2001).

When angered, his: Hubbard, *A General History of New England*, p. 111.

Standish brought a: Stephen Merrill Allen, *Myles Standish: With an Account of the Exercises of Consecration of the Monument Ground on Captain's Hill, Duxbury, Aug. 17, 1871* (A. Mudge and Son, 1871), p. 6.

The tribe's sachem: Nathaniel Philbrick, *Mayflower: A Story of Community, Courage and War* (New York: Penguin Books, 2006), p. 151.

Standish—whose head: Jenks, *Captain Myles Standish*, p. 201.

Wituwamat, Pecksuot, and: Edward Winslow, *Good Newes from New England* (Bedford, MA: Applewood Books, 1996), pp. 47–48.

94 Standish gestured for: Philbrick, *Mayflower*, p. 151.

When the latch: Winslow, *Good Newes from New England*, pp. 47 and 48.

Standish and his: Ibid.

When it was: Ibid.

His soldiers stood: Ibid.

Standish's longtime indigenous: Ibid.

Fellow colonists celebrated: Hubbard, *A General History of New England*, p. 63.

One Puritan who: Beale, "Captain Myles Standish."

Colonial leaders early: Ward, *Statism in Plymouth Colony*, p. 132.

95 French officers likely: Brenda Dunn, *A History of Port-Royal/Annapolis Royal 1605–1800* (Halifax, NS: Nimbus Publishing, 2004), p. 85.

I "now deliver: Ibid.

A flustered Edward: Edward Winslow, "Letter/Summons," dated August 31, 1644, Pilgrim Hall Museum archives.

Not only did: Dunn, *A History of Port-Royal/Annapolis Royal 1605–1800*, p. 13.

The area in: Ibid., p. 6.

D'Aulnay determined to: Emerson W. Baker, *American Beginnings: Exploration, Culture, and Cartography in the Land of Norumbega* (Lincoln: University of Nebraska Press, 1994), p. 219.

The Frenchman carved: Ibid., p. 225.

D'Aulnay's father had: William Arthur Calnek, *History of the County of Annapolis: Including Old Port Royal and Acadia* (London: William Briggs, 1897), p. 26.

D'Aulnay chose 1638: Baker, *American Beginnings*, pp. 220 and 223–24.

95 After receiving authority: Dunn, *A History of Port-Royal/Annapolis Royal 1605–1800*, p. 19.

96 The Frenchman christened: Ibid.

When war between: Davis, *Miles Standish*, p. 94.

Nonetheless, he good-naturedly: Ibid.

The Maquas tribesmen: Massachusetts State Archives collection, colonial period, 1622–1788, vol. 2, p. 333, May 16, 1653, Maquas Indians.

97 He counseled, "It: Richard S. Dunn, Laetitia Yeandle, and James Savage, eds., *The Journal of John Winthrop, 1630–1649* (Cambridge, MA: Harvard University Press, 1996), p. 260.

Recognizing the anger: Ibid.

Penowanyanquis's Narragansett allies: Felt, *The Ecclesiastical History of New England*, p. 353.

Arthur Peach and: Ibid.

Once, when writing: Mac Griswold, *The Manor: Three Centuries at a Slave Plantation on Long Island* (New York: Macmillan, 2013), p. 26; Massachusetts State Archives collection, colonial period, 1622–1788, vol. 2, p. 5.

He earned a: William Richard Cutter, *New England Families, Genealogical and Memorial: A Record of the Achievements of Her People in the Making of Commonwealths and the Founding of a Nation*, vol. 3 (Lewis Historical Publishing Company, 1913), p. 1250.

Coddington had been: Ibid.

98 He endorsed a: Felt, *The Ecclesiastical History of New England*, p. 353.

One Massachusetts Bay: Jere R. Daniell, *Colonial New Hampshire: A History* (Lebanon, NH: University Press of New England, August 2015), p. 31.

One group of: Ibid., p. 35.

Between swigs of: Ibid., p. 32.

As acrimony dragged: Dunn, Yeandle, and Savage, eds., *The Journal of John Winthrop*, p. 300.

The Piscataqua men: Ibid., p. 262.

99 But there was: Ibid.

Even wooly-haired: Dawn Dove and Holly Ewald, "Indigenous Life in Rhode Island: An Introduction, by Paulla Dove Jennings, as told to Holly Ewald," *Through Our Eyes: An Indigenous View of Mashapaug Pond* (Lulu Publishing, 2012), p. 37.

Broad stretches of: Observed by the author, April 8, 2017, Tomaquag Museum, Exeter, RI; on display.

Thick reeds at: Ibid.

The sharp smell: Russell M. Lawson, *The Piscataqua Valley in the Age of Sail: A Brief History* (History Press, 2007), p. 20.

A settler at: Ibid., p. 18; 17th Century Personal and Household Items collection: Wrestling Brewster's Rushlight Holder. Material: Pine base with wrought iron clip. Made in New England, from the home of Wrestling Brewster. Pilgrim Hall Museum. "Rushlights were the simplest and least expensive kind of lighting device. They were made from common meadow rushes which grew in the marshes. The outer skin of the rush was peeled away and the remaining pith was dried and then dipped in hot fat. After drying, the rush was placed in the jaws of the rushlight clip to burn. This particular rushlight holder also has a candle socket (on the left side in the picture), both to balance the rushlight clip and to serve, occasionally, as an additional lighting device." (Provides an example of portable fire source of the period.)

100 Thousands of shad: Lawson, *The Piscataqua Valley in the Age of Sail*, p. 18.

Crosse worked heartily: Ibid.

## 6. JURY SELECTION

101 Some fifteen years: Lysander Salmon Richards, *History of Marshfield*, vol. 1 (Marshfield, MA: Memorial Press, 1901), p. 47.

In canvassing this: Michael L. Fickes, "'They Could Not Endure That Yoke': The Captivity of Pequot Women and Children After the War of 1637," *New England Quarterly* 73, no. 1 (March 2000): 58–81, at 62, n. 14.

103 With the total: Ibid.

These were officials: Herbert Baxter Adams, *Norman Constables in America: Read Before the New England Historical Society, February 1, 1882* (Baltimore: Johns Hopkins University, 1883), p. 22.

Petty constables mirrored: Ibid., p. 14.

The Normans brought: Ibid., pp. 6 and 10.

The practice of: Jury Summons, May 18, 1695, Hillside Collection of Manuscripts, Pilgrim Society, Plymouth 1973, Pilgrim Hall Museum, references the earliest recorded jury summons, which might recall language similar to that which Governor Prence might have used. Signed by Governor Samuel Sprague.

The constable would: Ibid.; The Inventory of Thomas Prence, Plymouth Colony Archive Project. Plymouth Colony Wills 3:60-70, No. P205. April 23, 1673, references spectacles and case and great chair.

103 One of Prence's: Plymouth Colony Records, vol. 1, p. 86.

Contemporaries described the: James Cudworth to "his very loving and kind father," Dr. Stoughton, Scituate ("Citewat), December 1634, Colonial State Papers. Calendar Reference: Item 931, vol. 1 (1574–1660), p. 194.

He had escaped: Ibid.

104 The volumes in: Samuel Eliot Morison, *The Intellectual Life of Colonial New England* (New York: New York University Press, 1956), pp. 74 and 75.

Years later, Lothrop: Elijah Baldwin Huntington, *A Genealogical Memoir of the Lo-Lathrop Family in This Country: Embracing the Descendants, as Far as Known, of the Rev. John Lothropp, of Scituate and Barnstable, Mass., and Mark Lothrop, of Salem and Bridgewater, Mass., and the First Generation of Descendants of Other Names* (Boston: E. H. Lathrop, 1884), p. 34.

He went on: Ibid.

The idea of: Patrick Cheney and Philip Hardie, *The Oxford History of Classical Reception in England Literature*, vol. 2, 1558–1660 (New York: Oxford University Press, 2015), p. 464.

Cicero's call from: Morison, *The Intellectual Life of Colonial New England*, pp. 55 and 62.

This brand of: Ian Green, *Humanism and Protestantism in Early Modern English Education* (New York: Routledge, 2016), p. 11.

The philosophical movement: Ibid., pp. 14–15.

For colonists, the: Morison, *The Intellectual Life of Colonial New England*, pp. 55 and 62.

Many argue that: Green, *Humanism and Protestantism in Early Modern English Education*, p. 16.

Significantly, as one: Karen Ordahl Kupperman, *Indians and English: Facing Off in Early America* (Ithaca, NY: Cornell University Press, 2000), p. 27.

105 A Kentish observer: William Lombarde, *A Perambulation of Kent, Conteining the Description, Hystorie, and Customes of That Shire; Written in the Yeere 1570, First Published in the Year 1576, and Now Increased and Altered from the Author's Owne Last Copie*. Found under heading: 2, "The Estate of Kent" (London: Baldwin, Cradock, and Joy, 1820).

Through Lothrop's study: Morison, *The Intellectual Life of Colonial New England*, p. 164.

Lothrop became a: Ibid., p. 165.

When John Underhill: Margaret Ellen Newell, *Brethren by Nature: New England Indians, Colonists, and the Origins of American Slavery* (Ithaca, NY: Cornell University Press, 2015), p. 28; John Underhill and Paul Royster, eds., "Newes from America; Or, A New and Experimentall Discoverie of New England; Containing, A Trve Relation of Their War-like Proceedings These Two Yeares Last Past, with a Figure of the Indian Fort, or Palizado" (1638), *Electronic Texts in American Studies* 37, p. 35, digitalcommons.unl.edu/etas/37.

The most popular: Kupperman, *Indians and English*, p. 27.

Tacitus urged his: William E. Nelson, *The Common Law in Colonial America: The Chesapeake and New England, 1607–1660*, vol. 1 (New York: Oxford University Press, 2008), p. 50; Kupperman, *Indians and English*, p. 27.

106    In 1627, administrators: Kupperman, *Indians and English*, p. 29.

Tacitus's ideas unsettled: Ibid.

The English minister: Thomas Goodwin, *A Child of Light Walking in Darknesse* (London: R. Dawlman, 1643), p. 62. The edition attributed to Lothrop was in possession of his granddaughter, "Rebekah Lothrup—hir book." It is found at Sturgis Library in Barnstable, MA, along with a *nota bene* on the book's provenance that I have drawn from to explain Lothrop's connection to Goodwin's teachings.

Neighbors saw Turner: Richard M. Stower, *A History of the First Parish Church of Scituate, Massachusetts: Its Life and Times* (Scituate, MA: Converpage), p. 61.

His wife, Lydia: "A Genealogical Profile of Humphrey Turner," Plimoth Plantation, www.plimoth.org/.

107    By 1645, 130: Morison, *The Intellectual Life of Colonial New England*, p. 152.

In 1655, Harvard: Ibid., p. 135.

The departure of: Fickes, " 'They Could Not Endure That Yoke,' " p. 62, n. 14; "A History of Barnstable," www.town.barnstable.ma.us/.

"I desire greatly: C. F. Swift, *The Amos Otis Papers*, vol. 1 (Barnstable, MA: F. B. and F. P. Goss, 1888), p. 191.

108    Grizzlier legal methods: Edgar J. McManus, *Law and Liberty in Early New England: Criminal Justice and Due Process, 1620–1692* (Amherst, MA: University of Massachusetts Press, 2009), pp. 99 and 108 (quoting Professor John H. Langbein).

However, English jury: Ibid.

108 In criminal matters: James B. Thayer, "The Jury and Its Development," *Harvard Law Review* 5, no. 6 (January 15, 1892): 249–73, at 263.

In some ways: Clive Emsley, *Crime and Society in England: 1750–1900* (New York: Routledge, 2013), p. 206; Francis Hargrave, *A Complete Collection of State-Trials and Proceedings for High and Other Crimes and Misdemeanours: Commencing with the Eleventh Year of the Reign of King Richard II, and Ending with the Sixteenth Year of the Reign of King George III, with Two Alphabetical Tables to the Whole*, vol. 2 (Bathurst, 1776), p. 614.

Jurors contended with: James Masschaele, *Jury, State, and Society in Medieval England* (New York: Palgrave Macmillan, 2008), pp. 201–05.

Colony leaders resorted: Ibid., p. 204.

Jurors who "default[ed]: Massachusetts State Archives collection, colonial period, 1622–1788, vol. 40, pp. 318–19, jury selection, 1694–95.

By the early: Massachusetts State Archives collection, colonial period, 1622–1788, vol. 41, p. 67, jury fees, 1727, Plymouth.

That amount reflected: Massachusetts State Archives collection, colonial period, 1622–1788, vol. 41, p. 66, jury fees, 1727, Plymouth.

"Jurors are oftentimes: Ibid.

Jurors also expected: Massachusetts State Archives collection, colonial period, 1622–1788, vol. 38b, pp. 21–23, jurors want victuals paid.

109 Seventeenth-century grand: Massachusetts State Archives collection, colonial period, 1622–1788, "Northampton court 1696-7 grand jurors duty was to inquire into, and present, any breach of law within courts jurisdiction." This notation can be found in the "Courts" section of the Massachusetts State Archive index—it may represent a missing document.

Some years later: Massachusetts State Archives collection, colonial period, 1622–1788, vol. 40, p. 229, Suffolk county court jury fixing, 1685–86.

One law declared: Michael Dalton, *The Country Justice: Containing the Practice, Duty and Power of the Justices as Out of Their Sessions* (1648), chap. 47, p. 11, John Adams Library.

The author of: Ibid., chap. 136, 5H. An inventory of Prence's will notes two law books; *The Country Justice*, given its wide distribution at the time, was likely one of them.

The practice of: In one of the most notorious nineteenth-century American murder cases, a juror took over the job of prosecutor and aggressively questioned a witness about his testimony. Ronald B. Lansing, "The Tragedy of Charity Lamb, Oregon's First Convicted Murderess," *Oregon Historical Quarterly* 101, no. 1 (Spring 2000): 40–76, at 59.

110 In a moment: Masschaele, *Jury, State, and Society in Medieval England*, p. 24.

One English legal: Thayer, "The Jury and Its Development," p. 261.

Juries had varying: Ibid.

Parties agreed on: Ibid., p. 295.

"Special" juries were: Ibid., p. 300.

In London, epicurean: Ibid.

One legal commentator: Ibid.

As far as: McManus, *Law and Liberty in Early New England*, pp. 12 and 14.

Local land deeds: Jeremy Dupertuis Bangs, *The Seventeenth-Century Town Records of Scituate, Massachusetts*, vol. C-1 (Boston: New England Historic Genealogical Society, 2002), p. 249.

Former governor Bradford: William Bradford, *History of Plymouth Plantation 1620–1647*, vol. 2 (Boston: Massachusetts Historical Society), p. 268.

Ranulf de Glanville, a legal: Ranulf de Glanville, *A Translation of Glanville* (London: W. Reed, 1812), pp. 354 and 357.

111 While the colonists: McManus, "Law and Liberty in Early New England," p. 25; Nan Goodman, *Banished: Common Law and the Rhetoric of Social Exclusion in Early New England* (Philadelphia: University of Pennsylvania Press, 2012), p. 92.

The linen was: John Demos, *A Little Commonwealth: Family Life in Plymouth Colony* (New York: Oxford University Press, 1970), p. 54; Probate: Gyles Rickard Sr., Plymouth Colony Archive Project, www.histarch.illinois.edu/plymouth/.

Rickett traded the: Ibid.

Rough to the: Ibid.

Rickett carried out: Records of the Town of Plymouth, vol. 1, p. 16, February 10, 1643–44; Plymouth Colony Records, vol. 2, p. 34, March 1, 1641–42.

Trapping wolves meant: Alice Morse Earle, *Child Life in Colonial Days*, vol. 1 (New York: Macmillan, 1909), p. 315.

One of the: *New England Historical and Genealogical Register*, vol. 4, 1850 (New England Historic Genealogical Society, Heritage Books, January 1, 2000), p. 255; Earle, *Child Life in Colonial Days*, p. 315.

Rickett's track record: Adams, *Norman Constables in America*, pp. 22 and 25; Plymouth Colony Records, vol. 1, p. 86.

111 The makeshift prison: Ibid.

In the colonial: Jill Lepore, *Book of Ages: The Life and Opinions of Jane Franklin* (New York: First Vintage Books, 2014), p. 13.

112 Plymouth Colony constable: Adams, *Norman Constables in America*, pp. 22 and 25.

By law, the: Ibid.

One observer noted: Bradford, *History of Plymouth Plantation 1620–1647*, vol. 2, p. 364.

## 7. THE TRIAL

113 Next to it: Donna Petrangelo, "History of First Parish Church in Plymouth, Massachusetts," *Mayflower Quarterly* (June 2011). Petrangelo outlines the sources that reflect two opinions concerning Plymouth Colony's construction of a second meeting house. One historian argues that settlers built a second iteration of the meeting house in 1637, and the other scholar believes that it was completed in 1648. On balance, the author concurs with the argument of the latter academic, setting the events of the trial in Plymouth Colony's original meeting house.

114 Colonists strove to: Alice Morse Earle, *Child Life in Colonial Days*, vol. 1 (New York: Macmillan, 1909), p. 319.

On this front: William Bradford, *History of Plymouth Plantation 1620–1647*, vol. 2 (Boston: Massachusetts Historical Society, 1912), pp. 267–68.

115 Some years later: Margaret Ellen Newell, *Brethren by Nature: New England Indians, Colonists, and the Origins of American Slavery* (Ithaca, NY: Cornell University Press, 2015), p. 145.

One settler who: Mss. Misc. Boxes W. Number 86650, one folder, Roger Williams Papers, American Antiquarian Society.

Massasoit, a charismatic: Sydney V. James Jr., *Three Visitors to Early Plymouth: Letters About the Pilgrim Settlement in New England During Its First Seven Years—John Pory, Isaack de Rasieres, Emmanuel Altham* (Bedford, MA: Applewood Books, 1997), p. 30; Massasoit (Ousamequin) pictogram, as seen on March 23, 1649, land deed between the sachem and Miles Standish, Samuel Nash, and Constant Southworth, Plymouth County Registry of Deeds.

Intricate bands of: Chris Lindahl, "Wampanoag Work to Repatriate Remains, Artifacts," *Cape Cod Times*, April 14, 2017, www.capecod times.com/news/ (Images courtesy Wampanoag Confederation.)

Except for the: James, *Three Visitors to Early Plymouth*, p. 30.

His fur might: Observed by the author, April 8, 2017, Tomaquag Museum, Exeter, RI; on display.

116 In parts of: Keith Spence, *The Companion Guide to Kent and Sussex* (Boydell and Brewer Ltd., 1999), p. 81.

Its walls boasted: Ibid.

English town criers: Cotton Mather, *The Magnalia Christi Americana*, "Cotton Mather's Lives of Bradford and Winthrop," Old South Leaflets, no. 77, Old South Association, Old South Meeting-house, Boston, MA, p. 22.

Though all married: John Demos, *A Little Commonwealth: Family Life in Plymouth Colony* (New York: Oxford University Press, 1970), p. 54.

Juror Pontus may: "A Genealogical Profile of William Pontus," a collaboration between Plimoth Plantation and the New England Historic Genealogical Society, www.plimoth.org.

They were not: Jeremy Dupertuis Bangs, *The Seventeenth-Century Town Records of Scituate, Massachusetts*, vol. C-1 (Boston: New England Historic Genealogical Society, 2002), p. 240.

Juror Hatch had: Samuel Deane, *History of Scituate, Massachusetts: From Its First Settlement to 1831* (Boston: James Loring, 1831), p. 48.

117 Arriving among the: James, *Three Visitors to Early Plymouth*, p. 76.

Myles Standish kept: Edward Winslow, *Good Newes from New England* (Bedford, MA: Applewood Books, 1996), p. 48.

The skull was: James, *Three Visitors to Early Plymouth*, p. 31.

Standish added a: Ibid.

In defeated Ireland: Roxanne Dunbar-Ortiz, *An Indigenous Peoples' History of the United States* (Boston: Beacon Press, 2014), p. 38; James Wilson, *The Earth Shall Weep: A History of Native America* (New York: Grove/Atlantic, Inc., 2007), p. 64.

To colonists, the: James, *Three Visitors to Early Plymouth*, p. 76.

The Pequot, still: Bradford, *History of Plymouth Plantation 1620–1647*, vol. 2, p. 266.

118 Former governor Bradford: Ibid.

Those Englishmen and: Dennis Cerrotti, *Hidden Genocide, Hidden People* (Wellesley, MA: Sea Venture Press, 2014), p. 87.

Roger Williams simply: Roger Williams, *Publications of the Narragansett Club: The Letters of Roger Williams*, vol. 6 (Providence, RI: Narragansett Club, 1874), p. 111.

The "very austere": Edward Johnson, *Johnson's Wonder-Working Providence, 1628–1651* (New York: Charles Scribner's Sons, 1910), p. 220.

118 "Be careful on: Ibid.; ALS of Roger Williams to John Winthrop, August 14, 1638, Plymouth Homicides Project document.

The sachem promised: Roger Williams, *Publications of the Narragansett Club: The Letters of Roger Williams*, vol. 6 (Providence, RI: Narragansett Club, 1874), p. 116.

Former governor Bradford: Bradford, *History of Plymouth Plantation 1620–1647*, vol. 2, pp. 267–68.

While Prence focused: The Inventory of Thomas Prence, Plymouth Colony Archive Project, www.histarch.illinois.edu/plymouth/.

119 Prence would serve: Peter Charles Hoffer, *Law and People in Colonial America* (Baltimore: Johns Hopkins University Press, 1998), pp. 116–17.

During the early: Ibid.

Defendants advocated for: Ibid.

The accused had: Ibid.

These "gentlemen, &: Nathaniel Bradstreet Shurtleff, *Records of the Colony of New Plymouth, in New England: Court Orders. New Plymouth Colony. Massachusetts General Court*, vol. 1, 1633–1640 (Boston: Press of William White, 1855), p. 96.

Four years earlier: Joshua David Bellin and Laura L. Mielke, *Native Acts: Indian Performance, 1603–1832* (Lincoln: University of Nebraska Press, 2012), pp. 42–43.

On his return: Ibid.

Winslow's dear friend: Ibid.

120 The sachem had: Ibid.

Plymouth fell into: Ibid.

When settlers later: Ibid.

Massasoit determined that: Ibid.

No one would: Ibid.

Prence demanded that: Kim Baker, "Richard Derby of Plymouth," University of Virginia, Anth. 509, Fall 1996, Plymouth Colony Archive Project.

One of his most: David Pulsifer, *Records of the Colony of New Plymouth, in New England: Deeds, &c., 1620–1651*. Book of Indian Records for Their Lands, Massachusetts General Court (Barnstable County, MA: Press of W. White, 1861), pp. 20–21.

Less than a: Baker, "Richard Derby of Plymouth."

The colony would: Ibid.

121 In ancient English: James Masschaele, *Jury, State, and Society in Medieval England* (New York: Palgrave Macmillan, 2008), p. 125; Ronald B.

Lansing, "The Tragedy of Charity Lamb, Oregon's First Convicted Murderess," *Oregon Historical Quarterly* 101, no. 1 (Spring 2000): 40–76, at 47.

Though Sillis was: Jeremy Dupertuis Bangs, *The Seventeenth-Century Town Records of Scituate, Massachusetts*, vol. 3 (Boston: New England Historic Genealogical Society, 2002), p. 345.

Lothrop took note: Ibid.

The newcomer owned: David D. Hall, *Worlds of Wonder, Days of Judgment: Popular Religious Belief in Early New England* (Cambridge, MA: Harvard University Press, 1990), p. 40; John Von Rohr, *The Covenant of Grace in Puritan Thought* (Wipf and Stock Publishers, September 1, 2010), p. 78.

122 The very day: Shurtleff, *Records of the Colony of New Plymouth, in New England*, p. 96.

The upgraded status: Eugene Aubrey Stratton, *Plymouth Colony: Its History and People 1620–1691* (Salt Lake City: Ancestry Publishing, 1986), pp. 146–47.

Prence asked each: Massachusetts State Archives. Colonial Period Collection: 1622–1788. vol. 40: 539, 532 and 272.

Not only did: James B. Thayer, "The Jury and Its Development," *Harvard Law Review* 5, no. 6 (January 15, 1892): 249–73, at 374.

The forty-one-year-old: Probate: Gyles Rickard Sr., Plymouth Colony Archive Project, www.histarch.illinois.edu/plymouth.

123 "First kiss truth: Letter from Roger Williams, [1647]. Series II. Governor John Winthrop Jr. MSS 413, B2 F20, p. 269. Winthrop Family Papers, Phillips Library Reading Room, Peabody Essex Museum.

To prove the: Yasuhide Kawashima, *Igniting King Philip's War: The John Sassamon Murder Trial* (Lawrence: University Press of Kansas, 2001), p. 23; John Winthrop, *Winthrop Papers*, vol. 4 (Boston: Massachusetts Historical Society, 1944), p. 53.

Another problem was: Kawashima, *Igniting King Philip's War*, p. 23.

As the famed: Thayer, "The Jury and Its Development," p. 378.

124 Winthrop advised authorities: Mather, "Cotton Mather's Lives of Bradford and Winthrop," p. 12.

He argued that: Ibid.

He came "upon: Glenn LaFantasie, ed., *The Correspondence of Roger Williams*, 2 vols. (Hanover, NH: Brown University and University Press of New England, 1988), p. 172.

Each of the: Ibid.

125 Not long after: Edward Everett Hale Jr., *Note-book Kept by Thomas Lechford, Esq., Lawyer, in Boston, Massachusetts Bay, from June 27, 1638, to July 29, 1641* (Cambridge: John Wilson and Son, 1885), p. 4.

The peculiar volume: Ibid.

The book served: Margaret Aston, *John Foxe's The Acts and Monuments Online*. The Illustrations: Books 10–12, www.johnfoxe.org/.

Just possessing a: Daniel K. Davis, *Miles Standish* (New York: Chelsea House Publishers, 2011), p. 29.

Throckmorton took the: Hale, *Note-book Kept by Thomas Lechfor*, p. 4.

The author of: Aston, *John Foxe's The Acts and Monuments Online*.

Magnifying the religious: Ibid.

Peach's testimony brazenly: John Winthrop, *Winthrop's Journal, History of New England, 1630–1649*, vol. 1 (New York: Charles Scribner's Sons, 1908), pp. 273–74.

In fact, Peach's: Ibid., p. 273.

126 A member of: Dennis A. Connole, *The Indians of the Nipmuck Country in Southern New England, 1630–1750: An Historical Geography* (Jefferson, NC: McFarland and Company, 2007), p. 125.

The tribesman requested: Ibid.

While colonial leaders: Winthrop, *Winthrop's Journal*, vol. 1, p. 273.

He advised "to: Richard S. Dunn, Laetitia Yeandle, and James Savage, eds., *The Journal of John Winthrop, 1630–1649* (Cambridge, MA: Harvard University Press, 1996), p. 260.

"They could not: Ibid.

The passenger list: Peter Wilson Coldham, *The Complete Book of Emigrants: 1607–1660* (Surrey, England: Genealogical Publishing, 1987), p. 144.

A careful review: From Sec. Windebank to Robt. Earl of Lindsey, May 22, 1635. Calendar Reference: Item 1001, vol. 1 (1574–1660), Colonial State Papers, Widener Library. "The King expects that he will give every assistance to the bearer, Lieut. Robt. Evelin, who is on his return in the Plain Joan, to Capt. Yong in America, upon 'special and very important service,'" p. 208.

Yong, a grand: Elizabeth Mancke and Carole Shammas, *The Creation of the British Atlantic World* (Baltimore: John Hopkins University Press, 2005), pp. 75 and 80.

Some alleged that: The Aspinwall Papers, Collections of the Massachusetts Historical Society, Internet Archive, p. 83.

Yong had demanded: Mancke and Shammas, *The Creation of the British Atlantic World*, p. 76; Gideon Delaplaine Scull, *The Evelyns in America:*

*Comp. from Family Papers and Other Sour Ces, 1608–1805* (Private circulation, 1881), p. 58.

This group included: Scull, p. 57.

127 Evelyn carried with: The Aspinwall Papers, p. 100.

"The King expects: From Sec. Windebank to Robt. Earl of Lindsey, May 22, 1635, p. 208.

The adventurers sought: Mancke and Shammas, *The Creation of the British Atlantic World*, p. 76.

The English ruler: Ibid.

The king's orders: Scull, *The Evelyns in America*, p. 57.

Evelyn, with Peach: The Aspinwall Papers, p. 100; Edward Duffield Neill, *The Founders of Maryland as Portrayed in Manuscripts, Provincial Records and Early Documents* (Maryland: Joel Munsell, 1876), p. 60, n. 5; Charles Evans, *Oaths of Allegiance in Colonial New England* (Worcester, MA: Davis Press, 1921), pp. 4–6; John Camden Hotten, *The Original Lists of Persons of Quality, Etc.* (London: Chatto and Windus Publishers, 1874), p. 58.

The vast majority: Clive D. Field, *Religious Statistics in Great Britain: An Historical Introduction*, BRIN Discussion Series on Religious Statistics Discussion Paper 001 (Manchester, England: University of Manchester, 2010), pp. 2 and 3.

Some members of: Thomas Mansell, late of Michelstowne. Deposition, County Cork, August 23, 1641. MS 822, fols. 128r–129v.

128 By contrast, when: Richard Caulfield, *The Register of the Parish of the Holy Trinity (Christ Church), Cork, Ireland, from July, 1643 to February, 1668 with Extracts from the Parish Books, from 1664 to 1668* (Cork, Ireland: Purcell and Company Printers, 1877), p. 17.

Peach's English shipboard: Field, *Religious Statistics in Great Britain: An Historical Introduction*, pp. 2 and 3.

One corpse unearthed: Josh Fischman, "Catholic Spies in the New World? Relics Pose New Puzzle About Early American Colony," *Scientific American*, July 29, 2015.

They "ordered that: Joseph Barlow Felt, *The Ecclesiastical History of New England: Comprising not only Religious, but also Moral, and Other Relations* (Congregational Library Association, 1855), p. 597.

Once in the: Louise A. Breen, *Transgressing the Bounds: Subversive Enterprises Among the Puritan Elite in Massachusetts, 1630–1692* (New York: Oxford University Press, 2001), p. 132; Newell, *Brethren by Nature*, 82.

129 Evidence points to: William Sumner, *A History of East Boston; with*

*Biographical Sketches of its Early Proprietors, and an Appendix* (Boston: J. E. Tilton and Company, 1858), p. 80 (citing Winthrop's journal, August 3, 1636, vol. 1, p. 191); Newell, *Brethren by Nature*, p. 52.

129 No matter that: Sumner, *A History of East Boston*, p. 80 (citing Winthrop's journal, August 3, 1636, vol. 1, p. 191).

He described "the: Capt. William Claybourne, 1002i, Breviat of Capt. Claybourne's petition to the King, May 23, 1635, Elizabeth City, Virginia. Calendar Reference: Item 1002, vol. 1 (1574–1660), p. 208.

Another man bemoaned: Richard Frethorne to his father and mother, March 20, April 2, and April 3, 1623, Virginia Center for Digital History, Charlottesville, VA.

"With a fair: Beauchamp Plantagenet, *A Description of the Province of New Albion* (G. P. Humphrey, 1648), pp. 15–16 and 21.

And even better: *Proceedings of the Massachusetts Historical Society*, vol. 52 (Cambridge, MA: University Press, 1919), p. 330.

Such proved the: Kevin McBride and Ashley Bissonnette, "The Art of War: Early Anglo-American Translation, 1607–1643," *Drawdown: The American Way of Postwar*, ed. Jason W. Warren (New York: New York University Press, October 18, 2016), p. 32.

When colonial leaders: Charles Jeremy Hoadly and James Hammond Trumbull, *The Public Records of the Colony of Connecticut [1636–1776]. Records of the General and particular courts, Apr. 1636–Dec. 1649. Records of the General Court, Feb. 1650–May 1665. Records of wills and inventories, 1640–1649. Code of laws, established by the General Court, May 1650. Appendix* (Brown and Parsons, 1850), pp. 28 and 77.

Authorities also ordered: Ibid., p. 28.

But they did: McBride and Bissonnette, "The Art of War: Early Anglo-American Translation, 1607–1643," p. 32; Hoadly and Trumbull, *The Public Records of the Colony of Connecticut*, p. 77.

Captain John Mason: McBride and Bissonnette, "The Art of War: Early Anglo-American Translation, 1607–1643," p. 32; Hoadly and Trumbull, *The Public Records of the Colony of Connecticut*, p. 84.

130 Researchers have revealed: McBride and Bissonnette, "The Art of War: Early Anglo-American Translation, 1607–1643," p. 32; Kevin McBride, lecture at Mashantucket Pequot Museum and Research Center, June 24, 2017.

Furthermore, at the: John Franklin Jameson, *Original Narratives of Early American History*, vol. 12 (Scribner, 1912), p. 35.

On any other: Samuel Deane, *History of Scituate, Massachusetts: From*

*Its First Settlement to 1831* (Boston: James Loring, 1831), p. 46. "In 1696, 'The Town did enact, that every householder should kill and bring in six black birds yearly, between the 12th and the last day of May, on the penalty of forfeiting for the Town's use 6d for every bird short of that number"; "Early Families of Scituate," Scituate Historical Society Biography, scituatehistoricalsociety.org/.

131 The tribesmen nearby: Williams, *Publications of the Narragansett Club: Key into the Language of America*, p. 89.

He had already: William Richard Cutter, *New England Families, Genealogical and Memorial: A Record of the Achievements of Her People in the Making of Commonwealths and the Founding of a Nation*, vol. 3 (Lewis Historical Publishing Company, 1913), p. 1363.

Again Foster named: Ibid.

Soon enough religious: Lucy Loomis, *John Lothrop in Barnstable*, 2nd ed., rev. (Barnstable, MA: Sturgis Library, 2011), p. 26.

He diligently planted: James, *Three Visitors to Early Plymouth*, pp. 67 and 76.

The wedding marked: Cutter, *New England Families*, p. 1363.

The residents had: Isaac Mickle, *Reminiscences of Old Gloucester, Or, Incidents in the History of the Counties of Gloucester, Atlantic and Camden, New Jersey* (Philadelphia: Townsend Ward, 1845, p. 25.

132 The farmer-*qua*-juror: Jane Brox, *Clearing Land: Legacies of the American Farm* (New York: Macmillan, 2005), p. 35.

Whatever nostalgia Foster: Michael Zell, *Early Modern Kent, 1540–1640* (Kent: Boydell and Brewer, 2000), p. 230.

When he had: Deane, *History of Scituate*, p. 46.

133 The murdered tribesman: Bradford, *History of Plymouth Plantation 1620–1647*, vol. 2, p. 264.

The colonies survived: James, *Three Visitors to Early Plymouth*, p. 74; Harry M. Ward, *Statism in Plymouth Colony* (Port Washington, NY: National University Publications Kennikat Press, 1973), p. 41.

134 We do know: Winthrop, *Winthrop's Journal*, p. 236.

In response to: Ibid., p. 237.

What of "the: Ibid.

"A bramble," Schooler: Ibid.

No, he later: Ibid.

"But that could: Ibid.

He testified that: Ibid.

While Schooler admitted: Ibid.

135 He seized on: Ibid., p. 274.

As a nineteenth-century: Joseph Banvard, *Plymouth and the Pilgrims, etc., with Plates* (Boston: Gould and Lincoln, 1851), p. 179.

Each man gravely: Winthrop, *Winthrop's Journal*, p. 274.

Dr. James, whom: Bradford, *History of Plymouth Plantation 1620–1647*, vol. 2, p. 266; Henry Whittemore, *Genealogical Guide to the Early Settlers of America: With a Brief History of Those of the First Generation and References to the Various Local Histories, and Other Sources of Information Where Additional Data May Be Found* (Baltimore: Genealogical Publishing Company, 1967), p. 284.

He stated that: Bradford, *History of Plymouth Plantation 1620–1647*, vol. 2, p. 266.

But the Peach: Dunn, Yeandle, and Savage, eds., *The Journal of John Winthrop, 1630–1649*, p. 261.

136 Without a full: Edgar J. McManus, *Law and Liberty in Early New England: Criminal Justice and Due Process, 1620–1692* (Amherst, MA: University of Massachusetts Press, 2009), p. 110.

Plymouth Colony leaders: Kawashima, *Igniting King Philip's War*, p. 108.

As Governor Winthrop: Dunn, Yeandle, and Savage, eds., *The Journal of John Winthrop*, p. 261.

Every person at: Ibid.

The two Narragansett: Ibid.

137 Their vow to: Ibid.

The ancient story: Larry Spotted Crow Mann, *Drumming and Dreaming* (CrowStorm Publishing, 2017), p. 64.

"A large Cedar: Ibid.

To this day: Ibid., p. 65.

138 On his deathbed: LaFantasie, ed., *The Correspondence of Roger Williams*, p. 172.

As Williams described: Ibid.

"Good men . . . you: Peter Charles Hoffer, *Law and People in Colonial America* (Baltimore: Johns Hopkins University Press, 1998), p. 117.

## 8. Outside Influence

140 "True one wounded: Glenn LaFantasie, ed., *The Correspondence of Roger Williams*, 2 vols. (Hanover, NH: Brown University and University Press of New England, 1988), pp. 176–77.

In addition, Williams: Alvin Gardner Weeks, *Massasoit of the Wampanoags: With a Brief Commentary on Indian Character; and Sketches of Other Great Chiefs, Tribes and Nations; Also a Chapter on Samoset, Squanto and Hobamock, Three Early Native Friends of the Plymouth Colonists* (Norwood, MA: Plimpton Press, 1919), p. 123.

Exiled from Massachusetts: Ibid.

He owed his: Ibid.

Mary Williams may: Lori Stokes, Sarah Stewart, and Chris Peterson, *The Pleasure of the Taste: Recipes from 17th-Century Massachusetts* (Boston: Partnership of the Historic Bostons, Inc., 2015), p. 18.

141 The hearty dish: Ibid., p. 8.

Mary was able: Dawn Dove and Holly Ewald, "Indigenous Life in Rhode Island: An Introduction, by Paulla Dove Jennings, as told to Holly Ewald," *Through Our Eyes: An Indigenous View of Mashapaug Pond* (Lulu Publishing, 2012), p. 36; Sydney V. James Jr., *Three Visitors to Early Plymouth: Letters About the Pilgrim Settlement in New England During Its First Seven Years—John Pory, Isaack de Rasieres, Emmanuel Altham* (Bedford, MA: Applewood Books, 1997), p. 79; Stokes, Stewart, and Peterson, *The Pleasure of the Taste*, p. 18.

At the same: Bridget Champlin, "The Tour for Kids and Teens," First Baptist Church in America, Providence, RI, handout, and observed on tour.

The sachem forcefully: John Winthrop, *Winthrop Papers*, vol. 4 (Boston: Massachusetts Historical Society, 1944), p. 52; "Bronze Tablets Marking Site of Roger Williams House and Spring Landing Place," Providence Public Library. "Remains of wall and stonework which formed his hearth are found here," www.provlib.org/post-card-collection/.

"But one" alone: LaFantasie, ed., *The Correspondence of Roger Williams*, p. 176.

"True one wounded: Ibid., pp. 176–77.

142 He told Williams: Ibid., p. 177.

Standing on the: Caleb Johnson, *Here Shall I Die Ashore: Stephen Hopkins: Bermuda Castaway, Jamestown Survivor, and Mayflower Pilgrim* (Xlibris Corporation, 2007), p. 91.

The sachem was: Ibid.

He trudged up: Ibid., p. 93.

Likewise, Winslow found: Ibid., p. 94.

143 He further noted: Ibid.

His face was: Ibid.

Soon after, Winslow: Ramona L. Peters, "Consulting with the Bone Keepers: NAGPRA Consultations and Archaeological Monitoring in the Wampanoag Territory," *Cross-Cultural Collaboration: Native Peoples and Archaeology in the Northeastern United States*, ed. Jordan E. Kerber (Lincoln: University of Nebraska Press, 2006), p. 43, n. 2. I refer to Massasoit Ousameequin as Massasoit, as he is widely known. But as Ms. Peters notes, Massasoit is the term for a leader of the "greatest esteem among the Wampanoag"—not a name.

143 His fellow settlers: Edward Winslow, "Letter/Summons," dated August 31, 1644, Pilgrim Hall Museum archives.

The seal alluded: Willene B. Clark, *A Medieval Book of Beasts: The Second-Family Bestiary: Commentary, Art, Text and Translation* (Woodbridge: Boydell Press, 2006), p. 52.

The visitors lay: Margaret Ellen Newell, *Brethren by Nature: New England Indians, Colonists, and the Origins of American Slavery* (Ithaca, NY: Cornell University Press, 2015), p. 67.

Members of the: Ibid., p. 7; James, *Three Visitors to Early Plymouth*, p. 70.

Pious Winslow and: Alden T. Vaughan, *New England Frontier: Puritans and Indians, 1620–1675* (Norman: University of Oklahoma Press, 1995), p. 74.

144 He remarked on: Edward Winslow, *Good Newes from New England* (Bedford, MA: Applewood Books, 1996), p. 60.

Printer wrote, "Know: Amy Belding Brown, "Letter at the Bridge," Collisions: Natives and Puritans in Early New England blog, March 15, 2014, amybeldingbrown.wordpress.com/.

145 Printer, trained by: Ibid.

Winslow hastened to: Winslow, *Good Newes from New England*, pp. 32–33.

Before Winslow could: Weeks, *Massasoit of the Wampanoags*, pp. 85–86.

There is no: Ibid.

He pointed out: Ibid.

Winslow's presence undermined: Ibid.

On entering Massasoit's: Winslow, *Good Newes from New England*, p. 33; Caleb Johnson, "Massasoit Ousemequin," mayflowerhistory.com /massasoit/.

The Englishman was: Winslow, *Good Newes from New England*, p. 33.

The sachem's tribesmen: Ibid.

A "quire" of: William S. Simmons, "Conversion from Indian to Puritan," *New England Quarterly* 52, no. 2 (June 1979): 198–99.

Winslow later observed: Winslow, *Good Newes from New England*, p. 33.

"*Keen* Winsnow?: Ibid.; Johnson, "Massasoit Ousemequin."

"They cannot pronounce: Winslow, *Good Newes from New England*, p. 33.

"*Ahhe*, [Yes]," Winslow: Ibid.

146 "*Matta neen wonckanet:* Ibid.; Johnson, "Massasoit Ousemequin."

He had brought: Winslow, *Good Newes from New England*, p. 34; 17th Century Personal and Household Items collection: Edward Winslow's Mortar and Pestle. Material: Bronze. Made in England, 1600–50. Descended in the family of Edward Winslow. This mortar was probably used for grinding herbs for medicinal or cooking purposes. Pilgrim Hall Museum.

He used the: Winslow, *Good Newes from New England*, p. 34.

The great sachem: Ibid.

Winslow asked after: Ibid.

He had not: Ibid.

He could open: Ibid.

Winslow crouched down: Ibid.

Winslow paused in: Ibid.

"By two of: Ibid.

Winslow directed the: Ibid.

Winslow had also: Ibid.

He needed the: Ibid.

The messenger departed: Ibid., p. 35.

Winslow waited for: Ibid.

He reappeared with: Ibid.

The Englishman, sleep: Ibid.

Winslow did what: Ibid.

Perhaps surprisingly, Massasoit: Ibid.

147 The sassafras acted: John Moore Neligan and Rawdon Macnamara, *Medicines, Their Uses and Mode of Administration* (Dublin: Fannin and Company, 1867), p. 289.

The sachem's spirits: Winslow, *Good Newes from New England*, p. 35.

In short order: Ibid., p. 34; Johnson, "Massasoit Ousemequin."

He requested that: Winslow, *Good Newes from New England*, p. 35.

Quickly killing one: Ibid.

Massasoit refused to: Ibid., p. 36.

At this point: Ibid.

Massasoit would save: Ibid.

An indigenous pipe: 2018 Nipmuc Nation Powwow. Emcee: David Tall Pine White noted these details during a pipe ceremony.

147 Massasoit's pipe was: Chris Lindahl, "Wampanoag Work to Repatriate Remains, Artifacts," *Cape Cod Times*, April 14, 2017, www.capecodtimes.com/news/. (Images courtesy Wampanoag Confederation.)

Perched on its: Ibid.

Early on, when: Vaughan, *New England Frontier*, p. 81.

148 Penowanyanquis was "by: LaFantasie, ed., *The Correspondence of Roger Williams*, p. 177.

Williams replied tactfully: Ibid.

149 "He that doth: Ibid.

In this same: David Colclough, *Freedom of Speech in Early Stuart England* (Cambridge Cambridge University Press, April 7, 2005), p. 109.

## 9. THE VERDICT

150 Colonists worried, for: Mac Griswold, *The Manor: Three Centuries at a Slave Plantation on Long Island* (New York: Macmillan, 2013), p. 27.

The "witch amongst: Kupperman, *Indians and English*, p. 191.

Edward Winslow fretted: Ibid., p. 134.

151 Two years earlier: Robert Wilson Kelso, *The History of Public Poor Relief in Massachusetts, 1620–1920* (Boston: Houghton Mifflin, 1922), p. 31.

Plymouth Colony had: Adelos Gorton, *The Life and Times of Samuel Gorton: The Founders and the Founding of the Republic* (Philadelphia: George S. Ferguson Company, 1907), p. 14.

A 1638 Plymouth: George D. Langdon Jr., *Pilgrim Colony: A History of New Plymouth, 1620–1691* (New Haven, CT: Yale University Press, 1966), pp. 49 and 50.

Years later, Plymouth: Kelso, *The History of Public Poor Relief*, p. 31.

152 Colony records reflect: Plymouth Colony Records, vol. 1, p. 102.

Tellingly, not long: Ibid., pp. 41 and 42.

The nature of: Ibid., p. 42.

One Englishman, trying: Kupperman, *Indians and English*, p. 137.

Roger Williams, culturally: Andrea Robertson Cremer, "Possession: Indian Bodies, Cultural Control, and Colonialism in the Pequot War," *Early American Studies* 6, no. 2 (Fall 2008): 295–345, at 342.

153 He described Peach: William Bradford, *History of Plymouth Plantation 1620–1647*, vol. 2 (Boston: Massachusetts Historical Society, 1912), p. 264.

Peach was "a: Ibid.

Peach was "ring: Ibid.

154 Once in the: Nathaniel Bradstreet Shurtleff, *Records of the Colony of*

*New Plymouth, in New England: Court Orders. New Plymouth Colony. Massachusetts General Court*, vol. 1, 1633–1640 (Boston: Press of William White, 1855), p. 169.

When the colony: Ibid., p. 33.

155 Peach had earned: Bradford, *History of Plymouth Plantation 1620–1647*, vol. 2, p. 264.

Winthrop drew a: John Winthrop, *Winthrop Papers*, vol. 1 (Boston: Massachusetts Historical Society, 1944), p. 272.

The tavern owner had: Shurtleff, *Records of the Colony of New Plymouth*, p. 87.

156 In the relatively: The Last Will and Testament of John Winslow, Pilgrim Hall Museum, www.pilgrimhallmuseum.org/.

It is possible: Ibid.

He stipulated in: Ibid.

"She [Jane] shall: Ibid.

157 As one English: James B. Thayer, "The Jury and Its Development," *Harvard Law Review* 5, no. 6 (January 15, 1892): 249–73, at 378.

During the colonial: Peter Charles Hoffer, *Law and People in Colonial America* (Baltimore: Johns Hopkins University Press, 1998), p. 117.

This meant that: Ibid.

Governor Winthrop, adamantly: Richard S. Dunn, Laetitia Yeandle, and James Savage, eds., *The Journal of John Winthrop, 1630–1649* (Cambridge, MA: Harvard University Press, 1996), p. 260.

But then again: Bradford, *History of Plymouth Plantation 1620–1647*, vol. 2, p. 264.

158 Standish advised not: Edward Winslow, *Good Newes from New England* (Bedford, MA: Applewood Books, 1996), p. 9.

Having previously served: Plymouth Colony Records, vol. 1, p. 42.

159 Nor would his: John Demos, *A Little Commonwealth: Family Life in Plymouth Colony* (New York: Oxford University Press, 1970), p. 55; Bradford, *History of Plymouth Plantation 1620–1647*, vol. 2, p. 363.

As Dorothy searched: Demos, *A Little Commonwealth*, p. 56.

160 Traditionally, tribes tolerated: Ann Marie Plane, *Colonial Intimacies: Indian Marriage in Early New England* (Ithaca, NY: Cornell University Press, 2000), p. 5.

One young seventeenth-century: Ibid., p. 3.

"By his intisements: Ibid.

One concerned settler: Letter from William Paine, [April 21, 1640]. Series I. Governor John Winthrop Jr. MSS 413, B2 F5. Winthrop Family Papers, Phillips Library Reading Room, Peabody Essex Museum.

160 During the seventeenth: John Ruston Pagan, *Anne Orthwood's Bastard: Sex and Law in Early Virginia* (New York: Oxford University Press, 2002), p. 12.

161 As Holmes stood: Holmes Family, John Holmes Jr. Inventory, 1697, Pilgrim Hall Museum archives. (Items likely passed from one generation to the next.)

Thankful to be: "A Genealogical Profile of John Holmes," a collaboration between Plimoth Plantation and the New England Historic Genealogical Society, www.plimoth.org/.

In 1636, he: Ibid.

In 1637, eager: Eugene Aubrey Stratton, *Plymouth Colony: Its History and People, 1620–1691* (Salt Lake City: Ancestry Publishing, 1986), p. 181.

A new master: Ibid.

With his aged: Denwood Nathan Stacy Holmes, "The Black Sheep of Some Good Family," *New England Historical and Genealogical Register* 171 (Spring 2017): 85–92, at 86.

Eight months later: Ibid.

He received five: Ibid., pp. 86–87.

Holmes's father had: Ibid., p. 87.

Holmes's sister, Susan: Ibid., p. 88.

162 "If the said: Ibid.

The ugly fear: Ibid., p. 86.

Holmes focused on: Stratton, *Plymouth Colony*, p. 181.

Holmes unloaded the: Ibid.

163 Another seventeenth-century: Yasuhide Kawashima, *Igniting King Philip's War: The John Sassamon Murder Trial* (Lawrence: University Press of Kansas, 2001), p. 109.

164 At the front: Plymouth Colony Records, vol. 1, p. 97.

In a spectacular: Dunn, Yeandle, and Savage, eds., *The Journal of John Winthrop, 1630–1649*, p. 261.

## 10. DEATH AND SALVATION

165 "*Neenawun tabuttantamooonk newutche*: Nipmuc prayer, pinehawk .abschools.org/. Individual verses quoted at chapter headings 1–14.

"Upon the forementioned: William Bradford, *History of Plymouth Plantation 1620–1647*, vol. 2 (Boston: Massachusetts Historical Society, 1912), p. 364.

Before the execution: Nathaniel Bradstreet Shurtleff, *Records of the Colony of New Plymouth, in New England: Court Orders. New Plymouth*

*Colony. Massachusetts General Court*, vol. 1, 1633–1640 (Boston: Press of William White, 1855), p. 97.

The arbitrators' decision: Plymouth Colony Records, vol. 12, pp. 161–62.

Sillis was chosen: Ibid.

166 This type of: James Masschaele, *Jury, State, and Society in Medieval England* (New York: Palgrave Macmillan, 2008), p. 107; term defined by www.thefreedictionary.com/.

Pratt completed his: Natalie Zemon Davis, *The Return of Martin Guerre* (Cambridge, MA: Harvard University Press, 1983), pp. 92–93.

As Winthrop recorded: Richard S. Dunn, Laetitia Yeandle, and James Savage, eds., *The Journal of John Winthrop, 1630–1649* (Cambridge, MA: Harvard University Press, 1996), p. 261.

His father, Adam: Herbert Baxter Adams, *Norman Constables in America: Read Before the New England Historical Society, February 1, 1882* (Baltimore: Johns Hopkins University, 1883), pp. 3–4.

The work itself: Ibid.

The elder Winthrop: Ibid.

Reverend Lothrop embodied: Ibid.

167 Captain Myles Standish: Daniel K. Davis, *Miles Standish* (New York: Chelsea House Publishers, 2011), p. 8.

Issuing her proclamation: Arthur F. Kinney, *Elizabethan and Jacobean England: Sources and Documents of the English Renaissance* (West Sussex, UK: Wiley-Blackwell, 2011), pp. 85–90.

Just as Lothrop's: Karen Ordahl Kupperman, *Indians and English: Facing Off in Early America* (Ithaca, NY: Cornell University Press, 2000), p. 27.

The document outlined: Caleb Johnson, Mayflower Compact, mayflowerhistory.com/.

The English colonists: William E. Nelson, *The Common Law in Colonial America: The Chesapeake and New England, 1607–1660*, vol. 1 (New York: Oxford University Press, 2008), p. 49.

168 The Tacitus-like language: Davis, *Miles Standish*, p. 26.

American revolutionaries demanded: The Declaration of Independence, www.ushistory.org/DECLARATION/document/.

Their lives on: Ibid.

When the drafters: John A. Murley and Sean D. Sutton, *The Supreme Court Against the Criminal Jury: Social Science and the Palladium of Liberty* (New York: Lexington Books, 2014), p. 6.

168 The Boston lawyer: Alexander Bregman, *Reading Under the Folds: John Dickinson, Gordon's Tacitus, and the American Revolution*. Thesis or dissertation is available at ScholarlyCommons, repository.upenn.edu/.

Massachusetts Bay cultivated: Nelson, *The Common Law in Colonial America*, p. 92.

As John Adams: William E. Nelson, "The Lawfinding Power of Colonial American Juries," *Ohio State Law Journal* 71, no. 5 (2010): 1005.

169 "The jury are: Bernadette A. Meyler, "Substitute Chancellors: The Role of the Jury in the Contest Between Common Law and Equity," 2006, Cornell Law Faculty Publications 39, scholarship.law.cornell.edu/lsrp_papers/39, p. 2.

When juries made: Nelson, "The Lawfinding Power of Colonial American Juries," p. 1003.

With "the eyes: Thomas A. Green and J. S. Cockburn, *Twelve Good Men and True: The Criminal Trial Jury in England, 1200–1800* (Princeton: Princeton University Press, July 14, 2014), p. 214; John Tirman, *The Deaths of Others: The Fate of Civilians in America's Wars* (New York: Oxford University Press, 2011), p. 22.

Those jurors became: Green and Cockburn, *Twelve Good Men and True*, p. 214.

170 For example, when: Patricia Scott Deetz, "A Time of Quiet Change, 1640–1659," Plymouth Colony Archive Project, www.histarch.illinois.edu/plymouth/wampanoag.html.

The men stated: Plymouth Colony Records, vol. 1, p. 97.

Peach admitted that: Dunn, Yeandle, and Savage, eds., *The Journal of John Winthrop, 1630–1649*, p. 261; John Winthrop, *Winthrop Papers*, vol. 4 (Boston: Massachusetts Historical Society, 1944), p. 60.

Julian admitted to: Lawrence W. Towner, *A Good Master Well Served: Master and Servants in Colonial Massachusetts, 1620–1750* (New York: Garland Publishing, 1998), p. 1.

But Winthrop described: Dunn, Yeandle, and Savage, eds., *The Journal of John Winthrop, 1630–1649*, p. 261.

If this was: Ibid.

171 The soldier who: Ibid.

A convict who: Zemon Davis, *The Return of Martin Guerre*, p. 93.

Colony leadership recorded: Plymouth Colony Records, vol. 1, p. 97.

It likely took: Author interview with Professor J. Stanley Lemons, Rhode Island College professor emeritus of history, Providence, RI, December 19, 2017.

William Bradford noted: Bradford, *History of Plymouth Plantation*

*1620–1647*, vol. 2 (Boston: Massachusetts Historical Society, 1912), p. 268.

It was a matter: Plymouth Colony Records, vol. 1, p. 62, August 29, 1643.

He would have: Arthur Glass, *The Iliad* (Lulu Press, Inc., 2013), Book One, opening lines.

Over time, the: David Filipov, "The Mystery of Where Plymouth Got Its Start," *Boston Globe*, June 21, 2014.

172 Colonists tended to: Samuel Gardner Drake, *The History and Antiquities of the City of Boston: From Its Settlement in 1630 to the Year 1670. With Notes, Historical and Critical; Also an Introductory History of the Discovery and Settlement of New England* (Boston: L. Stevens, 1854), p. 149, footnote.

After she gave: Demos, *A Little Commonwealth*, pp. 31 and 131.

Plymouth leaders intervened: Plymouth Colony Records, vol. 1, p. 111.

The court demanded: Ibid.

None other than: Ibid., vol. 1, pp. 111–13.

A few years: Eugene Aubrey Stratton, *Plymouth Colony: Its History and People, 1620–1691* (Salt Lake City: Ancestry Publishing, 1986), p. 181.

Holmes and his: Plymouth Colony Records, vol. 1, p. 113.

The Holmes family: Holmes Family, John Holmes Jr. Inventory, 1697, Pilgrim Hall Museum archives.

Court records commonly: Richard M. Stower, *A History of the First Parish Church of Scituate, Massachusetts: Its Life and Times* (Scituate, MA: Converpage), p. 68; Bradley Chapin, *Criminal Justice in Colonial America, 1606–1660* (Athens: University of Georgia Press, 1983), p. 51.

Colony leaders reprimanded: "A Genealogical Profile of John Holmes," a collaboration between Plimoth Plantation and the New England Historic Genealogical Society, www.plimoth.org/.

173 Fulfilling the court's: Plymouth Colony Records, vol. 1, p. 127, June 4, 1639.

"Fainting in the: Ibid.

The equitable application: Tirman, *The Deaths of Others*, p. 22.

In 1638, England: James Truslow Adams, *The Founding of New England* (Boston: Atlantic Monthly Press, 1921), p. 209.

Not coincidentally, that: Susan Hardman Moore, *Pilgrims: New World Settlers and the Call of Home* (New Haven, CT: Yale University Press, 2007), p. 65.

174 After its founding: Ibid., p. 70.

174 The ideas reflected: Adams, *The Founding of New England*, p. 209.
Incredibly, the British: Ibid.
Life in the: Ibid.
Harvard's first class: Moore, *Pilgrims*, p. 70.
The new humanist: Stower, *A History of the First Parish Church*, p. 68.
The minister was: Ibid.
Others remained and: Moore, *Pilgrims*, pp. 64–65.

175 The ideas that: Jim Powell, "Edward Coke: Commonal Law Protection for Liberty," November 1, 1997, fee.org/articles/.
Three years after: Harry M. Ward, *Statism in Plymouth Colony* (Port Washington, NY: National University Publications Kennikat Press, 1973), p. 117.
While many "applauded: Ibid.

## EPILOGUE: AFTERSHOCKS

177 An exasperated Coddington: John Winthrop, *Winthrop Papers*, vol. 4 (Boston: Massachusetts Historical Society, 1944), p. 247.
Settlement leaders felt: Website for the Jailhouse Inn, jailhouse.com /content/our-story-0.
It remained a: Ibid.
In 1986, the: Ibid.
On their website: Ibid.

178 A twenty-three-year-old soldier: Mike Lockley, "Winson Green Prison Hangings: Murderers Who Were Executed at the Gallows," *Birmingham Mail*, November 29, 2015, www.birminghammail.co.uk/news /midlands-news/.
The year after: Nebraska State Bar Association, *Proceedings, Volumes 2–5* (Omaha, 1909), p. 147.
With the memory: William E. Nelson, *The Common Law in Colonial America: The Chesapeake and New England, 1607–1660*, vol. 1 (New York: Oxford University Press, 2008), p. 74.
Winthrop resolved to: Ibid.

179 The nineteenth-century Samuel: John Schwartz, "Who You Callin' a Maverick?" *New York Times*, October 4, 2008; biography of Samuel A. Maverick, samuelamaverick.blogspot.com.
It was this: Schwartz, "Who You Callin' a Maverick?"
Branding helped with: Ibid.
This unconventional, forward-thinking: Ibid.

180 It is called: Text from sign marking Hassanamessitt land of Nipmuc

Nation, abutting Grafton, MA, Massachusetts Bay Colony Tercentenary Commission.

On the rugged: William Arthur Calnek, *History of the County of Annapolis: Including Old Port Royal and Acadia* (London: William Briggs,
1897), pp. 28–29.

D'Aulnay's refined and: Ibid.

Legends recount that: Ibid.

He gamely presented: John Russell Bartlett, *Records of the Colony of
Rhode Island and Providence Plantations, in New England*, vol. 1 (Providence, RI: A. Crawford Greene and Brother, 1856), p. 44.

He offered, he: Ibid., p. 40.

181 This exercise ended: Ibid., p. 38.

When King Philip's: "Old Roger Williams Tries to Stop King Philip's
War," September 1, 2017, New England Historical Society. "With
thanks to Mayflower by Nathaniel Philbrick."

His home and: Ibid.

"This house of: Ibid.

The physician John: Caroline Frank and Krysta Ryzewski, "Excavating
the Quiet History of a Providence Plantation," *Historical Archaeology*
47, no. 2 (2013): 16–44, at 19.

Four years after: Ibid., pp. 17 and 19.

With a brick: Ibid., p. 25.

A more substantial: Ibid., p. 28.

Unlike his father: Ibid., p. 22.

He ate with: Ibid., p. 36.

Today, the waterfront: Ibid., p. 17.

Archeologists still carefully: Ibid., pp. 16–44.

182 Writing forcefully to: Jeremy Dupertuis Bangs, *The Seventeenth-
Century Town Records of Scituate, Massachusetts*, vol. 3 (Boston: New
England Historic Genealogical Society, 2002), p. 345.

Ever the diplomat: Amos Otis, *Genealogical Notes of Barnstable Families*, vol. 2 (Barnstable, MA: F. B. and F. P. Goss, 1890), p. 199.

And there was: Bangs, *The Seventeenth-Century Town Records of Scituate, Massachusetts*, vol. 3, p. 345.

Lothrop sold his: Plymouth Colony Records, vol. 12, p. 71.

The preacher and: Otis, *Genealogical Notes of Barnstable Families*, vol.
2204.

Lothrop had been: Edward Everett, *An Oration Delivered at Plymouth
December 22, 1824* (Boston: Cummings, Hilliard and Company, 1825),
p. 38. While researchers often note that this quote is attributed to

Lothrop in the "Winthrop Papers," no such reference exists. Staff at Sturgis Library in Barnstable, MA, point to the quote perhaps having been "passed down by word of mouth" as possible provenance linking the words to Lothrop.

182 As one historian: Lorenzo Sears, *American Literature in the Colonial and National Periods* (Boston: Little, Brown, 1902), p. 43.

183 Among Lothrop's progeny: Gaye E. Gindy, *The Underground Railroad and Sylvania's Historic Lathrop House* (Bloomington, IN: AuthorHouse, 2008), p. 57.

A historian tallied: Ibid., pp. 57–58.

Lothrop's copy of: Information on provenance provided by Cape Cod's Sturgis Library in Barnstable, MA.

At a time: Thomas Goodwin, *A Child of Light Walking in Darknesse* (London: R. Dawlman, 1643), p. 62. The edition attributed to Lothrop was in possession of his granddaughter, "Rebekah Lothrup—hir book." It is found in Sturgis Library in Barnstable, MA, along with a *nota bene* on the book's provenance that I have drawn from to explain Lothrop's connection to Goodwin's teachings.

In 1643, he: John Osborn Austin, *The Genealogical Dictionary of Rhode Island: Comprising Three Generations of Settlers Who Came Before 1690* (Genealogical Publishing Company, 1969), p. 200.

Governor Winthrop recorded: Ibid.

Those members of: Ibid.

Throckmorton survived and: Ibid.; Robert Charles Anderson, *The Great Migration Begins: G-O* (Boston: New England Historic Genealogical Society, 1995), p. 1073.

184 They dreaded the: Josh Fischman, "Catholic Spies in the New World?: Relics Pose New Puzzle About Early American Colony," *Scientific American*, July 29, 2015.

Spain hoped that: Ibid.

Attempts to impose: Robert Emmett Curran, *Papist Devils* (Washington, DC: Catholic University of America Press, 2014), p. 104.

Colonial leaders and: Confirmed by staff at the Rhode Island Historical Society.

While the ferocious: Margaret Ellen Newell, *Brethren by Nature: New England Indians, Colonists, and the Origins of American Slavery* (Ithaca, NY: Cornell University Press, 2015), p. 131.

185 In 1840, of: Thomas L. Doughton, "Unseen Neighbors: Native Americans of Central Massachusetts, a People Who Had 'Vanished,'" *After King Philip's War: Presence and Persistence in Indian New England*, ed.

Colin Calloway (Hanover, NH: University Press of New England, 1997), p. 228, n. 49.

When Reverend John: David D. Hall, *Ways of Writing: The Practice and Politics of Text-Making in Seventeenth-Century New England* (Philadelphia: University of Pennsylvania Press, 2012), p. 169.

In the seventeenth: Ibid.

In June 2004: Christopher J. Thee, "Massachusetts Nipmucs and the Long Shadow of John Milton Earle," *New England Quarterly* 79, no. 4 (December 2006): 637.

The OFA based: Ibid.

John Milton Earle: Ibid.

The OFA relied: Ibid., pp. 648 and 651–52.

Earle used an: Ibid., p. 642.

# Selected Bibliography

Apess, William. *On Our Own Ground: The Complete Writings of William Apess, a Pequot.* Amherst, MA: University of Massachusetts Press, 1992.

Bangs, Jeremy Dupertuis. *The Seventeenth-Century Town Records of Scituate, Massachusetts.* Vol. 3. Boston: New England Historic Genealogical Society, 2002.

Bradford, William. *Of Plymouth Plantation, 1620–1647.* Vol. 1. Boston: Massachusetts Historical Society, 1912.

Cave, Alfred A. *The Pequot War.* Amherst, MA: University of Massachusetts Press, 1996.

Cerrotti, Dennis. *Hidden Genocide, Hidden People.* Wellesley, MA: Sea Venture Press, 2014.

Connole, Dennis A. *The Indians of the Nipmuck Country in Southern New England, 1630–1750: An Historical Geography.* Jefferson, NC: McFarland and Company, 2007.

Demos, John. *A Little Commonwealth: Family Life in Plymouth Colony.* New York: Oxford University Press, 1970.

Dove, Dawn, and Holly Ewald, eds. "Indigenous Life in Rhode Island: An Introduction, by Paulla Dove Jennings, as told to Holly Ewald." *Through Our Eyes: An Indigenous View of Mashapaug Pond.* Lulu Publishing, 2012.

Dunbar-Ortiz, Roxanne. *An Indigenous Peoples' History of the United States.* Boston: Beacon Press, 2014.

Glanville, Ranulf de. *A Translation of Glanville.* London: W. Reed, 1812.

Goodman, Nan. *Banished: Common Law and the Rhetoric of Social Exclusion in Early New England.* Philadelphia: University of Pennsylvania Press, 2012.

Grandjean, Katherine A. *American Passage: The Communications Frontier in Early New England.* Cambridge, MA: Harvard University Press, 2015.

———. "The Long Wake of the Pequot War." *Early American Studies: An Interdisciplinary Journal* 9, no. 2 (Spring 2011).

Handsman, Russell G., and Ann McMullen. *A Key into the Language of Woodsplint Baskets.* Washington, CT: American Indian Archaeological Institute, 1987.

James, Sydney V., Jr. *Three Visitors to Early Plymouth: Letters About the Pilgrim Settlement in New England During Its First Seven Years—John Pory, Isaack de Rasieres, Emmanuel Altham.* Bedford, MA: Applewood Books, 1997.

Johnson, Caleb. *Here Shall I Die Ashore: Stephen Hopkins—Bermuda Castaway, Jamestown Survivor, and Mayflower Pilgrim.* Xlibris Corporation, 2007.

Kupperman, Karen Ordahl. *Indians and English: Facing Off in Early America.* Ithaca, NY: Cornell University Press, 2000.

LaFantasie, Glenn W., ed. *The Correspondence of Roger Williams.* 2 vols. Hanover, NH: Brown University and University Press of New England, 1988.

———. "Murder of an Indian, 1638." *Rhode Island History* 38, no. 3 (1979).

Langdon, George D., Jr. *Pilgrim Colony: A History of New Plymouth, 1620–1691.* New Haven, CT: Yale University Press, 1966.

Lenik, Edward J. *Picture Rocks: American Indian Rock Art in the Northeast Woodlands.* Hanover, NH: University Press of New England, 2002.

Lopenzina, Drew. *Red Ink: Native Americans Picking Up the Pen in the Colonial Period.* Albany: State University of New York Press, 2012.

Mancke, Elizabeth, and Carole Shammas. *The Creation of the British Atlantic World.* Baltimore: Johns Hopkins University Press, 2005.

Mavor, James W., Jr., and Byron E. Dix. *Manitou: The Sacred Landscape of New England's Native Civilization.* Rochester, VT: Inner Traditions International, 1989.

McManus, Edgar J. *Law and Liberty in Early New England: Criminal Justice and Due Process, 1620–1692.* Amherst, MA: University of Massachusetts Press, 2009.

Miller, Perry. *The New England Mind: The Seventeenth Century.* Vol. 1. Cambridge, MA: Harvard University Press, 1983.

Miller, Perry, and Thomas H. Johnson. *The Puritans: A Sourcebook of Their Writings.* Courier Corporation, 2014.

Mrozowski, Stephen, and Heather Law Pezzarossi. *The Archaeology of Hassanamesit Woods: The Sarah Burnee/Sarah Boston Farmstead.* Cultural Resource Management Study No. 69. Boston: Andrew Fiske Memorial

Center for Archaeological Research, University of Massachusetts Boston, October 2015.

Newell, Margaret Ellen. *Brethren by Nature: New England Indians, Colonists, and the Origins of American Slavery.* Ithaca, NY: Cornell University Press, 2015.

Senier, Siobhan. *Dawnland Voices: An Anthology of Indigenous Writing from New England.* Lincoln: University of Nebraska Press, 2014.

Spotted Crow Mann, Larry. *Drumming and Dreaming.* CrowStorm Publishing, 2017.

Williams, Roger. *Publications of the Narragansett Club: The Letters of Roger Williams.* Vol. 6. Providence, RI: Narragansett Club, 1874.

Wilson, James. *The Earth Shall Weep: A History of Native America.* New York: Grove/Atlantic, Inc., 2007.

Winslow, Edward. *Good Newes from New England.* Bedford, MA: Applewood Books, 1996.

Winthrop, John. *Winthrop Papers.* Vol. 4. Boston: Massachusetts Historical Society, 1944.

# Index

# ILLUSTRATION CREDITS

xi Map courtesy of Bill and Kristen Keegan.

22 Portrait of Edward Winslow. Courtesy of Pilgrim Hall Museum.

49 Nipmuc *manitou* stone. Photo by the author.

72 Replica Nipmuc dwelling at Fruitlands Museum. Photo by the author.

78 Portrait of Governor John Winthrop. Courtesy of the American Antiquarian Society.

79 Native American sachem, ca. 1700. Courtesy of the RISD Museum, Providence, RI.

84 *The Massacre of the Settlers*, engraved by Matthaus Merian after a work by Theodore de Bry, Frankfurt, Germany, 1634, black-and-white line engraving. Courtesy of the Colonial Williamsburg Foundation.

88 Lake County Tree. Courtesy of the Great Lakes Trail Marker Tree Society/Downes Studio.

92 Myles Standish. Courtesy of the Library of Congress.

102 Plymouth Colony Book of Laws. Photo by An LeFevre.

144 *The Mayflower Compact* by Jean Leon Gerome Ferris, 1899. Courtesy of the Library of Congress.

148 Statue of Massasoit by Cyrus Edwin Dallin. Courtesy of the Library of Congress.

A NOTE ON THE TYPE

This book was set in Adobe Garamond. Designed for the Adobe Corporation by Robert Slimbach, the fonts are based on types first cut by Claude Garamond (ca. 1480–1561). Garamond was a pupil of Geoffroy Tory and is believed to have followed the Venetian models, although he introduced a number of important differences, and it is to him that we owe the letters we now know as "old style." He gave to his letters a certain elegance and feeling of movement that won their creator an immediate reputation and the patronage of Francis I of France.

Composed by North Market Street Graphics,
Lancaster, Pennsylvania

Printed and bound by Berryville Graphics,
Berryville, Virginia

Designed by Betty Lew